D1180371

FIRST AID
AND CARE OF WILD BIRDS

Edited by
J. E. Cooper and J. T. Eley

DAVID & CHARLES
Newton Abbot   London   North Pomfret (Vt)

British Library Cataloguing in Publication Data

First aid and care of wild birds.
  1. First aid for birds
  I. Cooper, John Eric   II. Eley, J T
  639'.97'82   SF994

   ISBN 0–7153–7664–0

First published 1979
Second impression 1979

© J. E. Cooper 1979

All rights reserved. No part of this
publication may be reproduced, stored
in a retrieval system, or transmitted,
in any form or by any means, electronic,
mechanical, photocopying, recording or
otherwise, without the prior permission
of David & Charles (Publishers) Limited

Printed in Great Britain
by Redwood Burn Limited Trowbridge & Esher
for David & Charles (Publishers) Limited
Brunel House Newton Abbot Devon

Published in the United States of America
by David & Charles Inc.,
North Pomfret Vermont 05053 USA

Contents

Lugete, O Veneres Cupidinesque,
et quantum est hominum venustiorum.
Passer mortuus est meae puellae,
passer, deliciae meae puellae.

(Mourn, Loves and Cupids,
and all men of finer feeling.
My Lady's pet sparrow is dead
the sparrow of my dear lady.)
Catullus

List of contributors

J. E. Cooper BVSC, DTVM, MI BIOL, MRCVS
Huntingdon, Cambridgeshire

Margaret E. Cooper LLB, Solicitor
Huntingdon, Cambridgeshire

J. P. Croxall BA, PH D
Research Unit on the Rehabilitation of Oiled Seabirds,
University of Newcastle-upon-Tyne
(Now at the British Antarctic Survey, Cambridge)

J. A. Dall BSC, MRCVS
Southern Hospital Group, RSPCA, London

J. T. Eley MBOU
Bath, Avon

Lynne Eley SRN, SCMI
Bath, Avon

A. G. Greenwood MA, VET MB, MRCVS
Keighley, Yorkshire

D. C. Houston BSC, D PHIL
Department of Zoology, University of Glasgow

P. N. Humphreys MSC, MRCVS
Department of Zoology, University College, Cardiff

L. H. Hurrell MA, MB, B CHIR, MRCS, LRCP
Plymouth, Devon

C. G. Jones B SC
St Clears, Dyfed

R. E. Kenward MA, D PHIL
Edward Grey Institute of Field Ornithology, Oxford

P. T. Redig DVM
St Paul, Minnesota, USA

P. R. Richards MB, BS, MD, MRCS, LRCP, DPH, DIH, DTM&H, D OBST,
RCOG
Somersworth, New Hampshire, USA

D. Washington C ENG, MIERE
Wallington, Surrey

M. H. Williams BVSC, MRCVS
Upton-on-Severn, Worcestershire

Notes and Acknowledgements

This book would not have been possible without the help and advice of many people. In particular we are grateful to the authors of the various chapters for their contributions, and to Lynne Eley, who not only did the drawings but also helped in the checking of manuscripts. It gives us great pleasure to express our appreciation to Mrs Joy Adamson for writing the Foreword, and the Sylvanus Charitable Trust for providing financial assistance. We thank Tony Common and Patricia Ashbolt of the Wild Bird Hospital Society, who initiated this work and who gave support and assistance in the earlier stages, and Roger Scammell who enthusiastically and conscientiously assisted with the checking of chapters during the same period. We wish to thank the Editor of *Veterinary Practice* for his permission to reproduce sections of a paper first published in that journal in July 1970, and the Post Office for allowing us to reproduce part of the UK Regulations relating to the dispatch of pathological specimens. The paper 'Health hazards in volunteer bird hospitals' is reprinted, in a modified form, by permission of the American Association of Zoo Veterinarians. Plates 2 and 3 were first published in Volume 4, No 4 of *Pedigree Digest*, published by Pedigree Petfoods; Plate 20 is reproduced by permission of Dr Janet Kear of the Wildfowl Trust; and Miss J. Orsmond kindly allowed us to use Plates 14 and 15. Plates 22 and 23 were provided by Mrs Brenda Marsault, photographs by Clive Vickery and Colin Guy. Plate 21 is by kind permission of Mrs Eva Engholm, photograph by Mr I. Rumley-Dawson.

Several people were kind enough to read drafts of this book and to give us their comments and criticisms. We are grateful in this respect to B. C. Down, T. Hardy, P. E. Holt, J. W. Macdonald and M. A. Peirce as well as W. J. Jordan (of the Royal Society for the Prevention of Cruelty to Animals), C. Platt (of the International Society for the Protection of Animals) and P. Robinson (of the Royal Society for the Protection of Birds). We also wish to thank Mr F. H. Vowles, LLB, Solicitor, for his valuable advice upon the legal content of Chapter 2.

This book should, perhaps, be dedicated to those people, some of them laymen, some scientists and veterinary surgeons, who have worked with wild bird casualties over the years. Much of this work has gone unpraised and often it has attracted criticism; only in the past few years has its role in conservation and animal welfare been appreciated. One of us in particular (J. E. Cooper) owes much to the knowledge and expertise of such people and it is on their personal experience that some of the practical information in this book is based. We are grateful to them.

We must also thank Miss M. Smith, Mrs E. Thomsitt, Mrs J. I. Pyemont and Mrs A. Williamson for their help with typing of draft manuscripts and Mrs D. Suttie and Mrs J. Stevenson for completing the task. Last, but not least, we are indebted to our wives for their help in reading manuscripts and for their constant assistance and encouragement.

Huntingdon, October 1978   J. E. COOPER
                                                            J. T. ELEY

Foreword

When John Cooper asked me to write the Foreword for this book, I felt very honoured. However, I was also rather embarrassed because I was aware of my limited knowledge of birds, especially having watched John treating a wild Verreaux's eagle owl for a broken wing near my home in Kenya. I realised at that time how much there is to learn if we want to help an injured bird. I could not help but admire the way he handled this formidable owl, with utter tenderness and sympathy, during the six weeks that she had to be confined. She occupied a large enclosure and was nursed there until he could release her to live in the wild again.

I am writing here as a person concerned with the conservation of wildlife. Having lived in Kenya since 1937 and being the wife of a Game Warden, very close to nature, I have had unique opportunities to watch the decline of wildlife and, in recent years, the growing interest in preventing further destruction. Despite the heartwarming response of the general public towards the situation, and the intensive research by professionals into the protection and study of wild creatures, I feel that birds in general have been rather neglected in comparison with mammals.

Why is this? Are birds more elusive and more difficult to understand? Or, have we less opportunities to do research on, let alone rehabilitation of, birds than we have for similar work with mammals? The fact is that we still know far too little about birds and their care when sick or injured. Treatment of birds sometimes involves lengthy confinement which some people find inconvenient and expensive. One certainly requires more than just hygienic conditions, adequate feeding and medicines, since birds, like all sick creatures, need first and foremost a feeling of security. They must know that they are understood and affectionately cared for (to avoid the scientifically shunned word 'loved'), and in the case of young birds, that they are not left alone. It is a fact that 'fretting', which occurs when birds find themselves in unfamiliar surroundings amongst strangers, has sometimes nullified all medical treatment. It needs a sixth sense to approach such highly sensitive and vulnerable patients as birds, particularly birds of prey, which are equipped with powerful weapons with which they can defend themselves most efficiently. This sixth sense, combined with the best ornithological and veterinary experience, is the ideal foundation for a successful cure; however, even if that is achieved, the cured bird may then need rehabilitation before it can live in the wild again and this might be a long and complicated process.

The more we learn about the high mortality of birds living under natural conditions, the more we have to educate the public not only about the protection of healthy birds, but also about how we can help them when they are ill.

Wild birds are threatened in many ways. They are prone to injury or disease and are also vulnerable to man's interference by infringement of their territories for various development schemes, pollution of air and water, use of insecticides, the collection of eggs and feathers and many other destructive influences.

My own knowledge of the treatment of birds is limited but I know that I would most likely have lost the Verreaux's eagle owl had I not been lucky enough to find John Cooper to cure her. How very fortunate are we amateurs that he and his co-authors have now published their experiences and are sharing with us their knowledge of how to save sick birds. It is not difficult to foresee that this work will soon become a household book for those of us who not only love birds, but also want to help them whenever possible. I wish the authors all possible success.

Elsamere,
Naivasha,
Kenya.
October 1978

Joy Adamson

1 An introduction to the care of wild birds

J. E. Cooper

There has long been a need for a written guide to the care and treatment of wild birds. Each year tens of thousands of orphaned, sick or injured birds find their way into the hands of the general public; while many of these birds would die anyway, others succumb due to well-intentioned but incorrect treatment. However, it is not only the layman who needs guidance : many veterinary surgeons (unless they have experience of avian diseases) can offer little in the way of advice, and other professional people, for example wardens of nature reserves and field biologists, would find information on the care and treatment of wild birds of great practical value.

The paucity of literature on the care of wild birds is surprising. Ornithology is probably the most popular facet of natural history and there are very many first-class texts on birds. However, the information contained in such books is often not applicable to the care of captive birds. For instance, few ornithological books give the diet of the various species mentioned and as a result the person who finds, say, an injured plover, may have difficulty in ascertaining its correct food.

On the health side also, there is a shortage of data on wild birds. There are a number of veterinary books on poultry but only rarely are free-living birds mentioned; certainly there is nothing included on the clinical treatment of wild species. There are two books which[1,2] contain sections on wild bird casualties and oil pollution, but only a limited amount of information is given. A third[3], while providing extensive data on cage and aviary species, makes no specific mention of wild birds. There are scattered veterinary and medical publications on infectious and parasitic diseases of wild birds but these are usually based on post-mortem surveys and offer little or nothing on diagnosis or treatment. A US publication on the subject[4] provides some such information but is primarily aimed at the specialist and there are important omissions.

The question may be asked 'Why bother with wild birds; would it not be wiser and kinder to destroy those that cannot fend for themselves?' This is a justifiable question; many thousands of birds die 'naturally' each year and such a toll must be accepted. Most birds of prey, for example, suffer a 60–80 per cent mortality in their first year of life! There are arguments against saving wild birds – some, such as wood pigeons, are recognised agricultural pests; others may carry diseases which can affect people or domestic animals; many may be in pain or so sick or injured that the most humane approach is to kill them.

Against these arguments must be put some strong points in favour of the treatment and care of wild birds. First and foremost, the great majority of birds in the UK are protected by law (The Protection of Birds Act, 1954, and subsequent legislation) and it is an offence to 'kill, injure, or take, or attempt to kill, injure or take' protected species. The Act specifically permits the taking of a wild bird by a person 'if he satisfies the court before whom he is charged that the bird had been disabled otherwise than by his act and was taken or to be taken solely for the purpose of tending it and releasing it when no longer disabled'; but it also states that a person shall not be found guilty of an offence 'by reason of the killing of any wild bird if he satisfies the court before whom he is charged that the bird had been so seriously disabled otherwise than by his act that there was no reasonable chance of its recovering'. Hence the killing of a young blackbird is illegal unless, for example, the bird is so badly wounded that it is unlikely to survive.

The treatment of wild birds can be justified on other than legal grounds. Many species are declining in numbers and warrant full conservation measures. The threat of pesticides and oil pollution is already recognised but other factors may also be significant. For example, the number of birds killed on the road is enormous and could possibly contribute to the decline of certain species. Attempts to save some injured birds may well help to boost the numbers of these dwindling or threatened species. Individual birds can be released or, if permanent damage makes this impossible, used for educational purposes or breeding.

Furthermore, our knowledge of bird diseases is still sparse and more work is needed. There have been surveys in the past; some examples of publications are listed in the reference section at the end of this book. In a recent paper, Andrew Greenwood discussed the role that could be played by bird hospitals in monitoring the diseases of wild species[5]. Investigation of sick wild birds not only yields information on the diseases and parasites of free-living species; it may also help to improve our ability to treat aviary-bred birds and other species maintained in zoological collections.

A final point is that many members of the public are bird lovers and are anxious to save any sick or wounded bird. In general they appear disappointed with the response they get from the veterinary profession although it is appreciated that the treatment of such cases is rarely an economic proposition for a veterinary surgeon. As a result large numbers of wild bird hospitals have sprung up : the standard of these varies considerably but many are run efficiently and sensibly, and perform a very vital task.

It is difficult to know how to refer to a person who runs a wild bird hospital; since he may not always be the owner the word 'organiser' has been chosen. Similarly, for the sake of simplicity and concision, the organiser is referred to as he, although we fully appreciate that women as much as men may and indeed do run wild bird hospitals.

It is against this background that this book has been produced. Its aim is to help not only veterinary surgeons and others involved professionally, but also members of the public who may find themselves in need of advice. The latter often have only a limited scientific knowledge and with this in mind the text of the book has been kept relatively simple. However, care has been taken to ensure that it is accurate. Where scientific terms are used, they are either explained in detail or the more common layman's wording is inserted in brackets. The Appendices cover, among other things, drugs and their dosages and the scientific names of species mentioned in the text. The scientific names of British birds are not given; they are available in any standard ornithological book.

A number of authors have contributed to this book and, inevitably, there is a certain amount of overlap. In a few instances there may be divergence of opinion upon methods of treatment; the Editors apologise for this but they have felt it wiser to allow authors to express their own views and not to vet the individual scripts too closely. In this context it must be remembered that opinions on treatment vary considerably; in the field of oiled seabirds, for example, there are probably as many recommended treatments as there are people who tend birds. Each has its own devotees who, usually as a result of much investigation and experience, have found a particular method to be most satisfactory. This is not to say that other techniques are not recommended or are inapplicable; it must be remembered that the success of a particular treatment depends to a large extent upon such factors as the condition of the bird and the ability of the person carrying out the treatment.

This book does not cover every aspect of the treatment of wild birds. There are, inevitably, omissions and more emphasis on certain topics than others. This partly reflects the authors' own interests and expertise but is also attributable to the Editors' concern that the book should include those aspects of wild bird care less adequately covered elsewhere. Each author has contributed to his chapter a list of references and recommended reading. Books can usually be borrowed through any public library; scientific journals, on the other hand, may have to be obtained through a university library or one associated with a scientific institution.

This book has been produced with the assistance of the Wild Bird Hospital Society, a charitable organisation concerned with the co-ordination of work with wild birds throughout the United Kingdom. The Wild Bird Hospital Society and other organisations are approached for advice daily and it was largely as a result of this demand for information that this book was launched. As was outlined earlier, such important work has constantly been hampered by a dearth of literature on the subject of wild birds and their treatment. It is our hope that this book will go some way towards meeting such a need.

2 Wild bird hospitals and the law

Margaret E. Cooper

INTRODUCTION

Everyone involved in the work of a bird hospital is aware of the value of these hospitals, the demands on their organisers' time and resources and the responsibilities involved. One of these duties is to ensure that the hospital operates within the bounds of the law. There are no regulations laid down specifically to cover bird hospitals (as there are for veterinary or human hospitals), although a surprisingly wide variety of laws may affect their work.

Every effort has been made to apply general principles of law to the very varied size and scope of activities of wild bird hospitals, not to mention the interests of any other individual or organisation who may refer to this chapter. Much of the legislation discussed relates to the much broader category of 'animals' and the references to animals should be taken to include birds. Occasionally, the law distinguishes between domestic animals (for example, poultry) and wild animals; this chapter deals only with the latter.

Organisers of wild bird hospitals may find the ensuing selection of legal points useful. It is not possible to give the law covering every contingency nor to give every detail of the legal topics mentioned. This chapter is intended merely as a guide and anyone with a specific problem should consult a solicitor, a citizens' advice bureau or local authority. The law discussed is that applied in England and Wales at the time of writing; Scottish law may differ considerably.

Much of the law discussed in this chapter is to be found in Acts of Parliament and the statutory instruments (often called orders or regulations) made under the authority of an Act. Legislation which is enforced in a court by punishment such as a fine or imprisonment is known as criminal law. Other principles have been developed in the courts which enable a person who can prove that he has suffered some loss or injury by the infringement of certain rights to make a claim for damages from the person who caused the loss or injury; alternatively he may ask the court for an injunction ordering the infringement to cease. These laws comprise the civil law, much of which has been incorporated in Acts of Parliament such as the Occupiers' Liability Act 1957 and the Animals Act 1971.

CRIMINAL LAW

Some of the legislation, enforced as criminal law, which can affect wild bird hospitals, follows.

Protection of Birds Acts 1954–1967
These Acts of Parliament give protection to all wild birds, their eggs and their nests, subject to a number of exceptions for certain types of bird or in certain circumstances.

The provisions of this legislation are complicated and for detailed information reference should be made to the Acts or to the booklet, issued by the Royal Society for the Protection of Birds, called 'Wild Birds and the Law'.

The main provisions relevant to bird hospitals are as follows:
It is an offence:

1 deliberately to kill, injure or take any wild bird (or to attempt to do so);
2 deliberately to take, damage or destroy the egg of a wild bird or its nest while in use;
3 deliberately to disturb any nesting wild bird listed in the First Schedule (that is the more rare birds) although the Nature Conservancy Council can give permission for photography;
4 to ring or mark a wild bird without a licence;
5 to possess or have under one's control a wild bird recently killed or taken which cannot be proved to have been killed or taken legally. Thus a bird hospital accepting a wild bird for care should enquire about the circumstances of its capture and should obtain from the person handing over the bird a signed and dated statement that the bird was obtained legally; and
6 to sell certain live birds, dead birds, plumage and eggs.

The main exceptions to these provisions are:

1 specified educational, scientific, avicultural, sporting and pest control purposes, when permitted under licence.
2 It is of particular relevance to wild bird hospitals that it is *not* illegal to kill a sick or injured wild bird which is beyond reasonable hope of recovery (unless one caused the harm in the first place); likewise it is not illegal to take a sick or injured bird (unless one caused the harm) and to keep it in order to care for it. However, a wild bird must be released at the first suitable opportunity after its recovery from injury or illness.

It is justifiable to keep a permanently disabled bird and it is, of

16

course, a matter of experience, personal judgement and veterinary opinion whether a bird is fit for successful release. However, the use of a hospital to enable the organiser to build up a collection of wild birds once they have recovered would be illegal.

The Acts also require that a bird in captivity be kept in a cage or other receptacle in which it can stretch its wings freely, except when undergoing transport, being shown (for a maximum of 72 hours) or being treated by a veterinary surgeon.

The Schedules to the 1954 Act (which are amended from time to time) specify the extent of the protection afforded to various species of wild bird. Any species not mentioned in the First, Second and Third Schedules is protected all the year round. The Fourth Schedule lists the species which may not be sold alive unless they have been bred in captivity and close-ringed. The Schedules are liable to amendment from time to time and up to date information may be obtained from the RSPB.

The EEC is considering a directive as to the protection of wild birds. Although it is likely to be generally consistent with English law, it may, when issued, require a few changes to the Protection of Birds Acts.

Endangered Species (Import and Export) Act 1976
The import and export of certain species of bird is controlled by the Department of the Environment in conformity with the international standards set out in the 1973 Washington Convention on Trade in Endangered Species of Wild Fauna and Flora. Species requiring import or export licences include birds of prey, pigeons and most other orders.

Importation of Captive Birds Order 1976
This order deals with the import of captive birds and has the following effect :
1 all imports of captive birds and hatching eggs into Great Britain must be licensed by the Ministry of Agriculture;
2 on arrival in this country the birds are subject to a quarantine period of 35 days in approved premises under the supervision of the state veterinary service;
3 quarantine is replaced by rather less formal isolation requirements in the cases of : a) up to two caged pet birds accompanying a person entering the country on change of residence (customs officers may also waive the requirement of a licence in this case); and of b) imports of up to 12 birds from approved countries;
4 racing pigeons imported for release in the UK are subject to special regulations.

17

Protection of Animals Acts 1911–1964
These Acts make cruelty to animals (including tame or captive birds) a criminal offence and define cruelty as anything which causes an animal unnecessary suffering. This includes suffering caused by directly harmful acts, negligent omission, experiments not permitted by the Cruelty to Animals Act 1876, the manner of killing animals and any operation performed without due care and humanity. It is also an offence for the owner of an animal to permit someone else to cause unnecessary suffering to it or to fail to exercise reasonable care and supervision in protecting it from cruelty.

A bird hospital organiser may be asked to admit a bird which has been treated cruelly; he should report the matter to the police or one of the humane societies such as the RSPB or the RSPCA who may then take up the case if they consider that an offence has been committed.

The Abandonment of Animals Act 1960
It is an offence to abandon an animal, either temporarily or permanently, without reasonable cause, so that it is likely to undergo unnecessary suffering. The indiscriminate release of wild bird casualties without careful consideration of their chances of survival in the wild could amount to such an offence. When planning to release a bird it is necessary to balance the requirement of this Act with that of the Protection of Birds Act 1954, that a casualty should be released as soon as it has recovered from illness or injury. Within the context of the 1960 Act a genuine decision to release a bird would be a reasonable cause for abandoning it and, of course, a release should be conducted in a way designed to prevent or minimise any suffering to the bird.

The Protection of Animals (Anaesthetics) Acts 1954 and 1964
These Acts apply to operations on animals which interfere with sensitive tissues or bone structures. It provides that where any such operation is carried out without the use of an anaesthetic which is adequate to prevent pain to the animal it is presumed that the operation was performed without due care and humanity and is therefore punishable under the Protection of Animals Act 1911.

The 1954 Act excludes birds from the definition of 'animal,' but the Act is mentioned in order to prevent anyone making the assumption that it exempts them entirely from using anaesthetics in bird operations. Since the 1954 Act there has been a significant increase in availability and use of suitable drugs for operations on birds. Therefore, performing a major operation involving the soft tissues or bone structure of a bird

18

a wild bird hospital cage would be theft. Further, once a wild bird has escaped from captivity and can no longer be identified as someone's property, it is not theft for another person to take possession of it.

It is also an offence under this Act to advertise a reward for the return of a lost or stolen animal implying that no questions will be asked or that no prosecution will be made or that the purchase price will be reimbursed.

Criminal Damage Act 1971

It is an offence recklessly or intentionally to kill or injure any animal, including a tamed or captive wild bird, belonging to another person, without lawful excuse such as the protection of property, self-defence or consent of the owner.

Public Service Vehicles, Conduct of Drivers, Conductors and Passengers, Regulations 1936 (as amended)

One may not take an animal into a bus without the consent of the bus conductor or driver or place it anywhere other than where one is told to put it. Clearly most bus conductors and animal owners are reasonable about taking animals on buses but it is as well to know that the conductor has the final word on whether and how an animal travels on his bus. There are similar provisions affecting other modes of public transport.

CIVIL LAW

In many circumstances an owner of birds or someone else having them in his possession or control may become liable under the civil law for damage, injury or loss caused to another person or his property as a result of keeping birds. Conversely, a wild bird hospital organiser may have a claim in respect of harm caused to himself, his birds or hospital facilities.

The main remedies for a breach of the civil law are damages (financial compensation) and an injunction (a court order to stop wrongful activity). There are certain defences to a claim in civil law; for example, there is no liability for an unpredictable accident; nor where the person suffering loss had voluntarily taken the risk of that loss; nor where he is the sole cause of the loss; and where the loss was partly due to his fault he is only entitled to a proportionate amount of the compensation which he would otherwise receive.

Animals Act 1971

This Act deals with the liability of people looking after animals, including birds, for injury, loss or damage caused by those animals.

The Act puts responsibility for an animal upon its 'keeper'. This is the person who has it in his possession or control whether or not he be the owner of the animal. Where the keeper is under 16 years old the head of his household is also responsible. For the purpose of this Act the keeper remains responsible even after the animal has escaped or been abandoned until someone else becomes its keeper.

The degree of liability under this Act for damage done by an animal is much stricter than that for negligence or trespass (see below). It classifies animals as belonging to either a 'dangerous species' or a 'non-dangerous species'. It makes the keeper of a dangerous species responsible for any damage to person or property which it may cause, even when the keeper has done everything possible, including caging or other restraint, to avoid such damage or even if he has no knowledge or intention of its occurrence. In the case of a non-dangerous species this stricter liability of the keeper arises only where either (a) the damage is of a kind likely to be caused unless the animal is restrained, or, (b) the damage is a kind which is not likely to be caused, but which would, if it were actually caused, be severe. In both cases the damage must also be due to the animal's abnormal characteristics of which the keeper has prior knowledge. Where these criteria do not apply, a claim involving a non-dangerous species will have to be based on one of the other principles of common law discussed later.

A dangerous species is defined as one not commonly domesticated in the British Isles and whose adult form is likely, because of normal characteristics, to cause severe damage unless it is restrained. Any species not falling within this definition is classified as non-dangerous. In some cases (for example, lions) it is easy to recognise a 'dangerous species' but there is little authority as to how birds are to be classified. Therefore a wild bird hospital organiser should 'play safe' and take special care to prevent damage by birds which might be considered to belong to a dangerous species, such as swans or large birds of prey; likewise the keeper of non-dangerous species of birds, which to his knowledge have abnormal characteristics, such as aggressive poultry, will be liable for any damage done by them.

There is no liability for damage done by an animal to a trespasser, except where the animal is kept to guard premises without good reason. Thus, where a trespasser at a wild bird hospital is injured by one of the birds, the hospital organiser is not liable; nor is the organiser responsible if a trespasser is hurt by a guard dog kept to protect the hospital premises in reasonable circumstances. However, it may not be considered reasonable if an exceptionally fierce dog or some more unusual creature, such as a lion, poisonous snake, or golden eagle is used to guard the premises and in such cases a trespasser would be able to claim damages for injury caused by these unusual guards (unless perhaps there was some conspicuous notice warning of their presence and seen by the trespasser who could then be said to have voluntarily risked injury).

Negligence

Negligence, in this case, is the failure to exercise the care which is the duty owed by every citizen to those whom he can reasonably foresee might be affected by his actions or omissions. He has the duty to take the care which a reasonable person would take so that such people are not harmed and he will be liable for any damage or loss he causes which he should reasonably have foreseen. Consequently, a wild bird hospital organiser must take reasonable care for the safety of people and property either on the hospital premises or affected by the hospital's activities. Conversely, an organiser has a right to sue for compensation, injury or loss which he suffers as a result of someone else's negligence.

The protection formerly provided by notices and disclaimers excluding liability for injury or damage has been severely restricted by the Unfair Contract Terms Act 1977. It is no longer possible to exclude or restrict responsibility for death or personal injury caused by negligence and one can only limit liability for damage to property in so far as it is reasonable to do so.

It is still advisable to warn people of the presence of, for example, dangerous birds at a hospital by way of notices and, indeed, it could be negligent not to do this. However, an organiser could not rely on such a notice to absolve him from liability for harm caused by the animals.

Occupiers' Liability Act 1957

The Act provides that an occupier (whether or not he is also the owner) of premises owes a duty to all lawful 'visitors' to ensure that they will be reasonably safe when using the premises for the purpose for which they have been invited or permitted to be there. The Act applies to the state of land, buildings and structures; thus an injury caused by an insecurely built aviary or inadequate lighting would entitle the injured person to claim compensation. The term 'visitor' includes not only those specifically invited or permitted to enter the premises, but also those with a statutory right of entry, such as firemen putting out a fire and those with implied permission such as tradesmen or unexpected guests; naturally, it does not include a trespasser.

The occupier must be prepared for children to be more vulnerable than adults and to take care that anything particularly attractive to them, such as a deep hole or mound of building materials, cannot cause them harm even if they are trespassers.

The risk of liability can no longer be substantially reduced by the use of warning notices or of verbal or written agreements, as mentioned earlier.

Nuisance

There are two forms of nuisance, public and private. The former, often created by statute, such as the Public Health Acts, arises from some act which interferes with the life and comfort of some section of the general public. A public nuisance is punishable as a crime. However, if a private individual can show that he personally has suffered additional damage, he can sue in civil law for damages.

A private nuisance occurs when there is an unreasonable interference with an individual's use of his land – including his house and his general way of life. What comprises a nuisance is a matter of degree. In the case of a wild bird hospital someone might complain that the number of birds, their noise, smell or proximity to the person complaining amounted to a nuisance, bearing in mind the type of neighbourhood in which the hospital was situated. The converse can also apply – should someone set up an activity which materially interferes with the running of a wild bird hospital, it could amount to a nuisance.

In addition to seeking the usual remedies in civil law, the person suffering the private nuisance may personally take steps to 'abate' (stop or reduce) the nuisance. This last approach is inadvisable, certainly without taking prior legal advice.

The rule in Rylands v Fletcher

The principle of this rule is that the occupier of land who brings and keeps an animal on his property thus making unusual use of his land is responsible for any damage caused if the animal were to escape. Thus an urban wild bird hospital caring for a heron or raven may be liable for any damage which either bird caused if it escaped from the hospital premises.

However, in addition to the usual defences, there will be no liability if a bird escapes because of an Act of God, such as an exceptional storm, or because of the act of a third party.

24

Trespass to land

A trespasser is one who enters another's land or premises without his permission or lawful right. The latter is entitled to sue for damages for the mere act of trespass although he will only obtain nominal compensation (of, say, 5p) unless the trespasser caused actual damage which can be assessed in financial terms. A landowner may use reasonable force to remove a trespasser who refuses to leave on request.

Not only people but also animals are capable of trespassing and the owner or person in charge of captive wild birds is liable for the damage naturally arising from their trespass, whether or not it was intentional on his part. This liability lasts only while the bird is in captivity or, if not kept confined, while it shows an intention to return to its owner. For example, if a convalescing wild bird damages neighbouring farm crops or garden vegetables, the wild bird hospital organiser is liable for the damage done. He is also responsible for damage done by birds released after recovery from sickness or injury if they habitually return to the hospital for food. However, an organiser is not liable for the trespass of a bird which has become independent of his hospital after its release or escape.

A wild bird hospital may suffer trespass by man or animal but it should be noted that no one can be liable for the trespass of a cat. If a cat gets into a hospital and kills birds, the organiser cannot claim against the cat's owner for the trespass or any damage done. In the case of dogs, an owner who deliberately sends his dog into a wild bird hospital to harm the birds, or who allows a dog which he knows to have a penchant for birds to roam would be liable for the resultant damage; but he is not liable where the trespass occurs without his knowledge or any intention on his part. Trespass by any other domestic or captive wild animal is actionable whether or not the owner intended it to trespass.

MISCELLANEOUS LEGISLATION

Ownership of wild birds

In matters of ownership the law distinguishes between wild and domestic animals. The owner of the latter (the conventional farm and pet species) has the same rights and duties of ownership over them as he has over other goods which he owns. Likewise, a person has full ownership of wild animals while he holds them in captivity or while they show an intention to return to him, (for example, where doves are kept in a dove-cote or where former patients of a wild bird hospital are being helped to return gradually to the wild).

25

Once a captive wild bird has escaped permanently or has ceased to return to its owner, the latter's rights of ownership terminate and the bird may subsequently be acquired by someone else. However, the precise moment when ownership ceases is difficult to determine and the finder of a wild bird showing signs of ownership such as pinioning, close-ringing or leather jesses should make extensive enquiries for its prior owner and be very cautious about assuming that he is now the rightful owner. The question of theft, which has been discussed earlier, should be borne in mind in such cases. Subject to the Protection of Birds Acts, this would not, however, prevent him from caring for the bird until the owner was found.

Public health
When constructing aviaries (see Chapter 20) an organiser should check with his local authority that the design of his aviaries and the number of birds are not likely to lead to a health risk in the area. Smell, rubbish, disease and the attraction of vermin are potential risks to health. When the state of any premises, the place or manner of keeping any animal or the accumulation of rubbish is prejudicial to health or an interference with the normal comfort of people, a statutory nuisance (see p 24) exists. A local authority is required by the public health legislation to give notice to the person causing the nuisance to abate it and if he fails to do so, the local authority can obtain a court order requiring him to comply with the notice. Noise amounting to a nuisance can be similarly dealt with under the Control of Pollution Act 1974.

Local authorities have the power to make by-laws to prevent one keeping animals where this would be prejudicial to health; an organiser should make enquiries as to the existence and effect of these by-laws in his area.

Building regulations
Again, when planning aviaries, an organiser should consult his local authority as to the Building Regulations and ensure that his aviaries are constructed in compliance with them. Aviaries intended for private use on a moderate scale may be exempt from building control but this is unlikely to apply where a substantial hospital or major extensions are proposed.

Planning permission
This normally has to be obtained, in addition to building consent, before constructing a new building or altering the exterior of an existing

building. It is also required for a change in use, for example, from domestic to business use, even if there is no physical alteration to the premises. There are, however, a number of exemptions for minor building operations, one of which is of particular relevance to those keeping birds. To be found in the Town and Country Planning General Development Order 1977, this permits buildings of strictly limited size to be erected within the 'curtilage' (that is, usually, the garden) of a dwelling-house for a purpose incidental to the use of the house, including the keeping of birds, 'for the domestic needs or personal enjoyment of the occupants of the dwelling house'. However, any prospective builder of an aviary should enquire of the local planning authority whether he is within this exemption. Clearly someone establishing an extensive bird hospital would be outside the exemption whereas a single aviary for housing sick and injured birds kept for recuperation and personal enjoyment without charging fees might well be within it. A local planning authority also has power to restrict the operation of this exemption – another reason for making enquiries before starting to build since the ultimate sanction for a building erected in breach of planning legislation is an enforcement order requiring demolition of the building.

Restrictive covenants
The title deeds to a property should be examined to ensure that they do not include restrictions on keeping birds. In the case of older properties such restrictions may have ceased to be enforceable or it may be possible to have them discharged or modified. It is necessary to take legal advice on such matters. A tenant of rented property should also obtain his landlord's written consent to the building of aviaries before the work is commenced.

Employment
If a bird hospital organiser employs staff he must make the usual arrangements to deal with income tax and national insurance contributions. He should also be aware of matters such as the duty to notify staff of their terms of employment and of legislation relating to unfair dismissal, redundancy and equal pay. Under the race and sex discrimination laws it is an offence to discriminate against a person solely on the grounds of their race or sex in employment and certain other matters. Free information and leaflets on these subjects can be obtained from local employment offices of the Employment Service Agency.

Health and Safety at Work etc Act 1974
This Act applies to all people at work except domestic servants in a private household. It imposes a general duty upon an employer to ensure as far as is reasonably practicable, the health, safety and welfare of all his employees. A like duty is also owed to the general public and by employees towards their employers and co-workers. Thus an organiser should ensure that his bird hospital is run so as to avoid risks to the health and safety of himself, any employee, voluntary helper, visitors to the hospital and the general public.

CHARITABLE STATUS

A wild bird hospital not conducted for profit can be registered as a charity with the Charity Commissioners who will give advice upon its constitution prior to acceptance for registration.

Registration is not essential but has the advantage that it is conclusive evidence of the organisation's charitable status, which attracts the following benefits:

1 Exemption from income tax and corporation tax.
2 Reduction of rates: the General Rating Act of 1967 reduces rates by 50 per cent on premises wholly or mainly either used for charitable purposes or occupied by a charity, and the local rating authority has a discretionary power further to reduce rates on such property.
3 Value Added Tax: charities providing only free services are neither required nor allowed to register with HM Customs and Excise for Value Added Tax purposes. Where a charity charges for goods or services it must be registered; however, if its turnover is less than £10,000 per annum, it is entitled to exemption as a small trader.
4 Capital Transfer Tax: gifts to charities made a year or more before the donor's death are not subject to this tax; those made in a will or during the last year of a person's life are free of this tax unless the gift exceeds £100,000.
5 Capital Gains Tax: gifts to a charity are exempt from this tax, as are gains made on the disposal of an asset by a charity, providing the proceeds are applied to charitable purposes.

Anyone wishing to make a bequest to a bird charity will find a selection advertised in The Law Society's Gazette Charity and Appeals Supplement which is issued annually at Christmas. The chosen charity, either in their advertisement or on request, will supply a form of wording to be included in the will. A typical form is :

I hereby bequeath the sum of .... pounds (£...........p) free of duty to the (name and address of charity) for the general purposes of that charity and I direct that the receipt of the treasurer or secretary shall be a good discharge for such legacy.

Any taxpayer who wishes to make regular donations to a charity can benefit it greatly by making annual payments for a minimum of seven years by way of a deed of covenant. The donor makes payments out of his taxed income and the recipient charity, being exempt from paying income tax, is able to claim the tax originally paid by the donor.

A typical deed of covenant is as follows :

DEED OF COVENANT

I, ... (Full name)

of .... (Block capitals please)

Hereby covenant with the (name and address of charity), that for a period of seven years from this date, or during my lifetime, whichever period shall be the shorter, I will pay annually to the said (charity) the sum of .... net (£...............p) such sum to be paid from my general fund of taxed income.

Signed, sealed and delivered by ....

Date ....

Witnessed by :

   Signature of witness ....

   Address ....

   ....

Occupation of witness ....

Both the form of bequest and the deed of covenant are provided as examples only. The requirements of the law and of individual charities can vary and an intending donor should ask a charity for its preferred form before making his gift.

INSURANCE

Anyone organising a bird hospital should consider the advantages of taking out insurance, particularly against the possibility of personal injury, fire, theft, damage by or to the birds and civil liability to other people as a result of his or his employees' act. (An employer is, in certain circumstances, liable for the acts of his employee committed during the course of his employment.) Insurance against third party liability should be regarded as essential in view of the high amounts of damages sometimes awarded in such cases and the heavy cost of defending even an unsuccessful claim.

CONCLUSION

This chapter has covered the aspects of the law most likely to touch upon the life of wild bird hospitals. However, it cannot be over-emphasised that the subject matter has been treated very generally and that anyone with a particular query should seek advice on the specific aspects of their problem.

It is hoped that this chapter, besides being a starting point of reference for those with a legal problem involving wild birds, will also prove of general interest and value to those concerned with wild bird hospitals or, indeed, to anyone keeping birds.

3 Bird structure and function
R. E. Kenward

For a full understanding of disease diagnosis and treatment it is important to have some knowledge of anatomy and physiology. In this chapter, which is intended primarily for the layman, the basic features of avian structure and function are described. Readers may find it useful to refer to this section when anatomical or physiological terminology is used in subsequent chapters.

EXTERNAL FEATURES AND THEIR FUNCTIONS

The first birds appeared about 225 million years ago, and apparently evolved from small agile reptiles which already walked mainly on their hind-limbs and perhaps spent much of their time in the trees. The skeleton of the earliest known fossil bird, *Archaeopteryx*, contains teeth and a long bony tail, similar to that of the extinct reptile *Pseudosuchus*. The scales which cover reptiles had evolved into feathers covering much of the body of *Archaeopteryx*, forming fringes to turn the fore-limbs into wings and the tail into a steering paddle. The evolution of feathers must have been the single most important step in bird evolution.

Plumage
Feathers are composed mainly of keratin, a protein which is formed by the epidermis (outer layer) of the skin, as indeed are beaks, claws and leg scales. The keratin, which is produced by living cells, is itself dead, so damage to feathers, or the outer parts of a bird's beak and claws, causes no pain (see Chapter 14). Mammals, which evolved by a slightly different route from reptiles, also have a layer of keratin on the surface of their skin and special elements formed from this such as hair and nails. The smell of burning keratin, which probably owes much to its high sulphur content, is a feature of both scorched hair and scorched feathers.

The immediate obvious outer covering of adult birds is composed of contour feathers. These have a central shaft, hollow nearest the bird's body, to which are attached, at an angle, a large number of narrow elements, the barbs. Barbules (secondary processes) are found on either side of the barbs. Those barbules pointing towards the tip of the feathers

31

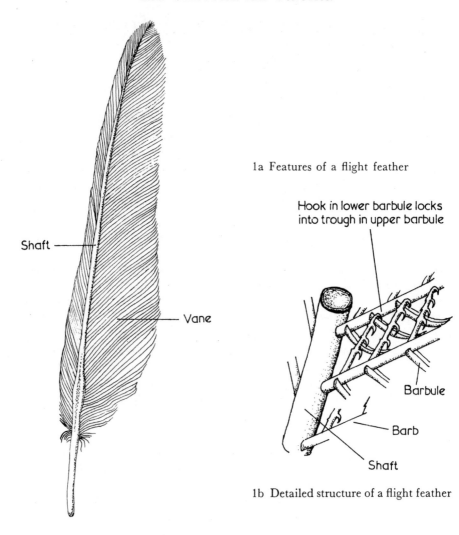

1a Features of a flight feather

Hook in lower barbule locks
into trough in upper barbule

Shaft

Vane

Barbule

Barb

Shaft

1b Detailed structure of a flight feather

have small hooks which engage ridges on the posterior barbules of the next barb towards the tip. This system acts rather like a fastener to hold adjacent barbs together into the vane (sheet) on either side of the shaft (see Fig 1a and b).

Down feathers differ from contour feathers in that their barbs are soft, and lack the fastening hooks-and-ridges (see Fig 1c). Filoplumes – the 'hair' that is singed off a bird after plucking – are little more than a fine shaft with a few vanes near the tip (see Fig 1d). The vibrissae,

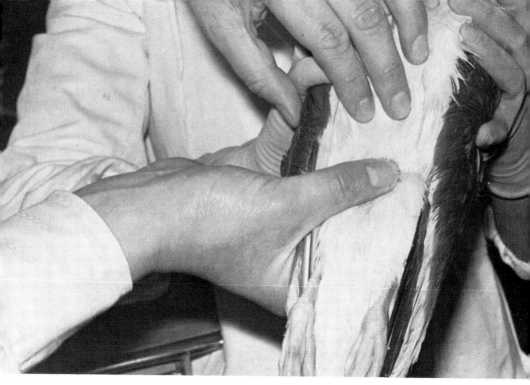

Plate 1
While one person holds an injured gull the veterinary surgeon carefully examines its body and gently palpates its abdomen

Plate 2
A wagtail is held in the hand while each limb in turn is examined for evidence of fractures

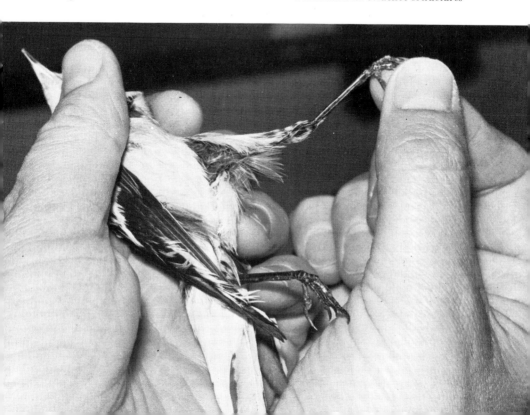

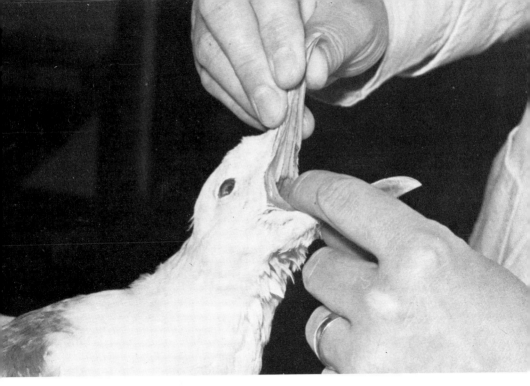

Plate 3
Force-feeding a gull: the bird's beak is held open while a piece of food is pushed over the tongue and into the oesophagus with one finger

Plate 4
Bacilli (rod-shaped bacteria) from a foot infection in a bird; the organisms have been stained and are highly magnified

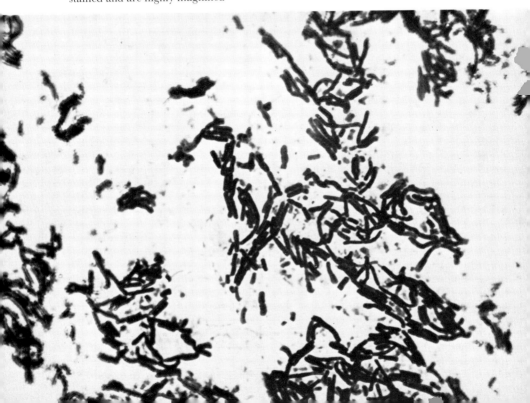

which are hair-like and are found around the nostrils and mouth of some birds, are much stiffer than filoplumes and probably have a sensory function.

The large contour feathers growing from the posterior edge of the wing are known as primaries if they originate on the final joint, and secondaries if they originate nearer the body. Passerine birds typically have nine primary feathers, grebes eleven, and most other birds ten. The number of secondaries varies with the shape of the wing : gulls have more than pheasants. Most birds have ten or twelve main tail feathers, which originate on the short, stubby, pygidium or 'parson's nose' (all that remains of the long reptilian tail). The smaller contour feathers grow in well-defined tracts which can best be seen on a plucked bird.

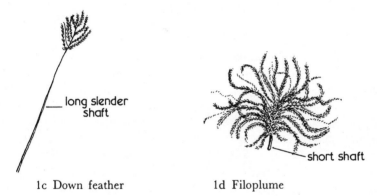

1c Down feather   1d Filoplume

Like hair, feathers are formed by cells at the base of a deep indentation of the epithelium. The formative region is circular, the shaft and barbs growing out from this as a tube which unfurls as it breaks free of its protective outer sheath. If the animal's metabolism is disturbed during feather growth, perhaps by nervous stress or shortage of nutrients, a discontinuity occurs in the formation of the shaft and each vane at that point (see Fig 2). This discontinuity may show as a line of weakness across the shaft and vanes, best called a fault bar, but also sometimes termed a fret mark or hunger trace. Sometimes the whole feather may 'pinch out' at this point (see Chapter 14). Fault bars are especially frequent in feathers grown in the nest, in which case they may occur at the same level across all the main retrices (tail feathers), a characteristic sometimes used to age birds whose first-year plumage differs little from that of later years. This condition can give rise to potentially handicapping feather breakage, a point to remember when subjecting nestlings or moulting birds to unusual conditions.

35

2 A feather showing a fault bar

Feathers are, of course, subject to wear and tear, and need to be replaced at intervals by moulting, in which case the start of new growth in the feather follicle causes the old one to drop out. New feathers will also usually grow if feathers are pulled out, or a growing feather 'pinches out'. Most birds moult their flight feathers once a year, although some larger species may take several years to complete each moult. A single moult may involve a short period of flightlessness, during which time all the main feathers grow at once (for example, in the case of ducks); birds which at all times depend on flight for their survival, have a longer period in which the primaries moult sequentially towards the wing tip and the secondaries towards the body. Birds eat more when they are moulting and the moult usually coincides with a period of high food availability.

Scales, claws and beaks
The scales found on the legs and feet of many birds are formed in the same way as those on the surface of a reptile, from the growth layer of epidermal cells beneath. Patches of the upper layer sometimes peel off, in much the same way that a reptile sheds its 'skin'. The scales are usually pigmented and may darken or even change colour completely with age. A decrease in colour, whereby the scales become translucent, and sometimes flaky, can be indicative of nutritional deficiency, specifically of certain carotenes which give rise to both vitamin A and yellow/red pigments. Feeding egg yolk or day-old hatchery chicks to birds of prey with abnormally pale legs, ceres (see p 37) and irides results in a gradual increase in the pigmentation of these parts. Some birds have replaced these scales by feathers and species which frequently walk on

ice and snow (for example, ptarmigan and snowy owl) even have feathered toes: this may aid heat conservation, camouflage, or grip on soft and slippery surfaces.

Claws are, in effect, modified scales which are grown by a very active layer of epithelium at their base. They are usually replaced after loss, although damage to the germinal epithelium may result in distortion of the new claw. In some grouse species they are even moulted. The upper portion may be grown slightly faster than the lower, causing the claw to curve downward as it grows, and differences in wear may produce the very short points of raptor talons. In captivity, lack of wear may mean that claws need to be trimmed, but birds that are dependent on their claws for survival should not be released with these badly blunted.

Beaks are formed in a similar fashion to claws, the keratin overlying and projecting beyond the maxillary (upper) and mandibular (lower) jaw bones. In some birds there is a well defined region, the cere, from which grows the base of the maxillary beak, and faster growth at the top of this region may result in the down-curve characteristic of parrots and birds of prey. In other birds the core of bone extends almost to the tip, and beak growth probably occurs outwards from this all the way along. The relationship of beak and scale formation is shown clearly in the puffin, whose coloured plates peel off from the beak sides at the end of the breeding season. Bird beaks are wonderfully adapted to their function: witness the short fine beaks of the insect-eating warblers, the more massive beaks of seed-eaters, the hooked tearing beaks of predators and the long probing beaks of waders (see Fig 4).

Other surface structures

The eyes, ears and other sense organs, although visible on the surface, will be considered in the section on the nervous system. It is, however, appropriate to mention the preen gland, the opening of which occurs on the upper surface of the pygidium. In preening, birds may be seen using their beaks to wipe the oily secretion from this gland over their feathers. The secretion assists in waterproofing the plumage so, hardly surprisingly, the gland is especially well developed in waterbirds.

Flight

The evolution of feathers gave birds the ability to form the large and yet strong light surfaces necessary for powered flight. During forward flight it is the downstroke of the wing that provides lift, while both the up and down strokes produce thrust along the axis of the body. Thrust during the downstroke is produced almost entirely by twisting the leading

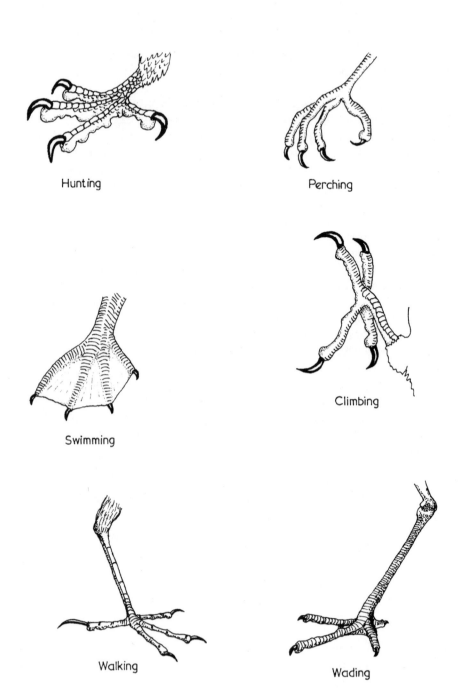

Hunting

Perching

Swimming

Climbing

Walking

Wading

3 Examples of feet showing how the structure is related to the bird's habitat and behaviour

edge of the wing below its trailing edge, so that some air is deflected backwards off the lower surface of the wing (see Fig 5a and b). During the downstroke the primary feathers are locked into a flat plane because the broad posterior vane, which is pushed upwards relative to the narrow anterior vane by the higher air pressure on its greater surface, overlaps below the anterior edge of the following feather. During the upstroke some thrust is obtained because the wing is tilted considerably, with the leading edge above the trailing edge, so that little 'negative lift' is generated but some air is deflected backwards off the upper surface, and also because of the backward deflection of air passing between the individual primary feathers.

As well as providing large surface areas for flight, contour feathers are also important in shaping a bird for flight. A bird's wing in cross-section has the convex upper surface and concave lower one, with tapering section towards the rear, which man uses for the wings of gliders to give high lift at low speeds. In other words, birds' wings are shaped for gliding flight too.

For balanced flight and maximum manoeuvrability a bird's body needs to be very short and compact, with no weighty extensions (imagine how much harder it is to turn a corner carrying a long plank than holding the same wood as neatly stacked one-metre lengths); hence the loss of that heavy reptilian tail and its replacement by a bunch of low-weight feathers, as well as shortening of the trunk. However, on the same principle, the long narrow (high aspect ratio) wings of some sea birds, which the flight surfaces of high performance gliders so resemble, have most of their weight towards the wing base, the outer ends being feather. Short compact objects create a lot of drag when moving at speed : feathers help overcome this by streamlining the body.

Primaries of many soaring birds have a narrow portion towards the tip, and they separate when the wing is spread. This slotting probably helps to smooth the air flow past the wing and further reduce drag. The bunch of feathers on the first digit, the alula or bastard wing, has a similar function, opening to smooth air flowing over the upper wing surface when low speed manoeuvres or sharp turns would create turbulence and stalling or loss of control.

The tail is used mainly for steering, although it may in addition provide some lift. Birds also steer by varying the depth of stroke and pitch of each wing.

Powerful beak for
tearing flesh

Long bill for catching fish
and frogs

Seed-eater

Bill designed for
'sieving'water

Insect-eater

Probing beak for finding small
molluscs and worms

4 The beak, like the feet, shows adaptations, depending on the type of food
eaten. Careful observation of such anatomical features may, in the absence of
a definite identification, help in the choice of diet for a captive bird

Heat conservation

Feathers give birds the efficient insulating layer which is needed by homeotherms (animals which keep their internal temperature above that of the surroundings). Poikilotherms (cold-blooded animals), such as reptiles, become sluggish at low temperatures, as all the chemical reactions which go to make up their metabolism slow down.

The layer of insulating air trapped between the feather surface and the skin allows birds to remain active and alert at times of day and in climatic extremes which would render reptiles unable to feed or hopelessly prone to predation. In cold conditions birds fluff out their feathers to increase the depth of this insulating layer and cover thinly feathered regions as much as possible. One leg may be drawn up into the body feathers, and the head tucked under a wing. The wing itself covers a more sparsely feathered region of the body and there are comparatively few feathers covering the skin on the lower surface of the wing itself. These sparsely feathered regions of the body are exposed in flight and probably help the bird lose some of the excess heat generated by the operating flight muscles. Feathers are also lost from regions of the breast during the breeding season, and the blood supply to the skin at these 'brood patches' is increased to assist in the transfer of heat to eggs and young chicks. Heat may be lost also by allowing more blood to reach areas of body surface bearing few, if any, feathers. The scaly legs and feet of a resting bird are normally cool but may become quite warm after flight or when illness has raised the bird's internal temperature.

When the bird's internal temperature is too high (for example, during an infection), feathers may be erected beyond the point at which insulating air is trapped, so that heat is lost directly from the skin, which is like a mammal's in structure but rather more delicate and containing no sweat glands. The withdrawal of heat from the body through the

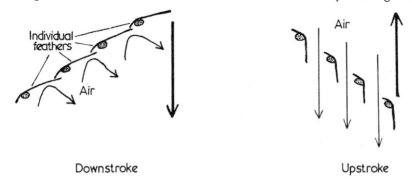

Downstroke   Upstroke

5a and b Action of the feathers during flight

41

evaporation of water is the most important source of cooling in birds, but occurs via the respiratory tract, and not the skin. Hot birds pant and lose heat through the evaporation of water across their respiratory surfaces; they can suffer from dehydration if drinking water is not available to replace this. It is, therefore, important to make water readily available to sick birds, and to replace excess fluid loss resulting from reduced respiratory control during anaesthesia.

Birds operate at higher temperatures than mammals, so that their metabolic reactions proceed at a faster rate. Body temperatures of around 41°C are usual, but exertion may raise this to as high as 44°C and a fall in temperature is often apparent at night. Environmental temperatures below the body temperature are tolerated far better than high temperatures, partly because birds find it easier to conserve heat in the cold than to lose it in hot conditions, and partly because they can tolerate a lowering of their body temperature better than a rise. Care should be taken not to overheat and dehydrate injured or sick birds by placing them in too high a temperature although, as will be mentioned later, the provision of warmth is an important part of treatment. The metabolism of birds is already running at the upper end of the temperature range conducive to life, but can be slowed down considerably. Indeed, the temperature of diurnal birds usually drops slightly at night, and the nestlings of nidicolous birds (which fledge their young in the nest) can become chilled quite markedly such that their body state resembles the cold-blooded condition of reptiles.

A small animal has more surface area relative to its volume than a large one. (Imagine cutting an apple in halves : each portion now has half the volume, but as well as half of the original skin, it also has the extra surface where the cut was made.) Since heat is generated according to volume, but lost through the surface, small birds lose more heat relative to their size than large ones, and need to eat a greater proportion of their body weight each day in order to keep up their temperature and remain alive. Very small birds may, like wrens, huddle together in old nests or holes at night, while hummingbirds give up the struggle to maintain a high body temperature and conserve their energy by chilling into a torpid state at night.

Colouration

Feathers may contain coloured pigments, or thin air spaces which produce iridescent colours in the same way that a thin film of oil does on a puddle of water. These colours may serve to camouflage the bird against its enemies or its prey, to serve as an advertisement during the breeding season and perhaps also, in the case of dark colouring on penguins and their chicks, to absorb as much of the sun's heat as possible.

THE SKELETON AND MUSCLES

The bird skeleton (see Fig 6) is like that of amphibians, reptiles and mammals. There is an axial skeleton consisting of a skull and vertebral column (backbone). Associated with the vertebral column is the appendicular skeleton, the bones of the fore- and hind-limbs. However, the whole structure has been much modified for fore-limb-powered flight.

Since the fore-limbs are modified as wings, they are not available for manipulation of food, nest materials, and so on. Apart from a few cases where food is held by the hind-limbs, and may even be transferred by these to the beak, birds rely on their mouth for food manipulation. The jaws, to the exterior portion of which the keratinous beak is attached, are hinged well back on the skull and are thus capable of a wide gape. In some birds the upper jaw, the maxilla, is attached fairly

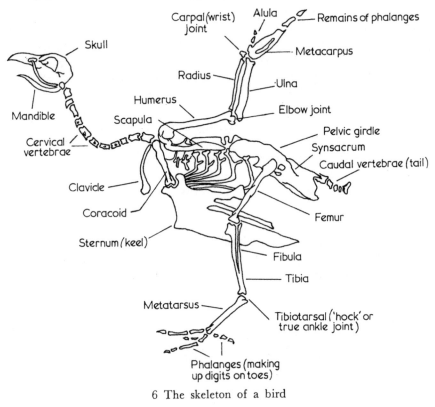

6 The skeleton of a bird

43

flexibly to the brain-case, so that its tip can be raised slightly relative to the rest of the skull. The tongue is supported by fine bones which, like the jaws, are derived from the gill arches of the first, fish-like, vertebrates. In birds such as woodpeckers, whose tongues can be greatly extended and used to extract food from crevices, the two support bones and their musculature are much enlarged and curve right round the back and top of the skull in a loop.

An animal moving rapidly forwards through its environment needs to be able to detect objects at a fair distance. For this purpose the most accurate sense is vision. The eyes of birds are much larger in proportion to the size of their heads than are those of other animals, and the bony sockets of the skull which protect them are correspondingly large, extending the whole width of the skull and separated by a very thin septum (partition) which is not always complete. The sense of smell is not of such great importance and the nasal passages connecting the external nares (nostrils – usually found at the base of the beak) to the back of the mouth are simple compared with those of many mammals. To handle the information received from the eyes and the balance centres of the inner ear, and to translate this into the appropriate movements of the complex musculature, requires a well developed brain. The brains of birds are much larger than those of reptiles, and require a large cranium to protect them. This part of the skull is behind the eye sockets, and low down, near the jaw articulations, is the aperture leading into the middle and inner ear. There are a number of perforations in the cranium through which pass the nerves from the brain, the largest of these being that for the spinal cord.

To provide the head with adequate agility it is attached to a long and flexible neck. This not only contains more vertebrae (up to 22) than that of a mammal (normally seven), but these are joined to each other and to the skull to give them greater vertical and lateral flexion. As in other vertebrates, the spinal cord passes through, and is protected by, the upper portion of each vertebra.

The chest or thorax is greatly strengthened to provide attachment for the flight muscles and to withstand the forces they exert. Most of the vertebrae in this region are usually fused together. Extending from these round the body cavity on either side are the ribs, which connect the backbone to the sternum. These have processes projecting backwards which are attached by ligaments to the rib behind for added rigidity. In birds the sternum is greatly expanded laterally, and possesses a central keel (see Fig 19b p92) which extends downwards and provides attachment for the main flight muscles. From the anterior outer edge

44

of the sternum on each side a coracoid bone passes forwards and out to a point where it meets with the scapula, a long thin bone stretching back over the ribs, and the clavicle, a bone which extends to the anterior edge of the keel where it fuses with its opposite number to form the 'wishbone'. At this point there is also a socket in the coracoid in which fits the ball-like head of the innermost end of the humerus. The humerus is thus effectively supported by a tripod of bones. A ligament from the smaller pectoralis muscle passes through the aperture where these three bones meet to the upper surface of the humerus, and acts as a pulley; contraction of this muscle raises the wing. The larger pectoralis muscle, which overlies this on the sternum, is attached to the lower side of the humerus and is responsible for the powerful downstroke. Other smaller muscles are used for fine control of flight.

The radius and ulna connect the humerus to the carpal bones which form the outer joint of the wing. The bones of the 'hand' and 'fingers' are much fused and only digits II, III and IV may be distinguished in the adult skeleton. Digit II supports the alula, digit III gives the length to the wing; digit IV is detectable as a vestige which is largely fused with III.

Since the fore-limbs are not available for supporting the animal's weight on the ground, the hind-limbs must do this. Shortening the trunk for flight has also brought the point at which these limbs support the bird's weight close to the centre of gravity, which reduces the tendency for birds to tip over frontwards. Many birds stand more erect at rest, which puts their weight even more directly over their legs. The legs are important not just for movement on the ground, but to give a push when leaving it, and to absorb the shock of landings. They are very strong and muscular, so it is not surprising that the vertebrae which support the three fused pelvic bones are themselves fused as the synsacrum. There are unfused vertebrae between the synsacrum and the fused thoracic vertebrae, which give some flexibility to the trunk; flexibility is given to the base of the tail by several more unfused vertebrae before the pygostyle which terminates the vertebral column.

The head of the femur fits deeply into its socket in the pelvis, allowing little lateral movement to a bird's leg. Below this is a composite bone which is mainly tibia, but with the remnants of the fibula more or less fused to its upper end and tarsal (ankle) elements fused at the lower end. Below this is the metatarsal bone, another composite bone formed from many fused elements. Most birds have four toes of which one points backwards and is normally opposed to the others. Woodpeckers have two toes pointing backwards, while a few birds have only three, or even two, forward-pointing toes.

In the same way that the weight associated with wing movement is kept near the trunk, so is that of the legs. Almost all of the musculature is associated with the femur and the tibiotarsus, while the upper region is covered by skin and feathers of the abdomen so that the knee joint is not readily visible. The metatarsus and digits contain virtually no muscle, and few blood vessels or nerves. The muscles higher in the leg are connected to these upper parts by long tendons which pass over pulley-like surfaces at the end of the metatarsus to clench the toes. This toe-clenching system is so arranged in perching birds that the folding of the leg, as caused by the bird's weight at rest, pulls the tendons sufficiently to attach the bird firmly to its perch without the expenditure of any muscular energy.

Many of the bones in a bird are either completely hollow, or contain bone formed with a sponge-like structure which is immensely strong but light. Some contain air and this feature, known as pneumatisation, can best be seen in the wing bones and skull. These characteristics can be seen in radiographs. Female birds soon to lay eggs often store extra calcium by laying down temporary medullary bone in the air spaces.

Bird muscles that have to operate continuously for long periods are much darker red in colour than those used infrequently (compare the breast muscles of a pigeon and a chicken).

NERVES AND SENSE ORGANS

Like mammals, birds have larger brains in relation to their size than reptiles, but the brain of a bird differs from that of a mammal in several respects. The parts associated with smell are small, while the vision centres are large. The cerebral hemispheres, considered to be important in learning, are relatively undeveloped, while the corpus striatum beneath them, considered to be the source of unlearned (instinctive) behaviour patterns, is well developed. As in mammals, the part of the brain associated with coordination of movement, the cerebellum, is large.

Sensory and motor nerves connect with the spinal cord at all levels, but the nerve supply at the level of the wings and legs is especially well developed. The cord conveys messages to the brain from the wings, legs and trunks and returns motor messages to their musculature.

Birds can distinguish certain flavours and may 'smell' some foods in the mouth. However, experiments whereby carcasses were covered to prevent sight, but not smell, have shown that even vultures use only their eyes to seek their food.

46

The eyes of birds differ from those of mammals in more respects than relative size. Like those of some reptiles they usually contain a ring of strengthening bony plates. The lens is relatively soft, and focussing is achieved by a ring of muscles that squeeze it into a more convex shape. Some birds can also increase the curvature of the cornea. The iris muscles are voluntary, so the pupil is capable of rapid expansion and contraction. The retina has comparatively few blood vessels, while the pecten, a fringed body which extends into the vitreous humour, is well supplied with these and may help nourish the retina. The retina usually contains both cone cells, associated with colour vision, and rod cells, although some owls lack cones and probably cannot see colours. Owls' eyes are elongated so that the lens casts a smaller, more intense image on the retina, and they can see far better than man in light of low intensities. The rod and cone light receptors are more densely packed in diurnal birds of prey than in the human retina, which probably accounts for their greater visual acuity.

Birds' eyes are relatively inflexibly fixed in their sockets, but the great agility of the head more than compensates for this. There is a third eyelid, the nictitating membrane, which is frequently drawn across the eye from its anterior corner. This action moistens and cleans the cornea, and also protects it from abrasion when, for instance, a hawk seizes its prey. The movable lower eyelid is used to close the eye relatively infrequently in healthy birds.

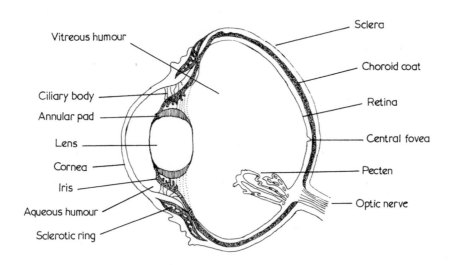

7 The structure of the eye

The outer ear is not equipped with a sound collecting trumpet; it is a simple tube passing into the head behind the eye. 'Ear' tufts on top of the head are nothing to do with hearing. At the base of the outer ear tube is the ear-drum. Sound is transmitted from the ear-drum to the cochlea of the inner ear by a single bone, the columella, as in reptiles. Cells in the cochlea translate sound vibrations into nerve pulses to the brain. The inner ear also contains fluid-filled tubules responsible for the sense of balance.

Birds are sensitive to much the same range of pitch as is man, but they are better able to detect rapid changes in the sound, such as occur in bird song. Most birds are probably not as well able to detect the direction of sounds as is man, partly owing to their lack of an external ear, and partly because their ears are so close together that they can get few clues from the difference in time between a sound reaching one ear and the other. The wide heads of owls, and the asymmetry of their ear openings, may improve matters for them, and they are able to strike rustling prey in absolute darkness.

The skin of a bird contains some pressure-sensitive cells, which may be important for responding to alterations in the position of the feathers. Other sensory cells are relatively sparse on the surface, and birds may not be very sensitive to locally applied heat, cold or pain.

BLOOD AND RESPIRATORY SYSTEMS

Blood is the transport medium of the body. It conveys heat, oxygen, waste carbon dioxide, dissolved nutrients, and the cells and molecules that combat foreign bodies and disease. It also contains special proteins which clot on exposure to the air and seal wounds; a bird's blood clots very quickly.

The heart pumps blood round the body. A bird's heart is relatively larger than that of a mammal, and maintains a higher pressure in the blood system. It is situated at the anterior end of the thorax, and in small birds may beat over 500 times a minute. De-oxygenated blood enters the right side of the heart, and is pumped from this to the lungs via the pulmonary arteries. It then returns from the lungs in the pulmonary veins to the left side of the heart, which is even more muscular than the right side and is pumped through the arteries to all parts of the body. As the arteries decrease in size the blood flow slows, and the fluid plasma (but not the red blood cells) enters the tissues by diffusion from very fine capillaries. The plasma then diffuses back into the capillaries, and flows more sluggishly to the heart through the veins.

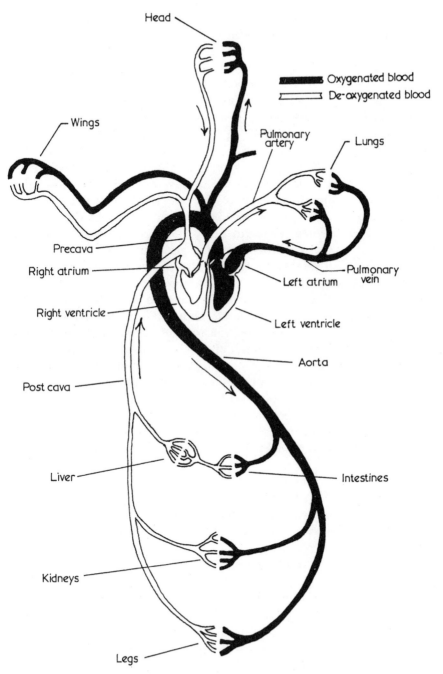

Head

Wings

Pulmonary
artery

Lungs

Oxygenated blood
De-oxygenated blood

Precava

Right atrium

Right ventricle

Left atrium

Pulmonary
vein

Left ventricle

Aorta

Post cava

Liver

Intestines

Kidneys

Legs

8 The blood system of a bird

49

Bird bone contains relatively little of the bone marrow which produces the red blood cells in mammals. In birds these cells are largely manufactured and stored in the spleen, an organ found in the abdomen near the gizzard.

The respiratory system provides the body with oxygen, and is important for cooling. At the base of the tongue is a valved opening, the glottis, which leads into the trachea. This can be seen when the bird's mouth is open and is important in wild bird treatment since one must ensure that food or liquids given forcibly do not enter the trachea. The trachea itself is a tube, ridged to maintain its shape, which passes down the neck and divides as it enters the thorax into two bronchial tubes. One bronchial tube enters each of the two lungs, which are pinkish bodies adjacent to the ribs and backbone in the thorax. In the lungs the bronchial tubes become finer and finer, and oxygen passes from these into the blood capillaries. Bronchial tubes also convey air from the lungs into a system of air sacs in the thorax, abdomen, neck, and some of the limb bones. At inspiration air is drawn into the air sacs through the lungs by muscle relaxation allowing the sternum to drop. At expiration muscles contract to draw up the sternum, and air from the air sacs passes again through the lungs and out through the bronchi and trachea. Fresh air is thus passing through the avian lungs continually during breathing, in contrast to the situation in a mammal where some stale air remains in the lungs because they cannot be emptied completely.

The large air sacs probably also help to cool the body, which is very important to avoid overheating during active flight. The testes, which require a lower temperature for sperm production, become almost surrounded by the abdominal air sacs when they expand during the breeding season.

Where the bronchial tubes meet at the trachea is the syrinx, the organ of sound production in birds. Sound is produced by the vibration of a membrane, the tension of which can be varied, as air passes over it. Birds do not have the sound-generating vocal cords of mammals.

THE DIGESTIVE SYSTEM

The digestive system is adapted for very efficient rapid utilisation of food to produce the energy required to maintain a high metabolism (see Fig 9). Animal or vegetable matter enters the mouth and passes over the glottis into the oesophagus. Birds which can eat faster than they can digest have a crop, which acts as a storage organ and allows them to retire to a safe perch to process their meal. Vegetarian species usually

Plate 5
A buzzard killed by electrocution: the feathers have all been charred

Plate 6
Normal beak of a crossbill: the structure of the bill is adapted to the bird's feeding habits

Plate 7
Legs of a magpie: the lower one shows a badly healed fracture which was probably the result of illegal ringing

Plate 8
Radiograph (X-ray) picture of a wing showing badly healed fracture of radius and ulna and a particle of lead shot. The soft tissues and flight feathers can also be seen

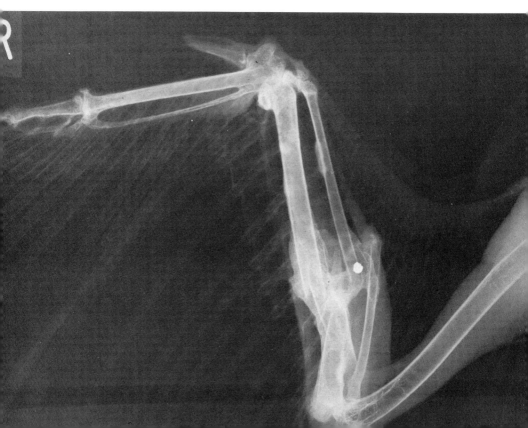

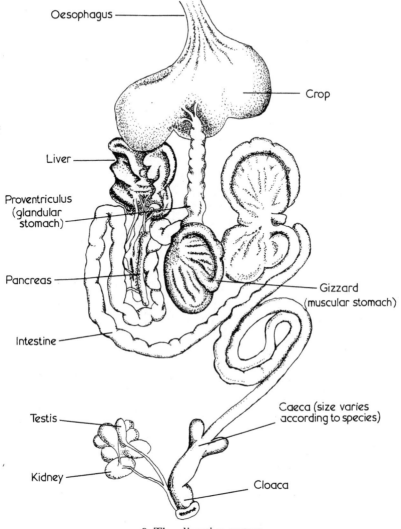

9 The digestive system

have crops, as do those that eat large animal prey; insect eaters, which spend some time obtaining each mouthful, have none. Beyond the oesophagus or crop is the proventriculus, a glandular region of the stomach which secretes digestive juices, whence food passes into the gizzard.

The gizzard is a very muscular organ with strong inner walls, which in many species contains grit or stones to assist in grinding up the food.

A turkey's gizzard is strong enough to roll up strips of iron sheeting, and tough enough to break up steel needles and surgical lancets! This organ allows a bird to turn hard food into an easily digested mash without the need for weighty jaw structures placed far in front of the centre of gravity. From the gizzard, food passes into the intestine, the first loop of which is the duodenum. The pancreas is a long, narrow, reddish organ lying in this loop and ducts carry digestive juices from the pancreas to the duodenum. Other juices enter this region via ducts from the gall-bladder, a blue-green globular body embedded in the liver.

The liver, which in healthy birds is a uniform rich red colour, is beautifully moulded to fit in the space between the gizzard, intestine, and posterior edge of the sternum, and is immediately obvious when a bird's abdomen is open. It is an important organ for the metabolism and storage of fats, vitamins, and carbohydrates. It also breaks down old red blood cells, and stores their pigments in the gall-bladder. These bile pigments give colour to the faeces (the dark part of the droppings), being obvious as a green colour when there is no food in the gut; they also dictate the colour of the shells of the eggs a bird produces.

Digestion proceeds as the food passes along the intestine, and nutrients are absorbed into the blood stream through its lining. Towards the end of the intestinal tract are two caeca (side branches) in many vegetarian birds. These assist with digestion, and in some birds (for example, grouse) may be as long as the rest of the intestine. The intestine terminates in the cloaca, whence the faeces are voided at intervals.

Some birds eat food containing totally indigestible parts, such as fur, feathers and insect exoskeletons. These parts are usually covered with mucus in the stomach and cast up by the mouth as a pellet.

EXCRETORY AND REPRODUCTIVE SYSTEMS

In metabolising protein, animals produce nitrogenous waste. Mammals eliminate this from the body as urea, in dilute solution. Birds form much more concentrated uric acid crystals and thus help conserve body water.

The organs of nitrogenous excretion are the kidneys, a pair of long, red-brown, partly segmented bodies under the backbone in the abdomen. From the kidneys, tubes pass to the cloaca, and convey the uric acid to the terminal region of the gut. This forms the white part of the droppings.

In mammals the excretion of excess salt occurs mainly in the kidneys, but birds have specialised nasal salt glands. These glands lie under the facial skin above the eyes, and produce a relatively concentrated salt solution which is flicked from the beak. They are best developed in marine birds and enable them to obtain body water by drinking the sea and excreting the excess salt; this procedure is impossible for mammals, the kidneys of which cannot produce a sufficiently strong salt concentration in the urine.

Male birds possess paired testes, oval whitish bodies which lie between the kidneys and the gut. These organs spend much of the year in an inactive state, their small size adding little to body weight during the non-breeding season. At the start of the breeding season the pituitary gland, a small body on the floor of the cranium beneath the brain, releases hormones which stimulate the male and female gonads to expand. The testes may increase over a thousandfold in size, and, as well as commencing sperm production, secrete testosterone, a hormone which activates courtship behaviour and produces other signs of breeding condition. Tubes convey the sperm from the testes to the cloaca, and may have an expanded region for sperm storage. There is no true penis in male birds, although the region of the cloaca where the tubes from the testes emerge may be slightly protrusible. At copulation the male presses his cloaca against that of the female, and sperm is transferred from one to the other.

In female birds it is usually only the left ovary that functions. It lies close to the kidneys, like the testes, and, outside the breeding season, looks like a bunch of tiny yellowish grapes. It too enlarges under the influence of pituitary hormones, and as the individual follicles (the grapes) enlarge and fill with yolk they become very prominent. The ovary produces hormones inducing breeding behaviour and preparation of the oviduct for egg-laying.

The oviduct has at its anterior end a funnel which opens into the body cavity near the ovary and collects the large yolk-filled egg cell as it is shed from its follicle. Fertilisation occurs at this stage from sperm which may have been stored, or freshly introduced, into the oviduct. The egg then passes down through a glandular region where first the albumen, and then the shell membranes, are added. In the final region of the oviduct, the uterus, the hard calcium carbonate shell is deposited and marked before laying.

To conclude, the bird is a highly specialised animal which shows a number of unusual anatomical and physiological features, many of which influence its care in captivity, particularly when sick or injured. Chief amongst these are the possession of feathers, high body temperature and a specialised respiratory tract structure. Although similar in some ways to both reptiles and mammals, birds are sufficiently distinct to warrant careful study of their biology by all those working with them.

4 Classification and behaviour of birds

D. C. Houston

Most people are more aware of birds than of other wild animals around them. This is chiefly because birds are active during the day and rely on the same senses as humans do – sight and hearing – while their sense of smell is usually poor or non-existent. One can therefore fully appreciate their displays and activities. However, most wild mammals are nocturnal; they rely heavily on their sense of smell and so live in a world that is very difficult to imagine. Birds give great attention and care to their young, so it is only too easy to assume that the mind of a bird is similar to that of a human. In fact, birds are more closely related to modern reptiles than to mammals.

The earliest ancestors of birds were clearly reptilian (see Chapter 3). The avian body, apart from the development of feathers and a warm blood system, has not changed very greatly from that of the reptile; for example, birds still have scales in the skin of their legs and feet. It is probable that during evolution, the feathers developed originally to give an insulated covering to the body and enable the reptilian ancestors to maintain a stable body temperature. This was a great advantage because it enabled the animal to be active irrespective of the weather conditions, while cold-blooded reptiles are dormant in cool conditions. Once feathers had been developed for this purpose they then probably became modified to assist in gliding and, later, in powered flight. Of course, it would be wrong to consider birds just as warm, feathery reptiles, but it would be equally erroneous to think of their behaviour as equivalent to that of mammals.

There are about 8,600 species of birds in the world today, but compared with most other groups of animals their basic structure varies very little from species to species. About half the world's species belong to an order called the Passeriformes or passerines – the perching birds – which are the most advanced groups of birds. They include most of our small land birds, sparrows, finches, crows, starlings, thrushes, and many others. There would be little point in listing here all the other taxonomic groupings by which modern birds are classified, since this can be found in any standard textbook and the reader is referred to those listed at the end of this book.

The classification of birds, like other animals and plants, is based on criteria which are recognised throughout the world. Two examples, the starling and the kestrel, are given below :

	STARLING	KESTREL
Kingdom	Animal	Animal
Phylum	Chordata	Chordata
Class	Aves	Aves
Order	Passeriformes	Falconiformes
Family	Sturnidae	Falconidae
Genus	*Sturnus*	*Falco*
Species	*vulgaris*	*tinnunculus*

It can be seen from the above that both birds are in the Animal Kingdom; they are both chordates (which can be roughly equated with their having a vertebral column); they are both in the class Aves (birds). Here, however, they begin to diverge since they are in different orders, families and genera and, of course, different species. A scientific name does more than just give a label to each species; it also indicates their relationship to each other. Species that are very closely related are placed in the same genera; if two species are placed in different families or orders it indicates that they have been separated for longer periods in their evolutionary development.

The correct scientific name for the starling is *Sturnus vulgaris* and for the kestrel *Falco tinnunculus*. Note that both words are italics – they should be underlined when written – and that while the generic name has a capital letter, the other does not.

This is only a simplified outline of classification; the subject is very complex and the reader who is interested in more detail should consult the International Code of Zoological Nomenclature.[1] It must be stressed that some knowledge of classification is useful for all those dealing with wild bird casualties since, often, food preferences and other factors differ considerably between species.

It is obvious to anyone handling birds that there is a great difference in the reactions of the different species; chickens, for example, are comparatively dim, while crows are extremely bright. To consider why the behaviour of birds varies we really need to understand what determines the way in which a bird will react in any situation. Virtually all the actions of birds serve a definite function; their behaviour patterns have developed so that they can feed themselves, find shelter, breed, and escape from their enemies.

A bird's behaviour in any particular situation may have developed in two ways. First, the behaviour pattern may be genetically determined, or instinctive. A sparrow flies away if it is alarmed – by, say, an approaching cat – and clearly the birds that are alert are more likely to escape than those that are inattentive. During evolution these instinctive behaviour patterns are selected in the same way as are the physical features of the birds. The patterns are usually very fixed – for example, all gulls scratch their heads in exactly the same way by bringing a foot up under the wing, while all sparrows scratch by bringing the foot above the wing. But birds can also alter their behaviour during their life, as they gain more experience, and this is a second method by which behaviour patterns may originate. A robin may learn that it can approach a man who regularly puts out food on the bird table, but that it is dangerous to approach small boys with catapults.

Until a few years ago many people considered that bird behaviour was largely determined by instinctive responses. Birds are still believed to be basically creatures of instinct but it is now clear that learning also plays a most important part in modifying most birds' behaviour. In man and the higher mammals much behaviour is learnt. A baby must learn for many months before it is able to walk; but a young bird does not need to learn how to fly – it has an inbuilt ability to do so. Young pigeons, reared with their wings restrained so that they cannot flap, are able to fly normally when they are fully grown. Once a bird has started to fly it will then start to improve on its skills by learning : this is particularly obvious in certain birds of prey where the young birds often spend many weeks learning how to soar and hunt.

A similar situation applies to nest building. Even the most complicated nests woven by weaver birds, which may involve many thousands of leaves intertwined together, can be built entirely by instinct and by young birds that have been reared without ever seeing a nest; but during its life, each bird learns how to build slightly better nests. Similarly with the songs of birds like the chaffinch the basic notes are instinctive, but birds rely on hearing their own voice and that of neighbouring birds if they are to learn to develop the normal song. However, the alarm calls of most birds are completely instinctive – it would be dangerous if these were not perfect first time. Most bird behaviour is therefore basically instinctive, although it may be modified considerably by learning.

Since man relies so heavily on learnt behaviour, we often find it surprising that very complicated activities in birds can be completely instinctive. An obvious example is shown by migration. A young cuckoo is abandoned by its parents in the middle of summer. Several weeks after its parents have left, the young bird will start to prepare for its own migration by storing fat. It will know instinctively when to start the migration, how to navigate over many thousands of miles to Africa, when to stop the journey, and what type of country it should live in when it reaches Africa. In some species of birds the young travel with the older birds, and there is some opportunity for the young birds to learn features of the migration route; but in the case of the cuckoo this extremely complicated task depends purely on instinct for its completion. A practical aspect of migration for anyone keeping an injured bird in captivity is the problem of when to release a migrant species once it has recovered. An important factor to remember is that, in order to complete a migration successfully, a bird needs to be more than just healthy. The journeys involved are extremely demanding and all migrants have to prepare themselves for migration by laying down extensive fat deposits in their bodies; they probably need a considerable period to develop the physiological condition necessary to undertake the journey. It is probably pointless to release a recently recovered bird immediately prior to its migration time, since it would be very unlikely to survive the journey if it did not have a sufficient period to build up its body condition. If a bird cannot be released several weeks before the normal migration time it is perhaps better to attempt to keep the bird in captivity and then release it when the wild birds return. This often results in practical difficulties – swallows and martins in particular often do not survive the whole winter – and more research is needed on the effects of depriving such birds of their migration.

Instinctive behaviour patterns are also involved in general maintenance behaviour, such as preening and bathing. In birds these activities do more than just keep the bird clean from mud and grime. The feathers of birds are very delicate and can easily become damaged. They require regular attention to ensure that the feather barbs remain interlocked and that the feathers lie in an orderly way. Preening also helps to maintain the boundary layer of air which is trapped below the feathers and which provides the insulation properties of the plumage, as well as playing a part in the removal of fleas and feather lice from the plumage. During grooming birds collect oil from the preen gland and smear it over the surface of the feathers. This probably helps to lubricate the feathers, gives a waterproof property to the plumage and it has also been shown that, under sunlight, the secretion produces vitamin D; the latter can be absorbed into the body either through the skin or when the bird preens and swallows old preen oil.

It follows that any bird that is injured so that it cannot preen normally will be unable to keep the plumage in good order. The most obvious consequence of this in captive birds is usually an increase in the number of feather parasites, which may build up to a level where they may weaken the bird or hinder its recovery (see Chapter 11). An injured bird which cannot preen regularly may develop very scruffy and tattered feathers which it may be unable to restore when it finally recovers. If the damage to the feathers is extensive the bird is probably best kept in captivity until it moults and a new plumage develops but this, as is mentioned in Chapter 14, may result in a prolonged period of confinement.

Birds often bathe before they start to preen, and wetting the plumage may help to clean the feathers and assist with the application of the preen oil. Birds usually bathe and preen themselves instinctively whenever a shallow pool of water is available. Many bathe very enthusiastically, even in cold weather, and it is important to ensure that when they are kept in cages they have a warm area in which they can dry off. Wild birds in captivity are often reluctant to bathe at first, probably because this is an activity where they are rather vulnerable to predation. They are only likely to bathe when they feel secure in their surroundings.

Birds also have instinctive signals for communicating information to each other. The elaborate threat and courtship displays of most birds are instinctive and many of the bright colours in a bird's plumage are intended to stimulate a response in other birds; for example, a robin will become aggressive at the sight of the red breast of another robin within his territory. Some of these interactions obviously have importance when wild birds are brought into captivity. Many birds which feed in flocks, such as chickens, pigeons, and rooks, have a social hierarchy in which each bird knows its position in relation to its neighbours. The strongest and most aggressive individuals always select the best perches and take the pick of the food, while weaker individuals are relegated to less favourable areas. When birds first collect into a flock the hierarchy is established. Once the peck order has developed the social position of each bird often remains fairly stable: each individual will know which birds are dominant over itself and it will not attempt to challenge them. In this way constant squabbling and fighting is avoided, and the flock develops into a clear social grouping.

During food shortages in the wild it is probably the birds at the bottom of the social hierarchy that cannot find enough food and therefore die, leaving the other more dominant birds, still obtaining sufficient food, in good condition. It is also the subordinate birds that are likely to show clinical or post-mortem evidence of stress (see Chapter 14). These hierarchies can be clearly seen in many groups of captive birds, and obviously care must be taken to ensure that they do not prevent some individuals at the bottom of the peck order from feeding. If any individuals seem to be weakening in such a group they would probably stand a better chance of survival if they were caged on their own, away from the competition of other birds.

All these instinctive behaviour patterns are modified by learning, and different species of birds rely on instinct and learning to different extents. Birds are capable of considerable feats of learning. Sparkie Williams, a budgerigar, could recite several complete nursery rhymes and had learnt 550 words; in laboratory mazes many birds learn to find the correct path as effectively as small mammals. In the wild most birds learn how to search for food efficiently; they learn to watch where other birds are feeding and to copy any new feeding techniques. In many parts of Britain tits have learnt to peck through the foil caps of milk bottles to drink the cream. This is a trick that a few birds discovered, and many others saw them feeding in this way and copied the technique. When we consider that one bird is more 'intelligent' than another we usually mean that if the two birds are placed in a new situation, such as finding a new food supply, one of them may take less time than the other to alter its behaviour in order to take advantage of the new surroundings. We might then consider one to be more 'intelligent' than the other, but we really mean that it learns faster.

The most intelligent birds are probably found in the crow family, especially the crows, jackdaws and ravens (see Chapter 17). In the wild these birds are very quick to exploit and investigate any change in their surroundings. They are therefore relatively easy to keep for short periods in captivity. They will quickly adopt a great variety of foods, so that there is usually no problem over their feeding. Parrots are probably very near the crows in their learning ability. It is rather surprising to find that birds of prey are comparatively unintelligent. They therefore need slightly more consideration to ensure that they are correctly caged and that appropriate food is properly presented.

Among the small birds, some, such as tits, are naturally very inquisitive and learn comparatively fast, while others seem to be slower to alter their normal behaviour. When we put a wild bird into a cage we are placing it in a completely strange environment. A bird that relies heavily on instinctive behaviour may repeatedly fly against the wire trying to escape, or refuse to eat the food that it is offered. This is not because the bird is 'stubborn', but because in the wild it does not need to alter its behaviour rapidly and so it cannot adjust quickly to the new surroundings. Its behaviour may appear to be irrational, but this is because its

61

behaviour patterns have evolved to be effective in the wild, not in the artificial conditions of a cage.

So, when we bring a wild bird into captivity the ease with which it will settle down to its new life depends on how rapidly it can alter its behaviour. An obvious example is that in the wild all birds are adapted to avoid predators, and most birds include man in that category. When we take them into captivity we subject them to the regular close approach of people. The majority of birds have a definite flight distance for each of their predators, this being the minimum distance they will permit the predator to approach before flying away. Most cages are obviously far smaller than the normal flight distance from man in the wild; the bird constantly wants to retreat whenever someone approaches, but is unable to do so. When an animal's normal behaviour is thwarted in this way it is under stress and this can be a major factor in determining the speed of its recovery from injury.

In the case of recently caged birds it is therefore important to reduce the flight distance rapidly, and this can be done in two ways. First, the flight distance for most animals is considerably reduced if there is dense cover available so that the bird is not always fully visible: so, clearly, cages should contain dense, leafy branches where birds can hide. Second, the flight distance can be reduced by taming so that the bird no longer wishes to escape. The speed with which a bird becomes tame will depend on how rapidly it can learn that man no longer represents a threat, and this will vary between individuals as well as between species. But clearly all wild birds must be approached with slow movements and great care should be taken not to alarm them unnecessarily. Birds that are very slow to tame are best kept in very spacious aviaries where they can maintain a large distance from people; if this is not possible, it is preferable to keep them in small darkened boxes for a few days rather than to introduce them directly into a small cage where they may injure themselves. This and other aspects of cage and aviary design are discussed in more detail in Chapter 20.

Finally, there is a special type of learning which is known as imprinting and which is most commonly found in the young chicks of ducks and geese and other birds that normally leave the nest within a few hours of hatching. It is found that these young chicks learn to follow any moving object and form a permanent attachment to it. Normally, of course, the first moving object they see is their mother, and they become imprinted on to her and follow her wherever she goes. The unique property of this type of learning is that it is largely irreversible; the learning can only occur during a short period after hatching. If the chick does not attach itself to its mother during this time then it may never associate itself normally with other animals. There have been many experiments made in which young chicks have been imprinted on to humans, other species of birds or even cardboard boxes. If these are the first moving objects which the young birds see they will form attachments to them and will follow them as if they were their mothers. One of the subsequent results of this imprinting on to a foster mother of another species may be that when they grow into adult birds they may attempt to mate with birds of the foster mother's species and not their own. If very young chicks are brought into captivity they may imprint themselves on to humans or a foster mother and this may have a long-term effect on their behaviour when they become adults.

It should be apparent from the foregoing that an understanding of bird behaviour is most valuable if casualties are to be nursed and treated in captivity. Many of those who deal with wild birds have learnt by trial and error and are putting into practice the points outlined in this chapter. The whole field of animal behaviour is expanding rapidly and many researchers are involved in studies on free-living and captive birds. It is to be hoped that this work, coupled with the practical experience of aviculturists and bird hospitals, will result in improved standards of care and management.

5 Finding and examining wild birds

J. A. Dall

The circumstances under which birds are found requiring assistance vary with the time of year and the state of the weather. During the spring and early summer many fledglings may appear to be abandoned or lost. Exhausted, semi-starved or damaged migrants arrive in the spring and autumn while moulting birds are occasionally found in poor condition between July and September. During the winter, after prolonged periods of frost and snow, aquatic birds in particular may be encountered in distress, frozen on ponds or simply unable to obtain enough food. At all times of the year there are the road accidents, the shot birds and those that fly into walls, windows and power lines.

YOUNG BIRDS

Fledglings that appear abandoned are often picked up by over-zealous people. It is possible that these birds have either fallen from the nest or 'crash-landed' during their initial flight; they certainly are, in some cases, in danger of being attacked and damaged by cats.

If, after examination, the young bird is found to be uninjured and strong, it should be returned to the area where it was discovered, placed in bushes as high as possible near the nest (if this can be located) and left. In some instances the bird may be put in a wire cage or small box which should be hung out of reach of cats and sheltered from direct sun or heavy rain. The parents are quite likely to find the bird and will almost certainly continue to feed it. If necessary the cage can be brought in at night and put out early in the morning. The youngster can be released when it has gained sufficient strength and one is certain that the parents are feeding it. If the bird is put back in bushes or undergrowth it is always advisable to check later to ensure that the parents have actually found it.

The importance of returning healthy baby birds to the wild cannot be over-emphasised. A poster jointly sponsored by the RSPCA and RSPB puts this succinctly in its caption: 'If you see a young bird please leave it alone – its parents will return to feed it when you have gone.'

64

Far too many young birds are 'rescued', only to die later as a result of inadequate care.

Not all young birds can be immediately returned to the wild: some may be sick or injured or the parents may have been killed. It is fortunate that a young bird does not object to being handled as much as the adult does; as a result a thorough examination can be made without causing too much distress. If the bird is injured a decision must be made at once as to whether it is likely to recover or not, and if the injuries are severe then it should be destroyed quickly and painlessly; a veterinary surgeon or RSPCA clinic will do this (see Chapter 15).

If a decision is made to rear the fledgling every effort must be expended to identify it. One should at least decide whether it is an altrichial (nidicolous) species – that is, one which remains in the nest and is fed by the parents – or precocial (nidifugous) – one which leaves the nest, follows the hen and is capable of feeding itself. Nestlings without feathers require heat and temperatures of 27–32°C; once the feathers begin to grow, the heat may be reduced and eventually need only be supplied in very cold weather.

Nestlings are ideally kept in an abandoned nest. This must be checked for parasites before being used for them, as frequently red mites and other ectoparasites remain in old nests for some period after use (see Chapter 11). Alternatively, an artificial adaptation of a nest can be made.

10a Altrichial and precocial birds: a newly hatched passerine chick on the left and a wading chick on the right

This should be placed in a cardboard box over which can be hung an infra-red lamp, or failing this, a 60-watt lightbulb. These sources of heat must be positioned so that they offer a suitable temperature range and the bird should be placed where it appears most comfortable. This method is satisfactory for most nestlings, but birds nesting in holes, such as woodpeckers, should be kept out of a bright light and a dull-emitter lamp or bottom heat must be used.

The young should be fed each hour from dawn to dusk. Up to about two weeks of age they will gape whenever anything is offered so little difficulty will be experienced in feeding them. However, if they are older, they may require to be fed forcibly until they will accept food; fortunately nestlings will not usually overeat so they may be fed to capacity. The food must be of high quality, readily digestible with adequate protein and without too much fibre.

10b Fledgling mistle thrush 'gaping' for food

In the wild the young of both hard- and softbills are fed by their parents mainly on an insectivorous diet of spiders, insects, grubs and caterpillars. Substitute foods such as mealworms (very rich and digestible), earthworms and chopped snails are useful in captivity. Maggots can be used, with caution (see Chapter 8). Hard-boiled egg, (boiled for about thirty minutes to make it digestible) should be passed through a sieve and, when cold, mixed with four times its volume of sweet biscuit. A pinch of salt should be added and the mixture made crumbly moist with water. This mixture must be used reasonably quickly as it goes stale. It may be stored in a refrigerator but must not be fed chilled. Insectivorous foods are available commercially (see Chapter 8) and these can be used moistened initially. Canary-rearing mixture or tinned baby foods are also useful. The food may be rolled into pellets and fed with blunt forceps. The moisture contained in the food should supply sufficient fluid for the nestlings.

When the fledgling attempts to leave the nest it should be put in a suitably constructed cage and given a bowl of food; if necessary it should be fed from this bowl until it will feed itself. A *shallow* dish of water, which cannot easily be tipped up, must be available.

Young birds that hatch as active chicks not attached to their nest or mother fall into two groups: one of these comprises those able to feed themselves, such as pheasants, ducks and geese, and the other those that are fed by the hen, such as coots, grebes and herons. Both groups require a source of heat until they are fledged; initially this must be continuous but as they grow older it is only required in very cold weather and at night. An artificial brooder (such as is used for poultry-rearing) is ideal as the central source of heat; the birds can then run about, feed and return to the warmth as necessary. They should have adequate floor space for exercise and the floor can be covered with a layer of sand and newspapers.

Suitable accommodation can be made from a large box with a 60-watt electric lightbulb which is hung off-centre and covered with a sleeve of wire netting. In this way the chicks will be able to get as much warmth as required. Strips of cloth may be used to simulate the feathers of the hen, thus giving an extra sense of security. The top of the box must be covered with netting to prevent escape. Youngsters that feed themselves require only food and water in addition to warmth. Turkey or chick crumbs are satisfactory with the addition of a few mealworms or maggots which may be chopped for very small birds.

It may be necessary to stimulate the birds at first by imitating the mother's pecking and scratching; the presence of moving maggots on top of the food also arouses their interest and may start them feeding. Earth or a turf should be supplied; it will give the birds added interest and activity as well as helping supply the fine grit which is necessary for proper digestion. Water is necessary but care must be taken that the chicks do not get wet. An exception to this is the aquatic chick which will nuzzle in the water. It is the author's experience that the head and eyes of these species should be wetted regularly to prevent eye trouble arising. Nevertheless, the orphaned chicks of aquatic birds lack the necessary oil in the down and should not be allowed to bathe or swim as they will remain wet and may become chilled.

Those chicks that are fed by the parents present a real problem as they require constant feeding; coots and grebes feed from the mother's beak so food must be dangled in front of them, imitating to as great an extent as possible the parent's action. Worms, aquatic plants, insects and strips of fish can be offered with forceps. However, it may be necessary to force-feed them initially and this and other techniques are discussed in Chapter 7.

Gulls regurgitate food in front of the chicks but here again force-feeding may have to be resorted to initially; a diet consisting of a crumbly mash of raw fish, brown bread, cod-liver oil and milk is suitable. Food should normally be presented from above the bird so that it will raise its head, as this is the natural position for feeding. Attempts to imitate the mother's call will often arouse otherwise uninterested chicks.

Raptor chicks do not appear to require the same amount of heat as others and can often be kept successfully in a cardboard box. Their food consists of small pieces of mice or chicks or even pieces of raw beef or chicken (see Chapter 16). It should be offered on blunt forceps raised and lowered in front of the bird, which will then usually open its beak. If the food is not taken it can be gently forced into the mouth. It may be necessary to touch the bristle-like feathers at each side of the beak to stimulate the feeding reaction. Once a young bird of prey is feeding it will often call when hungry and can be fed to capacity. When it is four or five weeks old it will usually accept food placed in its talons or on the floor of the box.

The problems of releasing hand-reared fledglings is dealt with in more detail elsewhere. Often it is more difficult to return the bird successfully to the wild than to rear it.

ADULT BIRDS

Adult birds which allow themselves to be caught by humans are usually in dire straits. Such birds are often shocked, stunned, have fractured bones or are in an exhausted, semi-starved or dehydrated state; they may even be suffering from an infectious disease.

Waterbirds, such as coots and grebes, will sometimes land by mistake on wet roads or shiny roofs; they may then appear unable or unwilling to move and are liable to be hit by a car or attacked by cats. A sudden heavy thunderstorm will beat swifts to the ground and soak their plumage. As it is impossible for these birds to take off once they are grounded they are easy prey for predators or quickly become chilled and starved. Prolonged periods of rain will also adversely affect swallows, martins and swifts and can reduce them to a semi-starved condition in a few days. Other birds may become trapped in garden netting or entangled in nylon fishing line, string or cotton. Deserted buildings are frequently a trap for sparrows, wrens, blackbirds and starlings looking for nesting or roosting places; although they have got into these places they cannot necessarily get out again.

Birds are difficult to catch single-handed. They object to hands approaching them and prolonged chases will cause damage and distress. In an attempt to capture a wild bird it is better that it is cornered and dealt with rapidly. A fishing net is a very useful gadget as is a light cloth, which can be thrown over the bird. The capture of oiled seabirds is discussed in Chapter 13.

Immediately the wild bird is caught it should be put in a dark box and taken to where it can be examined. The transport of large water-fowl, such as swans, is best achieved by putting the body of the swan in a sack and then tying the neck of the sack around the base of the swan's neck; in this way they appear to travel reasonably comfortably and do not attempt to struggle.

EXAMINATION

It is always better to observe the bird initially without handling it; one can then note any deformity, unusual position of wings or lameness, as well as the bird's sense of balance and ability to see and respond to stimuli. In some cases it may be useful to observe the bird attempting to fly as well as standing and walking. Without exception adult birds object strongly to being handled and invariably struggle, using a great deal of energy and producing excessive rises in blood pressure, which in a sick or injured bird can quite easily be fatal; they are liable to cerebral and other haemorrhages. Excessive pressure on the body of a small bird can produce asphyxia due, in this instance, to the anatomical structure of the respiratory system.

Handling must therefore be positive and firm yet gentle; the wings must quickly be controlled close to the body for the pectoral muscles are so powerful that they can fracture or otherwise damage the wing bones.

All small birds can be picked up with one hand over the back and the head restrained between the first and second finger; the other fingers and thumb will then be able to control the wings and the legs. By turning the hand over, the under-side of the body, legs and wings can be examined.

Larger birds with strong beaks and talons require more care, preferably with one person to hold and another to examine. It is wise to slip an elastic band over the beak to keep it closed; a stab is not so painful as a pinch. The strength of the beak and feet is quite amazing and, together with the sharpness of the claws, can cause considerable pain

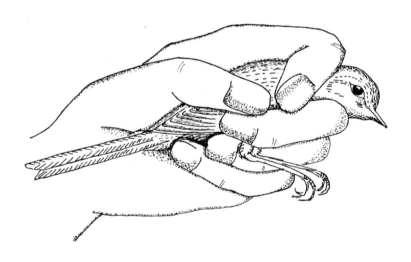

11a Holding a small bird

to the handler; this applies particularly to jays, magpies and other corvids. Gulls and seabirds also have sharp beaks and will require similar treatment although their feet are not so dangerous. Ducks are best picked up over the back using both hands to restrain the wings. Swans and geese strike out with the wings as a mode of defence; these are extremely powerful, and can inflict a painful blow to the handler. It is, therefore, imperative that the wings be immobilised immediately.

Raptors' talons are normally their means of defence; frequently these birds will lie on their backs and use their feet to defend themselves. In such circumstances, it is best to use strong gloves or apply a cloth for them to grip. If the head is covered they become very much more docile; this also applies to geese, swans and most other birds. All diurnal species will be quietened if handled in darkness or subdued light.

Examination must be thorough and rapid. Body condition should be assessed by the size of the pectoral muscles and dehydration by the movement of the skin over these muscles and elsewhere – the skin of a dehydrated bird appears adherent to the underlying muscles. Wounds are not easily found on the body but they should be suspected if a matting of the feathers is noted; however, it must be pointed out that the actual wound may be some distance from the matted feathers. Eyes, nostrils and mouth should be examined for injuries or abnormalities and any discharge noted. Opening the mouth of a bird is not always easy; sometimes it can be done manually or with the aid of a pair of forceps. Alternatively, if the bird will bite at an object – for example, a small flat piece of wood – this can be used gently to lever the jaws apart. It is advisable to examine the vent region for evidence of soiling as this may indicate diarrhoea, cloacal infection or prolonged recumbency (see Plate 1).

The wings should be investigated separately and in detail. Each wing is released from the encircling grip by extending the carpal (wrist) joint. The wing can then be spread out and primary and secondary feathers checked. Damage to the primary feathers on one side is likely to be due to damage to that wing or leg; in the case of the latter, because the bird is using an outstretched wing to balance itself. However, if a bird has been in someone else's hands for a few days, plumage damage may reflect its previous care, particularly if it has been kept in a cage. Examination may also reveal ectoparasites or skin wounds. The bones and joints are palpated for fractures or dislocations which are identified by abnormal mobility, marked swelling and bruising. In the case of fractures there is often deformity and crepitus (a grating sound as the bone fragments rub). Strangely, and in contrast to mammals, evidence of pain is often lacking in birds.

71

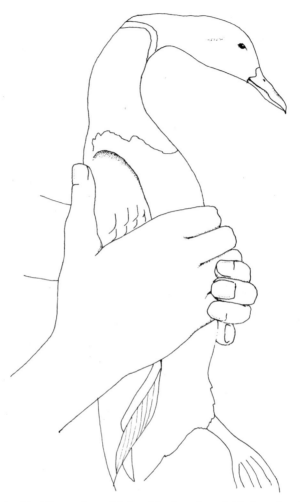

11b A method of holding a large bird, with the wings folded against its side

Examination of the legs follows that of the wings and a similar routine is followed (Plate 2). The digits should be examined carefully but this is not always easy since the bird tends to clench them; flexing and extending the tibiotarsal joint may help open the foot.

Each wing and leg is treated separately and the examined member is returned before releasing the other except when making a direct comparison (often a useful diagnostic aid) between them. It may be that one or both wings or legs is completely flaccid yet no fracture or dislocation is detectable. In this case the trouble is probably nervous in

72

origin and may be due to a body, back or head injury. The backbone may be fractured by a shot wound or a blow to the area resulting in spinal cord damage and paralysis. Swellings within the abdominal cavity will often cause flaccid paralysis of a leg by pressure on the nerves. In some instances similar clinical signs are associated with excess stretching of the nerves due, for example, to the bird being suspended from a fence or telephone wire for a prolonged period. Accurate records of the patient's history may help determine such factors.

If a bird is obviously unwell but no injury can be detected, it may have internal damage. This is discussed in Chapter 9. Alternatively it may be suffering from an infectious or parasitic disease or the effect of a poison. Specific diagnosis of these conditions is never easy; a guide is given in subsequent chapters. Such birds must be isolated in order to reduce the risk of transmission to other birds and supportive treatment (nursing, food and water) provided until a tentative diagnosis can be made. Specific symptomatic therapy can then be attempted.

FIRST AID

The initial aim of the examination is to ascertain whether the bird should be destroyed or kept alive. In the case of the latter, one must then make a provisional assessment as to the likelihood of the patient being returned to the wild; if this is unlikely, it will have to remain in captivity.

The last alternative may be considered with relatively uncommon birds where there are adequate facilities to keep them and where there

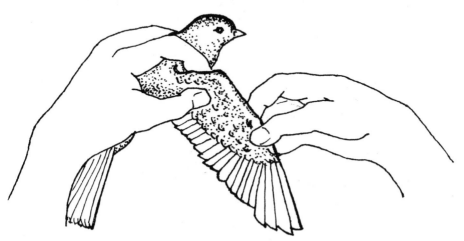

12 Examination of a bird's wing

is a likelihood of their breeding; or, it may be justifiable when the birds are likely to prove of scientific or educational value. If neither of these options is likely the bird should be humanely destroyed (see Chapter 15).

Once a decision has been made to treat the bird, the first task is to cope with shock, stress, hunger and thirst.[1] The bird should be placed in a darkened box or cage and kept warm. If the plumage is wet the patient can be wrapped lightly in cotton wool or enclosed in a sock; the latter will also help quieten it. At this stage the bird should be left alone and only examined occasionally. The high metabolic rate of birds creates a high body temperature and there is danger of respiratory disease if they have been chilled or exposed for an undue length of time, particularly without food (see Plate 23).

When the bird appears more active, food and water can be offered. Diurnal birds will feed only if it is light. If the patient is unwilling or unable to feed itself, force-feeding will be necessary. Small quantities of solid food can be placed in the mouth and gently pushed over the back of the tongue (see Plate 3) or a liquid food administered by crop or stomach tube. Alternatively a 'feeding stick' (such as the stick from an ice lolly) can be used to push food over the tongue. If forceps are used they should be blunt-ended; pieces of rubber tubing attached to the ends will help prevent damage to the bird's mouth. The aim should be to feed little and often. At a later stage, particularly during convalescence, it may be possible to hand-feed a bird : the patient is offered food from the hand but no attempt is made to open its beak.

Thirst, due to dehydration, may also be a problem. Normally birds will drink readily and the provision of a glucose saline solution (available from a veterinary surgeon) rather than pure water will help counteract shock. Some people recommend milk but in sick birds it may result in diarrhoea; if it is to be used two parts should be diluted in one part water. The water container must be chosen carefully. It should not be able to spill nor should the bird be able to get into it and drown or become chilled. Even the shape is important – for example, a heron will not drink from a saucer and should be provided with a bowl or deep container.

Some birds found unable to fly will recover completely if kept in the warm overnight. The diagnosis in such cases is probably concussion, exhaustion or shock following a minor injury. Birds which are half-starved – for example, redwings after an exceptionally prolonged cold spell – will also respond dramatically to 24 hours of nursing including food and water. Such cases are, however, usually the exception; most wild bird casualties have more severe problems.

If there are skin wounds the feathers should be clipped exposing the affected area. Wounds may be cleaned with a dilute solution of a suitable antiseptic (for example cetrimide), salt and water (two teaspoonfuls of salt to a pint of water), or potassium permanganate made up in water to a dark pink colour. If a wing is broken or dislocated it should be held in the natural resting position while it is taped to the body with sticky tape or brown paper. An encircling band is wrapped round both wings and body just behind the wing butts. The ends of the flight feathers can then be taped together. This may cause the bird to lose its balance, but will maintain the fractured wing in such a position that no further damage can be done. Broken legs can be temporarily splinted, using a thin light splint.

The points made above deal with initial first aid only; the layman confronted with an injured wild bird may need to follow these guidelines before professional advice is sought. The treatment of wounds and fractures is covered in greater detail in Chapter 9 and other topics, such as oil pollution and poisoning, are also dealt with separately.

One final point must be emphasised. As Dorothy Yglesias wrote : '. . . wild birds only allow themselves to be caught when their condition is pretty desperate; therefore, the number of complete cures is bound to be relatively small and the number of deaths great.'[2] The attempted care and treatment of wild birds is a satisfying task but one that is frequently fraught with disappointment. Casualties often die despite intensive care and the best possible veterinary attention. Such work is, however, never wasted; valuable experience is gained and this serves to improve the techniques for the care of future patients.

6 Diagnosis of disease

J. E. Cooper

The diagnosis and treatment of disease in animals is strictly the domain of the veterinary surgeon. In Britain it is covered by the Veterinary Surgeons Act and this is discussed in Chapter 2. In this chapter the diagnosis of disease will be considered with the following objectives: to explain to the layman the principles of a veterinary diagnosis; and to guide the layman as to which clinical observations or samples would be of value to a veterinary surgeon called in to see a sick bird.

Correct diagnoses are important in order to reduce spread of disease to other birds; to minimise the risk of infection to humans tending, or coming into contact with, the birds; and, to ensure that correct treatment is implemented, thus discouraging the misuse of antibiotics and other drugs.

Diseases naturally transmissible to man from vertebrate animals are termed 'zoonoses' and a number involve birds. They are discussed in Appendix 6 in an article by the author reprinted from the *Proceedings of the American Association of Zoo Veterinarians*. All those working with wild birds should be aware of the existence of zoonoses and should ensure that hygienic precautions are always followed.

Disease diagnosis can be conveniently divided into clinical diagnosis – where the bird is still alive– and post-mortem diagnosis – where the bird has died. The various facets of each of these are as follows:

1	Clinical diagnosis:	observation
		examination
		clinical aids to diagnosis
		laboratory tests
2	Post-mortem diagnosis:	macroscopical findings
		laboratory tests

CLINICAL DIAGNOSIS

Much useful information on a bird can be obtained by careful visual examination. The experienced layman will quickly detect such clinical signs as lameness, a drooping wing or a swollen eye. Similarly, careful

76

observation will enable the bird that is not feeding or that is passing abnormal droppings to be picked out before its condition deteriorates. In this context it is important to be able to recognise normality – the faeces of birds vary from species to species.

Clinical examination necessarily involves handling the bird. This in itself may result in undesirable effects, such as fright and increased heart rate, and is the reason why visual observations must always precede examination. Once a bird is in the hand, certain other procedures can be followed. The beak should be opened and the mucous membranes inside examined for evidence of pallor or other changes. Similarly the body can be palpated for evidence of fractures or swellings. Unnatural sounds may be heard, as for example in crepitus when broken bones rub against each other, while the use of a stethoscope will permit study of heart and lung sounds.

There are many clinical aids to diagnosis. The stethoscope, mentioned above, is an example. A more sophisticated technique is the use of radiography (X-rays) to assist in diagnosis. Radiography not only helps in the diagnosis of fractures and skeletal abnormalities; it also permits the detection of lead shot and other foreign bodies. It may be used to diagnose soft tissue abnormalities; an example is in the fungal infection aspergillosis (see Chapter 10) where distinct nodules may be visible, often accompanied by a decrease in size of the air sacs. It is not within the scope of this book to discuss radiography in detail. It is the province of the veterinary surgeon who should be consulted whenever

13 A finch with a drooping left wing, indicative of an injury

an X-ray examination is deemed desirable.

If X-ray facilities *are* available, they can be of great value in wild bird work. Although some injuries can be diagnosed satisfactorily by palpation alone, the treatment of many is improved if radiological examination has revealed such features as the extent of the damage or the relative apposition of the broken bones. However, there is the disadvantage that radiography of small birds may be difficult without considerable restraint or anaesthesia. The latter need not be as traumatic as it sounds and a number of anaesthetics can be used relatively safely for such purposes.[1]

Laboratory tests within the following specialities are proving of increasing value in the diagnosis of avian diseases:

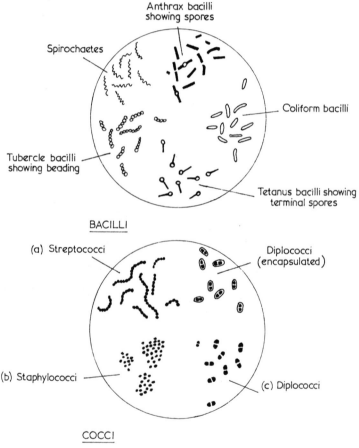

14 Diagrammatical representations of various types of bacteria. Note the variation in shape and appearance

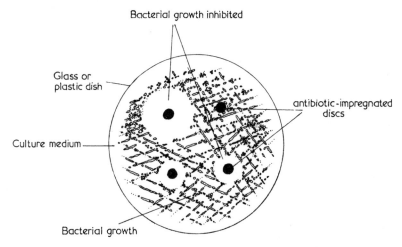

Bacterial growth inhibited

Glass or plastic dish

antibiotic-impregnated discs

Culture medium

Bacterial growth

15 An antibiotic sensitivity test. Each disc is impregnated with a different antibiotic; a clear area around the disc implies inhibition of bacterial growth

1 *Microbiology* Diseases due to micro-organisms can often be best diagnosed if the causal agent is demonstrated or grown. For example, if a bird has a swollen foot which is exuding pus, bacteriological culture of the pus may yield the bacteria involved and appropriate treatment can then be implemented. Even a smear of the pus may, if appropriately stained, reveal clusters of bacteria (see Plate 4). Antibiotic sensitivity tests can be performed on the bacteria isolated in order to help ensure that the correct antibiotic is used. Other types of organism, such as viruses, mycoplasmas and chlamydiae can also be grown in the laboratory but these involve more sophisticated techniques which are often not practicable with wild birds. Even the electron microscope can be used on exceptional occasions; for example, the author has used it to diagnose avian pox, a highly infectious disease of captive birds.

2 *Parasitology* Parasites are discussed in Chapter 11 and will not, therefore, be covered in detail here. Suffice it to say that the correct identification of parasites will help in the diagnosis and treatment of parasite-associated disease. In some cases this may amount only to the examination and identification of, say, a flea or tick. A strong hand lens or simple microscope can be used for this purpose in a bird hospital. At other times, more sophisticated techniques may be required – in the detection of parasite eggs in faeces, for example. A straightforward suspension of faeces in physiological saline will permit the identification of many parasites, but the detection of certain species, and the counting of worm eggs, will necessitate the use of special solutions, in which

79

parasite eggs will float, and of glass counting chambers. Such techniques will, in most cases, have to be performed by a veterinary surgeon or diagnostic laboratory although a suitably trained person at a larger bird hospital can do it himself.

3 *Haematology* Although the examination of blood is a recognised diagnostic aid in mammals, its use in birds has, until recently, been restricted. This has been due to a number of factors, not least among them the difficulty of obtaining adequate quantities of blood from small birds and the unusual properties of bird blood compared with that of mammals. In addition, there has been very little information on the normal blood values of birds and therefore the veterinary surgeon examining blood has had little or nothing with which to compare his results. The situation has now changed and in recent years a number of papers on the subject have appeared.[2,3] Blood samples should be taken only by a veterinary surgeon or by someone trained in the technique. Blood smears can be prepared by close-clipping a claw but for full haematology a sample should be withdrawn from the brachial (wing) vein. Useful haematological tests include PCV (packed cell volume) and haemoglobin and these and others are discussed in more specialised publications. Blood smears should always be examined for bloodborne parasites (see Chapter 11).

4 *Histology* Histological examination permits microscopical changes in the tissues of an animal to be seen and may aid diagnosis. In the case of live birds this involves the removal of a tiny piece of tissue, usually the skin, under appropriate anaesthesia. The tissue (biopsy) is fixed in a 10 per cent formalin or formol-saline solution before being subjected to a rigorous set of procedures, including immersion in alcohols, embedding in paraffin wax and cutting of fine slices. The slices thus cut can be stained with a variety of dyes – some to demonstrate bacteria, some to differentiate between types of cell, and so on – before being mounted on a glass slide with a coverslip. The finished product can be examined microscopically and kept for reference; further sections can be cut from the original paraffin wax block. This technique is only of limited value in the live bird and, as was mentioned above, is usually restricted to cases where there are skin lesions, but is of inestimable value in post-mortem diagnosis (see later).

POST-MORTEM DIAGNOSIS

As a general rule, a post-mortem examination should only be performed by a veterinary surgeon or by a person with adequate facilities and safeguards against infection. There is a recognised procedure for the post-mortem examination of a bird but it will not be described in detail here. Basically it consists of opening the body cavity to expose the internal organs *in situ* before they are removed for more detailed examination. Sometimes it is possible to make a definite diagnosis on the macroscopical (gross) findings alone; a ruptured liver, for example, is unmistakable and requires no further investigation. In other cases, a probable diagnosis can be made – yellowish-white nodules in the liver of an emaciated bird are strongly suggestive of avian tuberculosis but bacteriology and/or histology is needed to confirm the diagnosis. In other cases, the organs may appear normal macroscopically and no diagnosis can be made until other tests have been completed. This fact is often overlooked by lay people who keep birds. They submit a carcass for post-mortem examination and are disappointed to hear that 'there were no significant lesions – laboratory tests are continuing'. They also forget that such tests may take several days or even weeks to complete.

The success of a post-mortem examination is strongly influenced by the state of the carcass and how quickly and efficiently it has been packed and despatched to the laboratory. The bird should be sent fresh, as soon as possible after death. If there is any delay it should be chilled. While the prime aim should be to ensure rapid delivery and safe arrival of the specimen, the possible hazards to those handling the package must also be borne in mind. The UK Post Office Regulations relating to the posting and packaging of pathological specimens are reproduced in Appendix 7.

Laboratory tests have already been discussed in some detail. They play an invaluable role in the post-mortem examination of birds. However, their value will be influenced by the way in which the carcass has been preserved; deep-freezing, for example, will usually render histology and haematology useless. As a general rule a dead bird should be kept chilled, at normal refrigerator temperature, prior to examination.

A laboratory test that was not mentioned under 'Clinical Diagnosis' is toxicology or the examination for poisons. This subject is discussed in detail in Chapter 12. It is worth emphasising that a laboratory cannot just 'look for poisons'. There are many hundreds of possible poisons and their analysis is extremely expensive; the person who suspects poisoning, therefore, must state which poisons are a possibility so that the appropriate tests can be performed.

81

The various laboratory diagnostic procedures have been outlined in order to acquaint the layman with some of the techniques that are used. Specimens for laboratory examination will usually be the responsibility of a veterinary surgeon but from time to time, especially in established bird hospitals, it may be necessary for an unqualified person to take samples. These may be clinical specimens from live birds or, occasionally, tissues from a bird at post-mortem examination. The actual techniques will not be described here – a veterinary surgeon should be asked to demonstrate – but it may be useful to discuss some of the principles involved.

Strict hygiene precautions should be followed whenever pathological material is being handled. It is a wise safeguard to wear gloves and a pair of kitchen gloves, which can be washed after use, is quite adequate.

Specimens for microbiological examination must be handled with clean, perferably sterile, instruments. If this is not done contamination may occur. When dealing with tissues for histopathological examination, (histology) clean instruments are advisable but need not be sterile.

Any post-mortem material should be as fresh as possible – preferably taken immediately after death. If there is any delay, tissues can be stored (wrapped, or in a bottle) in a refrigerator at 4°C.

When selecting material for histopathology a portion containing both normal and pathological tissues should be taken – for example, a piece of lung on the *edge* of an area of discolouration or consolidation. If an organ such as the liver shows several discrete nodules or foci, the piece submitted should contain at least one such lesion but normal tissue must also be present.

Preservation of specimens for subsequent examination is of the greatest importance. As was mentioned earlier, freezing an animal or its tissues renders it virtually useless for histological examination. This method of storage should be reserved for the preservation of tissues for toxicology (analysis of poisons) only.

Tissues for bacteriology should be stored in a refrigerator at 4°C prior to examination or despatch. Alternatively, swabs can be taken and stored in Stuart's Transport Medium (STM). The latter must be obtained from a laboratory.

Tissues for histopathology should be fixed in 10 per cent formalin or formol-saline; this is available from a chemist or veterinary surgeon. Only small 1cm cubes of tissue are required. If the material is larger than this, cuts should be made in it to ensure penetration of formalin. Specimens should not be squashed or squeezed through the necks of bottles. Whenever material is preserved in formalin there should be at least five and preferably ten times as much formalin as tissue present in the container. If this is not possible, the formalin should be changed at least twice over a 96-hour period, the first change being made 12–24 hours after taking the tissues.

The submission of specimens to a laboratory is also an important consideration. Specimens must be wrapped well and fully labelled; an explanatory letter, giving a full history, should be included. Many laboratories have their own submission forms and will also supply containers for specimens.

Perhaps the most important aspect of diagnosis, whether clinical or post mortem, is the keeping of records. All wild bird cases should be documented. Each bird, on arrival, should be given a reference number and a record card should be issued for it. Simple suggested formats are shown below. At the larger bird hospitals such data as food consumption and behaviour are collated[4] but this is not always feasible. Our knowledge of bird diseases is increasing but there is still a dearth of information on wild species. The keeping of records, however brief, will go a long way towards remedying this.

CLINICAL RECORD CARD

Ref no   Species   Sex   Age   Ring number or other
                                            means of identification

Source   Weight on arrival   Condition on arrival

Initial findings   Preliminary diagnosis

Treatment and laboratory tests

Subsequent history

Fate – died/released/retained

Final diagnosis

The veterinary surgeon will probably have his own forms for post-mortem examination but the following format may prove useful for the layman who wishes to keep a summary of the findings :

POST-MORTEM RECORD CARD

Ref no   Species   Sex   Age

Clinical history

Date, time and circumstances of death

Date and time of post-mortem examination

Weight   External features

Summary of post-mortem findings

Laboratory tests

Diagnosis/significant features

7 The control of disease

J. E. Cooper

TREATMENT

The treatment to be adopted in any particular case depends on the disease present and its cause. There is no such thing as a panacea that will treat all diseases and the choice of a drug, or a method of treatment, is a skilled task, learnt only by careful training coupled with considerable experience.

Most laymen know little or nothing about drugs and find it difficult to assess when a particular treatment should be used. All too often one hears such statements as 'Terramycin is good for sick birds'. It is true that this brand of antibiotic is frequently successful in treating a wide range of infectious diseases but its action is limited (it will not, for example, have any direct effect on parasites or fungal infections) and neither it nor any other drug should be prescribed for sick birds in general.

In order to comprehend the basis of treatment one must have some understanding of the changes that take place when a bird is sick or injured. A healthy bird has a normal metabolism; that is, its organs function and work together to achieve a relative equilibrium. For example, the temperature of a healthy bird remains constant (usually at about 41°C) even when the temperature of its environment varies. The bird's internal organs operate together to ensure that the cells of the body receive a supply of oxygen and nutrients and that waste products are carried away. Thus, for example, a healthy respiratory tract means that air can be inhaled into the lungs, and there oxygen can pass across the lung surface and enter the blood stream; oxygenated blood flows round the body and supplies the tissues. A rather more complex tie-up concerns the liver and kidneys which, together, ensure that waste substances are excreted from the body. The liver is responsible for the production of waste materials which are filtered from the blood by the kidneys and passed out as the urate (white) portion of the droppings.

If a bird is sick or injured the intricate balance described above begins to suffer and tissues show changes associated with damage. For instance, if the lungs are diseased, oxygenation of the tissues is impaired; if liver or kidneys are damaged, excretory products may accumulate. When a bird receives a skin wound, the tissues are damaged and cells begin to die; damage to blood vessels results in haemorrhage and injury to nerves can cause paralysis or pain. If the wound heals satisfactorily, the cells regenerate and the area may revert to normal. If bacteria do enter the wound they can cause a localised infection or they may enter the blood-stream and result in an infection elsewhere. When bacteria (or other micro-organisms) multiply in the body they can cause disease and such agents are called pathogens. However, disease is not inevitable since the body has its own defence mechanisms which can isolate or kill invading organisms. The body defence mechanisms can themselves produce clinical signs of disease; the swelling and redness seen around a skin wound are manifestations of the body's inflammatory reaction whereby the blood supply has been increased, and the protective white blood cells mobilised, in order to meet the challenge.

It should therefore be apparent that the treatment of a sick bird must, wherever possible, be based on a diagnosis of the bird's condition. There is little point in treating a bird for parasitic roundworms if its diarrhoea is due to protozoa, bacteria, or an injury, none of which will be affected by anthelmintic (worm) treatment.

Occasionally therapy must, unfortunately, be empirical but as a general rule a provisional diagnosis should be made before treatment is started. Failing this, treatment should be symptomatic. For example, a bird may be presented which is thin, weak and dehydrated but which has no obvious diagnostic signs. In such a case it is logical to treat the bird by feeding it well (to improve its condition) and by administering fluids (to counteract its dehydration).

It is not possible to cover the wide range of drugs available and their application in avian medicine. Detailed information on this subject in the field of infectious diseases is given in Chapter 10. All that can be done here is discuss the main methods of treatment that can be adopted. From the outset it must be emphasised that many drugs are available on prescription only; it is assumed that they will be prescribed by a veterinary surgeon and used under his supervision. The legal implications relating to drugs are discussed in Chapter 2 and a table of drugs and their dosages is in Appendix 3. It must always be remembered that most drugs can prove toxic if administered at an incorrect dosage or to the wrong species and it is vital to consult the manufacturers' instructions.

The treatment of wounds is based upon minimising tissue damage and its effects and is discussed in Chapter 9. The wound is cleaned (and, frequently, dressed) and an antiseptic or antibacterial substance applied in order to discourage the multiplication of bacteria. If there is haemorrhage, pressure may be applied; if there is dehydration, fluid replacement (by the administration of glucose saline) is indicated.

Bacterial infections may be local or general. In either case the aim is to kill the bacteria or so reduce their numbers that the body can deal adequately with them. For local infections, cleaning with a mild antiseptic will suffice but for general infections, a course of an antibacterial drug, such as an antibiotic or sulphonamide, is warranted. It is important that such a course covers several days (as a general rule, more than three and less than seven) and that adequate therapeutic doses are given; if this is not done, treatment may prove ineffective and a build-up of resistant bacteria can occur. One must also remember that not all bacteria are affected by all antibacterial substances and in order to obtain the best results a 'sensitivity test', which can be carried out by a medical or veterinary laboratory, is strongly advisable. Nor are all antibiotics recommended for use in birds; the administration of some, such as procaine penicillin, streptomycin and neomycin, can prove fatal (see Appendix 3). A final point is that even when an infection has been controlled, recovery may not result. A bacterial infection produces considerable tissue damage and this may be irreparable or take a long time to heal, even when the causal organisms have gone.

There are many types of parasite which can cause disease in birds and drugs are available to kill most of them. However, it must be remembered that in general such drugs are specific – a drug that will kill nematodes (roundworms), for example, will usually be ineffective not only against protozoa but also cestodes (tapeworms) and trematodes (flukes). Once again, therefore, careful diagnosis is important and it may be necessary to solicit help from a laboratory in order to identify the parasites.

Nutritional diseases may either necessitate changes in diet or direct therapy. Vitamins may need to be administered and this can be done by injection or by mouth. Additional vitamins can also prove valuable as a supplementary form of treatment in other conditions – in wounds, for example, where the healing of tissues may be delayed if vitamin levels are low. Care should be taken not to administer vitamins or other nutritional additives in excess (see Chapter 14).

Anti-inflammatory drugs, such as cortisone, may be useful in some diseases but these agents are dangerous and they should only be administered under the direct supervision of a veterinary surgeon. Although they will very effectively reduce inflammation and tissue damage they also cause a decrease in the body's defences and the bird can easily succumb to infection.

Of all the methods of treatment, nursing is the most important. In many cases it can make the difference between a live and a dead bird. In these days of potent therapeutic agents it is easy to underrate nursing, although its value is evidenced by the success of many dedicated organisers of bird hospitals, some of whom have published accounts of their techniques.[1] Its importance is also emphasised in many chapters in this book. As a general rule good nursing cannot be taught but is acquired through experience; it demands patience and dedication. There also seems little doubt that some people nurse animals better than others. The principles of nursing birds are to make the patient comfortable, to encourage it to feed and preen and to carry out palliative (supportive) treatment. Many of these points will be discussed in detail in succeeding chapters, but brief mention should be made here of the importance of warmth.

Birds have a high metabolic rate and a high temperature; if they are maintained in a cold environment they expend energy in order to keep themselves warm. The optimum temperature for sick birds is at last 25°C and this can be raised to 32°C in severe cases. Higher temperatures should not, generally, be used for the reasons outlined in Chapter 3. There are various sources of heat that can be used but the important features are that the method should be a reliable one that will not burn the patient and that any temperature fluctuations are gradual. Hot-water bottles, wrapped in a towel to prevent overheating, are simple but effective[1] and domestic heating appliances can also be used; an airing cupboard conveniently combines the features of warmth and darkness. Of particular value for small birds are the heated hospital cages used by aviculturists. Whichever source of heat is used, care should be taken to insulate the bird by using materials such as newspaper, polystyrene and foam rubber. The techniques of treatment are taught best by practical demonstration but some notes would not be out of place.

First and foremost birds must be handled correctly and the author makes no apologies for briefly repeating the points made in Chapter 5. The wings in particular should be held close to the body and not allowed to flap. Large birds are best held with both hands taking great care to ensure that the bird cannot peck, or in the case of birds of prey, strike with their talons. A pair of gloves is useful and those of thin, but strong, leather and which also offer protection to the arms are particularly recommended. Small birds can usually be held in one hand, the fingers being parted in order to secure the head.

Oral administration of drugs is particularly convenient. Often the drug can be mixed in the food or dissolved in the water. Capsules can be

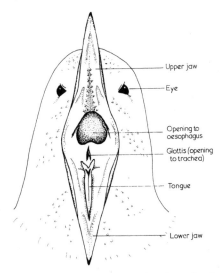

Upper jaw

Eye

Opening to
oesophagus

Glottis (opening
to trachea)

Tongue

Lower jaw

16 Bird with beak open showing glottis

secreted in a piece of meat or a dead mouse and fed to species such as birds of prey and corvids. Some birds have an uncanny knack of locating such a capsule and refusing it. In such cases force-feeding may be necessary and this is done by opening the bird's beak with the fingers and pushing the capsule down. Care much be taken to avoid the glottis which lies on the floor of the mouth and which opens and closes rhythmically as the bird breathes. The capsule should be placed behind the trachea and can usually be pushed further down the throat with the fingers (see Fig 16).

In some cases it may be necessary to use an oesophageal or stomach tube, either for the administration of a liquid medicine or for force-feeding. This consists of a piece of rubber tubing, boiled before use and lubricated with liquid paraffin, which can very gently be pushed down the oesophagus until it enters the crop or stomach. If necessary it can be attached to a syringe. Fluids can then be poured or pumped gently down the tube directly into the oesophagus, crop or stomach.

Although oral administration of drugs is often convenient, it is not always reliable. Birds may regurgitate the drug or its absorption into the body may be retarded by the presence of much ingesta or by hypermotility of the intestinal tract. As a result injections are often more satisfactory. There are four main injection routes employed in birds: subcutaneous – under the skin; intramuscular – into a muscle; intravenous – into a vein; and intraperitoneal – into the body cavity. Of these

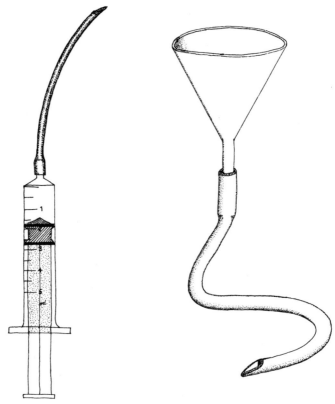

17a Syringe with oesophageal tube attached
17b Equipment for tube-feeding larger birds

the intramuscular is the most important and is used for the majority of injections of antibiotics and other drugs. Subcutaneous injections are employed for vaccination and for administration of fluids. Intravenous and intraperitoneal injections are not recommended in inexperienced hands and will not be discussed further although both are mentioned in other chapters.

Subcutaneous injections are given by lifting a fold of skin and injecting under it (see Fig 18). The most popular site for such an injection in birds is in the back of the neck; but in the author's opinion this is not the best place since there are many feathers in the region and it is often impossible to ascertain if the needle has in fact gone under the skin. It is preferable to use a piece of skin on the leg or over the pectoral muscles where it is possible to see the needle *in situ*. To facilitate this, a few small feathers can be plucked and the area wiped with spirit; the latter will

90

both clean the skin and make the injection site more visible. When a subcutaneous injection has been given successfully the skin will swell: this is quite normal and the swelling will subside as the drug is absorbed.

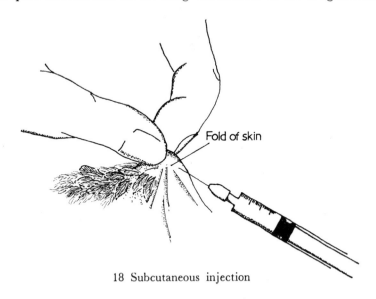

Fold of skin

18 Subcutaneous injection

Intramuscular injections are given in either the leg or pectoral muscle. In both cases the needle can, with confidence, be inserted quite deeply – for example up to 1·5cm in a crow. One of the best positions for a leg injection is the back of the leg, in the middle where the area is very fleshy, although the front can also be used (see Fig 19a). In the case of the pectoral muscle injection, the prominent keel (a sharp protruding part of the sternum) should first be felt and then the injection given a few millimetres on one side of it (see Fig 19b). If several injections are to be given it is advisable to alternate sites so that one area does not become too damaged by repeated needle puncture; for example, the right leg can be used for a first injection, the left for a second, the right for a third and so on. When giving any injection it is advisable to draw back the plunger before actually injecting the drug; if blood enters the syringe this means that a blood vessel has been pierced and it is advisable to reinsert the needle elsewhere. Such a precaution prevents a drug being inadvertently inoculated into a blood vessel, possibly with harmful results.

The techniques of filling and handling a syringe must be learnt practically and the layman is strongly advised to consult his veterinary surgeon for advice.

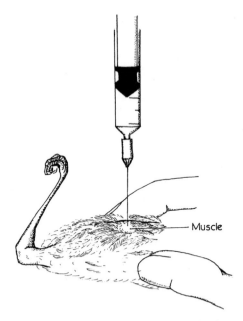

19a Intramuscular injection into the leg

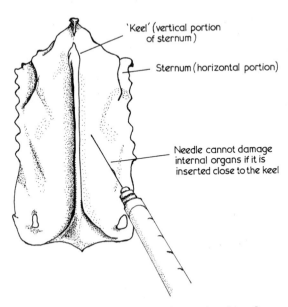

19b Intramuscular injection into the pectoral muscles (the figure also shows the structure of the sternum)

Other techniques of treatment can be mentioned only very briefly. Whenever a drug is applied to any part of the body care must obviously be taken to ensure that it comes into contact with the infected area. In the case of a foot infection, for example, nothing is gained by applying an ointment to a layer of dirt overlying the wound; it is vital that the area is first cleaned. If necessary, feathers should be clipped or plucked but some care should be taken here if there has been severe haemorrhage since the removal of feathers may dislodge a scab and reactivate haemorrhage.

Administration of drugs to the eyes needs some experience. Far too often an ointment is applied to the eyelids and not to the eyes themselves. It is important to ensure that the ointment actually touches the cornea of the eye; when the eyelids and nictitating membrane close they will effectively spread the drug across the eye (see Fig 20).

Application of a therapeutic agent to the cloaca is also sometimes necessary. This is best achieved if the bird is restrained on its front and the tail lifted – the opening to the cloaca should then be visible. A syringe or nozzle of an ointment tube can be gently eased into the cloacal cavity.

PREVENTION

The old maxim 'Prevention is better than cure' should be the rule in any wild bird hospital. Unfortunately, the admission of wild bird casualties can easily be a potent source of introduced disease and full preventive measures are rarely practicable.

The use of prophylactic vaccines is a well recognised part of poultry husbandry and the intensive conditions under which such birds are kept are not too dissimilar to those in a busy wild bird hospital. The close

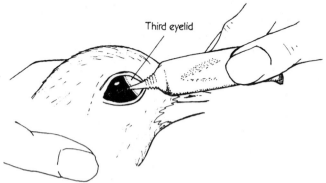

Third eyelid

20 Application of ophthalmic ointment. Note that the drug is placed directly on the surface of the eye

proximity of birds can result in rapid spread of bacteria and viruses and under such circumstances even some relatively innocuous organisms may assume a pathogenic role. It would be tempting, therefore, to extend the analogy and suggest that vaccination has an important part to play in disease prevention in bird hospitals. Unfortunately, there has been little work carried out on the vaccination of wild birds. Galliform species, such as pheasants, can usually be vaccinated with vaccines intended for domestic poultry but veterinary advice should be sought on this. The author has used an inactivated Newcastle-disease vaccine in birds of prey[2] and the safe use of an attenuated vaccine has also been reported in these birds.[3] Pigeon-pox vaccine might prove useful and effective in the protection of birds against avian pox – for example, if an outbreak should occur in a crowded bird hospital. Research is urgently needed into the role of vaccines in the prevention of disease in non-domesticated birds. Whatever vaccine is used, the aim is to produce antibodies in the bird so that it is able to resist a natural challenge; it must be emphasised that vaccination has no curative powers whatsoever.

The other aspects of preventive medicine that are of paramount importance are hygiene and good management. If hygiene is good, pathogenic organisms will be few and if management is good the birds will be better able to resist infection. Unfortunately the care of a disabled wild bird often necessitates its restraint in a small cage and the build-up of droppings is then a problem. Young birds that are being hand-reared are particularly liable to contaminate their environment. Hygiene involves not only the regular cleaning of cages and equipment but also personal hygiene. Hands should be washed after handling a bird in order to prevent the spread of disease not only to other birds but also, in some cases, to humans. If in doubt rubber gloves, that can be washed and disinfected, should be worn when handling a sick bird. Some examples of disinfectants are given in Appendix 3. If disinfecting agents are not available soap and hot water should be used. It must be remembered that the longer an object is exposed to hot water or a disinfectant the more organisms are killed. Disinfection will be hampered by the presence of organic material and therefore thorough cleansing, *before* the application of a disinfecting agent, is vital.

When a cage becomes empty it should be cleaned and disinfected before re-use, even if the previous occupant showed no signs of infectious disease.

In an attempt to maintain high temperatures many bird hospitals tend to keep their avian patients in poorly ventilated rooms. As a result the build-up of pathogens is facilitated and airborne infection becomes a hazard. It is also possible that exposure to bird droppings and feathers in such an environment may predispose human beings to the allergic disease 'bird fancier's lung' (see Appendix 6). One should therefore try to ensure adequate ventilation, preferably through the use of fans set in the walls or windows. Advice should be sought on the positioning of such fans since draughts must be avoided. If sophisticated ventilation is not available windows and/or doors should be opened on warm days. Drastic drops in temperature should, in general, be avoided but a gentle fluctuation will usually be harmless and will help patients that are recovering to acclimatise.

All examination and treatment of birds must be carried out as hygienically as possible and, in particular, all syringes and instruments should be sterile. The greatest care should be taken to ensure that only clean needles are used to withdraw fluids from bottles and that a different needle is used for each bird.

One important way of preventing the introduction of disease to a bird hospital is to quarantine incoming birds. Ideally, new patients should be kept in a separate cage well away from existing patients and tended separately, but rarely is such an approach practicable, usually because of insufficient space. In addition, it is sometimes desirable to put a newcomer with others of the same species to encourage it to feed, preen or bathe (see Chapter 13). Nevertheless, in most cases some attempt at isolating a new bird should always be made. Its cage can perhaps be placed in a corner of the room some distance away from the others and the bird fed and handled last, or dealt with separately. It is difficult to state how long a quarantine period should be – as a general rule, the longer the better – but seven days is a useful guide. If any clinical signs of disease occur during this time the quarantine period can be extended.

The prevention of disease in wild bird casualties poses several problems and there are many unanswered questions regarding the transmissibility of infections and variations in species' susceptibility. Some light is likely to be thrown on certain of these as a result of recent legislation controlling the importation of birds into the UK and other countries. Quarantine is a statutory requirement and, as a result, the veterinary authorities have drawn up guidelines on a number of subjects. In addition, in Britain at least, the Ministry of Agriculture has approved certain disinfectants for use against avian (and other) pathogens. The bird hospital organiser would be well advised to seek advice from the Ministry of Agriculture, through his veterinary surgeon, on this and other topics relevant to disease prevention.

95

8 Feeding birds

D. Washington

The information in this chapter is based on avicultural experiences. It deals with the requirements of birds with healthy appetites. The author has not included special diets for birds with digestive disorders as they really form part of specific treatments and will vary from case to case; many are mentioned elsewhere in the book. Birds of prey, seabirds, waders and waterfowl are also special cases which are not covered in this chapter.

Emphasis in the chapter is placed upon the practical aspects of bird feeding and not upon such theoretical nutritional data as protein and fat levels and digestibility. Such data are of little practical value to the layman who finds himself with a wild bird to feed.

Excluding the examples mentioned above, most bird hospitals are involved with seed-eating, insectivorous and omnivorous species. Aviculturists find it convenient to label small seed-eaters as 'hardbills', and lump the other two together as 'softbills'. This explains why advertisements of bird food manufacturers often list 'softbill food' which is a proprietary mixture suitable for insectivorous and omnivorous birds.

In feeding, as in other forms of bird care, opinions vary as to the best methods. It is therefore likely that some readers may not agree with all of the advice given here. Those who have better methods should stick to them. This chapter offers help to the inexperienced and is not intended to arouse controversy among those who are already competent.

In captivity both hardbills and softbills require two basic types of food, a staple diet of prepared food and a supplement of a live variety. Minerals and vitamins may also be desirable in small quantities. Useful advice is to be found in a number of books on aviculture.[1]

Seed-eating birds are the easiest to cater for. Their main food consists of a good quality, clean seed mixture such as, in Britain, Haith's 'British Finch Mixture' (see Appendix 4). Various brands are advertised in the weekly publication *Cage and Aviary Birds*; an up-to-date list should be consulted as prices are prone to considerable variation at times. Many pet shops sell similar mixtures, but it is best to avoid seeds sold specifically for budgerigars and canaries as these lack variety and provide an unbalanced diet for wild birds.

Most finches will take seed readily from a dish; some may not immediately recognise the source of food, but often they can be induced to try it if a quiet, harmless bird, such as a canary, is put in their cage to show them how. Another method is to disguise the food so that it is similar to something the bird normally eats in the wild. One example of this is the use of teasel to feed goldfinches. A few spent heads of this plant can be kept until needed, and goldfinches will readily probe them looking for seeds. They are extremely fond of a small narrow black seed called niger so a pinch of these can be sprinkled over each teasel head so that they drop into the holes previously occupied by teasel seeds. The gold-finch can then be encouraged to sample the seed dish by sprinkling niger over the standard mixture. Niger is related to the sunflower and con-tains a lot of oil, so it should not be used as the staple diet.

Pigeons and pheasants are also seed-eaters but they require larger seeds than finches. Pet shops and merchants usually sell seed mixtures for their species: in Britain, Haith's 'Dove and Pheasant Food' is a suitable brand. Wheat with some millet added can be used as an emergency ration for short periods in the absence of a well-balanced mixture.

Dry seeds are deficient in certain vitamins, but these can be supplied by providing fresh natural greenfood. This has the added advantage that the bird is given food with which it is normally familiar. One of the most versatile plants is chickweed, and most species enjoy eating the tender green leaves as well as the tiny seeds. This is a most popular plant among aviculturists and should not be neglected by those caring for sick and injured birds. Other useful foods are the seeding heads of sow thistle, groundsel, grasses, dandelion (especially for goldfinches), shepherd's purse and dock. Young tender leaves of dandelion and groundsel will also be enjoyed but care should be taken to see that the latter is not contaminated with an orange-coloured fungus which grows on some groundsel plants. There are many other useful plants, and those who want to explore this area in more detail should read the little book by Morse.[2] He gives the medicinal properties of most plants and for some of the more common seeds an analysis of their contents is included. Good ornithological textbooks should not be neglected either as they sometimes cover the special foods that certain birds like; for example crossbills are fond of fir cones.

A caution is desirable before leaving the subject of greenfood, and this concerns the use of toxic sprays. Clearly one does not want to risk poison-ing the birds, so care is needed to pick plants from places where sprays are not used (one's own garden for example) and, just as a precaution, the plants can be washed as well.

97

Grit should be offered as a digestive aid and as a source of minerals. This is not important when a bird is to be looked after for only a few days, but long-term patients will benefit from a supply. Grit is particularly important for some of the larger seed-eating birds such as pheasants and pigeons as they do not break the husks from seeds before eating them, but swallow them whole instead. Grit is also swallowed to help break down the seed prior to digestion. Suitable grit can be obtained from most suppliers of bird seed. It should be noted that certain birds, such as raptors, do not ingest grit.

Insectivorous and omnivorous birds are more difficult to feed than seed-eaters and, generally speaking, the specialised feeders are the most difficult to cater for; for example, flycatchers present a greater problem than thrushes. There are two aspects to consider: one is to provide an adequate artificial food and the other is to persuade the bird to eat it.

There are a number of proprietary softbill foods on the market, but some of the more experienced aviculturists prefer to use mixtures of their own.[1] F. Meaden, Secretary of the Association for the Study and Propagation of European Birds in Aviaries (ASPEBA) has kindly provided the following advice. The mixture he recommends is made from readily available items and will keep any small insectivorous bird in good condition for many months. A hand-operated or electric mixer is used to prepare a mixture from the following ingredients: the base consists of any cereal product. To this is added a variety of other ingredients such as soya flour (or soya beans ground to a meal), honey, a solid type of cheese such as Cheddar (grated or minced), cooked liver (lightly steamed if possible) and similar quantities of the following: grated carrot, celery, currants, raw cabbage, figs, dates, apple, nuts (or even peanut butter), dried milk and powdered baby or invalid foods such as Farex in the United Kingdom.

Other items can be profitably added to this basic mixture, especially left-overs such as roast beef and sausages. Even the heads from fresh fish, a few prawns or a couple of sardines may be minced and mixed with the basic diet. The consistency of the mixture should be crumbly and light. It is important to remember that where perishable items are used, no more than one or two days' supply should be prepared at a time. It is advantageous to offer the bird a multivitamin supplement when using this diet. Abidec liquid may be added to the drinking water or Vionate powder sprinkled into the mixture; both of these supplements are available through the larger chemists in the United Kingdom.

It is unlikely that the insectivorous bird will recognise the mixture as food, so some persuasion is needed. This process is known to aviculturists as 'meating off' and a useful paper on the subject has been written by Meaden.[3] The basis of the technique is to add live food to the artificial mixture to arouse the interest of the bird. A few active maggots are useful in this respect; they should be prevented from crawling away by using a shallow food container with an inturned lip around the edge (such as a sardine tin). Associated with this technique should be the immediate introduction of mealworms to the bird's diet. Meaden considers the mealworm to be the important food for bridging the gap between an insect diet and an aviary diet. He considers that a small insectivorous bird that has eaten six mealworms before roosting will survive the night, and a similar quantity in the morning will ensure a good start to the day. Diced mealworms should be placed in the mixture with the active maggots.

Another method is that used by Hanley on nightingales.[4] Mealworms are enclosed in a small corked glass tube which is laid in the food. On pecking at the mealworms the beak slips off the glass into the mixture, some of which is then swallowed. The meating off process may take only a day or two, or as long as several weeks. Once the bird is seen regularly taking the mixture, maggots and mealworms may be offered in separate containers.

There is some controversy over the use of live maggots since they may, on occasions, cause stomach irritation and disorders; it is therefore perhaps a wise precaution to pierce the cuticle or to kill the maggots by scalding before offering them as food. A more sinister threat is that of botulism (see Chapter 12), reported in captive birds at the London Zoo when they had been fed on commercially produced maggots.[5] Some aviculturists and veterinary surgeons believe that depriving maggots of meat for a few days prior to feeding them to birds will reduce the risk and such a step, although not proven, may be a useful precaution.

Living foods are extremely varied and birdkeepers have their own preferences. Most use maggots and mealworms and suppliers of these advertise regularly in the specialist press. Maggots may also be obtained from many fishing-tackle shops during the open season although the safety of these is likely to be even less certain than those from recognised suppliers. Other livefoods tend to be less convenient on a small scale, but if required in large numbers it may be worth establishing cultures. One group which has received attention over recent years is the locusts.There are several species available, but probably the most useful is the African migratory locust because it has the shortest hatching and growing time (it is possible to produce as many as five generations in a year). The main requirements are warmth (from a lightbulb), fresh grass daily for

99

food, moist sand for egg laying and cleanliness. Hunter-Jones has produced a comprehensive guide on housing and all aspects of maintaining locusts which should be read by anyone who plans to use them.[6] The smallest hoppers, as hatched, are fly-sized and suitable for such birds as warblers, whereas adults are several centimetres long and are ideal for starlings and crows.

In a useful series of notes on culturing insects[7] the following species were covered : wax moth (greater and lesser), Mediterranean flour moth, flour moth, fruit fly, whiteworm, rust-red flour beetle, house cricket and mealworm. In another issue of the same journal is a brief note on culturing house flies.[8] For those who have the time there is nothing better than collecting one's own wild insects. The author has successfully used an inverted umbrella held under overhanging shrubs and bushes whilst the branches were banged with a stick. The contents must be quickly transferred to a closed container to prevent too many escapes. Because of the many twigs and leaves this is not suitable material to feed from a dish, but it may be spread over the cage floor. Many aphids, green caterpillars, spiders and bugs can be collected in this way.

Another livefood which has recently been used by aviculturists is small fish fry[9] which can be offered in shallow dishes of water. A most unusual variety of species has been seen to eat fish daily in captivity, namely blackbird, song thrush, yellow, grey and pied wagtails, great-spotted woodpecker, chaffinch, greenfinch, whinchat, rock pipit, crossbill, yellow-hammer and reed bunting. In addition, in *The Field* of 17 February 1972 there was a report of a wren seen entering a trout hatchery and feeding on brown trout fry.

Before leaving the subject of animal food it is perhaps worth noting a paper by Hitchin and Harrison[10] on improving maggots. Maggots bought in shops have been removed from their food a day or two earlier and thus have used part of their body material without replacing it. Additives have been fed to such maggots, making them more suitable as bird food. They have even been fed on strained creamed spinach to provide chlorophyll and create a substitute for green caterpillars; such procedures may also help reduce the risk of botulism.

Larger omnivorous birds tend to be easier to feed than insectivores. Corvids will do well on a staple diet of soaked puppy biscuit (providing it is a well balanced one such as Saval No 1 in the UK). To this can be added meat meal or meat chips (25 per cent meat, made by Lowe's Animal Products in the UK – see Appendix 4), household scraps, softbill mixture, corn, layers' pellets (as used for poultry) and similar items. More detailed information on the care of corvids is given in Chapter 17.

Plate 9
Foot of a finch showing 'scaly leg' due to a mite infestation

Plate 10
A blood smear (highly magnified) showing two microfilarial worms. Note that the red blood cells surrounding the worms have a nucleus: this is a feature of avian blood

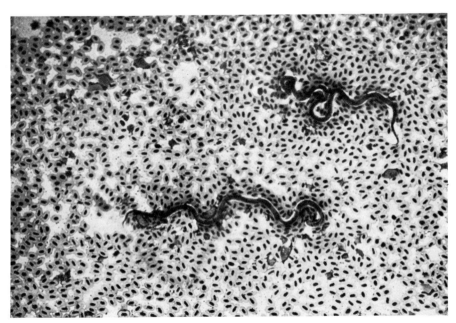

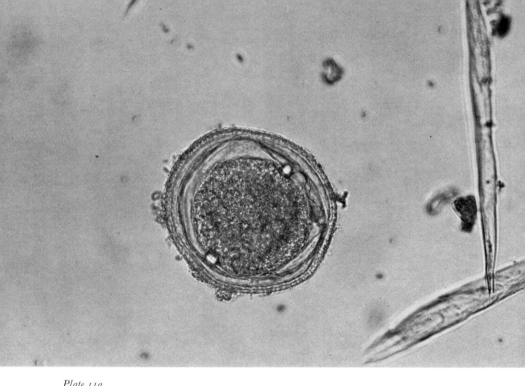

Plate 11a
A roundworm egg (ascarid type) as seen under the microscope. The structures on the right are pieces of vegetation in the faecal sample

Plate 11b
A highly magnified section of intestine showing four roundworms (ascarid type): these fill most of the cavity of the intestine. Such an infestation can occur in birds in poor condition

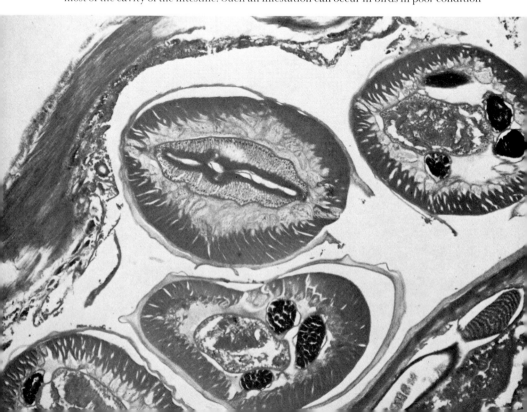

Fruits and berries are foods which have not been mentioned earlier, mainly because they are suitable for both hardbills and softbills. Many species will eat sweet apple, either sliced or by pecking at pieces fixed to the cage. Once a bird is seen to eat apple it is worth trying other fruits to give as wide a variety as possible to the diet. Berries, when they come into season, are invaluable. Elderberries will be eaten by warblers, finches, thrushes and tits and blackberries are almost as acceptable. If one uses berries, the best choice are those seen being eaten by the wild birds. There are some berries that, although attractive, are unpalatable to birds or have to hang on the bush for a long time before birds find them desirable. Fruits and berries should be used only as a supplement to the seed or softbill mixture, not as the main diet.

The author has left until last a brief section on handrearing because he has limited personal experience of this. He would, however, like to draw attention to two reference works. The first is a book by Ivor[11] which should be read by all those who have anything to do with running a bird hospital. The many photographs are a testimonial to Ivor's skill in bird care and there is a wealth of good advice in the text. He suggests the following ingredients for a rearing food which he finds highly successful for all songbirds, especially insectivorous species:

1 $3\frac{1}{2}$ oz tin strained beef heart
2 tablespoons mashed potatoes (not salted)
1 tablespoon mashed or finely grated carrots
2 tablespoons butter
1 teaspoon honey
4 drops liquid vitamin concentrate

As yet the author has been unable to trace a source of supply of tinned strained beef heart in the UK, but he gives this recipe for those who would like to experiment with a substitute. Ivor also gives full details of feeding techniques (he prefers a feeding stick to a syringe) and all aspects of caring for fledglings at various stages of growth.

The other publication is a scientific work describing a technique for rearing passerine birds from the egg.[12] The authors developed a technique for incubating and hatching song-bird eggs and rearing the young to maturity in their laboratory at the Kalbfleisch Field Research Station of the American Museum of Natural History in Huntington, New York. Their rearing mixture uses honeybee pupae as one of the main constituents. They also give a recipe for a softbill mix which they claim is used extensively for insectivorous birds in aviaries and zoological parks.

9 Wounds and injuries

J. A. Dall

Traumatic injuries are among the most common causes of debility in wild birds. They may result from gunshot or trap wounds, predation by wild or domesticated animals or collisions with motor vehicles or stationary objects. Many prove fatal but in some cases the bird is only injured.

Although the treatment of simple wounds may be carried out by laymen, more severe cases often necessitate surgery and sophisticated diagnostic aids, such as radiography. In this chapter, therefore, the methods of treatment are described in fairly basic terms. Many will be outside the scope of a member of the public but will help him or her understand the techniques used by the veterinary surgeon. They will hopefully also be a guide to members of the veterinary profession with little experience of birds.

WOUNDS

A wound is defined as a break in the continuity of the skin or the lining tissues of an internal organ.

There are many types of wound. Incised wounds are caused by a sharp object or edge slicing cleanly through the skin and, in some instances, the underlying muscles. Lacerated wounds are torn wounds of an irregular shape through the skin and into the underlying tissues. Punctured wounds are deep with a small skin wound but penetration into the tissues; they are often caused by shots or bites from a predator. Contused wounds are those wounds where, in addition to the break in the skin, there is considerable bruising. In birds bruising appears blue initially but later (after 72 hours) becomes green as the blood is broken down. A contaminated wound is one where foreign material is present and an infected wound is one which has already developed sepsis.

Healing of wounds

A number of specific terms are used in connection with wound-healing and these will be used in this chapter. First-intention healing is said to take place when there is no sepsis and there is a minimum amount of granulation tissue formed; the healing occurs by growth of protective epithelium over the wound. Second-intention healing occurs when the wound becomes filled with granulation tissue following infection, severe damage or bruising. The granulation tissue satisfactorily protects the wound but epithelium may not form, to complete the healing, until some time later.

Treatment of wounds

The wound should be examined gently to ascertain the type and extent of the injury. If there is still haemorrhage this must be controlled. On no account should any clot of blood be removed since this may result in further bleeding. Blood loss is likely to predispose to shock and therefore treatment for shock is also important *before* detailed attention is paid to the wound itself.

Control of haemorrhage

A clean incised wound tends to bleed to a much greater extent than a lacerated, punctured or contused wound. The blood volume of a bird lies somewhere between 10 and 15 per cent of its body weight. It is higher in small and young birds, so that a bird weighing 250g will have a total volume of 400 to 500 drops. Haemorrhage can therefore be of prime importance as a small bird can afford to lose no more than a few drops of blood. It is fortunate that avian blood tends to clot rapidly so preventing excessive bleeding.

The immediate control of haemorrhage is best achieved by applying local pressure, preferably with a piece of surgical gauze, to the bleeding point. Seeping haemorrhage may be controlled with styptics such as a silver nitrate pencil, alum crystals, tincture of ferric perchloride or a wafer-thin wisp of cotton wool placed over the area. These will all hasten the clotting process.

If bleeding is coming from the cut end of a vessel it may be necessary to use artery forceps to pick up the bleeding point and to ligate this with a suture material such as catgut, cotton or nylon. If there is haemorrhage from several points each should be treated in a similar manner. Such attention will probably necessitate veterinary assistance.

Internal damage is common in wild bird casualties, especially if they are struck by vehicles. Control is not easy and even diagnosis may be difficult. A bird with severe internal haemorrhage usually has pale mucous membranes and may show panting respiration. There may be abdominal distention and careful examination of the abdomen (by blowing the feathers in order to part them) may reveal bruising – a dark blue colour – through the skin and/or muscle layers. Fresh blood

105

is sometimes coughed up, regurgitated or passed from the cloaca. The prognosis in such cases is poor and death usually supervenes rapidly. In milder cases there may be a response to fluid therapy and other treatment for shock (see below). In large birds, such as waterfowl, it is sometimes possible to perform emergency surgery; the abdomen is opened and the haemorrhage controlled.

Treatment for shock

The condition arises from a marked drop in the volume of circulating blood following frank haemorrhage, internal haemorrhage or tissue damage. Extensive injuries are a common cause, the degree of shock depending upon the amount of haemorrhage or tissue damage. Pain, fear, exposure, thirst and hunger all further exacerbate the condition. Although some birds show few clinical signs of shock, the majority appear weak and listless, are cold to the touch and have rather pale mucous membranes. The heart beat is slower than usual – in small birds it may even be possible to count the beats. A bird with shock should be kept warm and quiet; it is wise to place it in a darkened box. Glucose saline may be injected subcutaneously at the rate of 0·5–1·0ml per 30g of body weight. This injection can be repeated every 4–6 hours if necessary. Oxygen may also be used, particularly in cases where there is marked respiratory distress.

It is preferable to prevent shock rather than treat it. All wild birds with injuries are liable to develop shock, often as much as 24–36 hours after the incident, and the provision of warmth and fluids will help prevent this. If in doubt detailed examination of the bird or its injuries should be delayed.

Attention to the wound

Following the arrest of haemorrhage and shock the wound can be examined further. A contaminated or infected wound should be cleaned with a dilute non-toxic antiseptic such as cetrimide. Care must be taken not to dampen the feathers too much as this can cause hypothermia and predispose to shock. Shot wounds must be examined as feathers are invariably taken in with the pellet or bullet. Round shot does not gather feathers to the same extent. It may be necessary to enlarge the wound to ascertain whether all foreign material has actually been removed. However, if radiography shows multiple shot in the body, it is *not* necessary to remove every piece. Particles lodged in muscles do little harm and are best left alone.

Any dead or necrotic tissue should be removed. An unpleasant smell may indicate gangrene and antibiotics must be given in such cases to control the causal organisms (bacteria). After thoroughly cleansing the wound, an antibiotic preparation or sulphonamide powder should be applied sparingly. Too much may retard healing. The cleaning and local application are repeated daily. It is generally true that sepsis is less common in birds than in mammals. This is probably due to the high body temperature and to certain inherent qualities of the avian defence mechanism. Nevertheless, hygienic precautions must always be taken when dealing with traumatic injuries in birds, especially open wounds.

The surgical repair of the wound can now be attempted but only large incised or lacerated wounds require suturing. During this operation the bird should be anaesthetised. This and other surgical procedures should be referred to a veterinary surgeon and, under normal circumstances, not attempted by laymen, but a brief summary of the approach is given below.

Suturing materials and instruments should be as delicate as possible; they consist of dressing forceps, artery forceps, sharp- and blunt-ended scissors, small surgical needles and needle holders, surgical thread and catgut (preferably with an attached needle). The instruments are sterilised before use. The operator's hands are washed in a mild antiseptic solution and clean cloths are used to cover the body of the bird, leaving the wound exposed. The exposed area is swabbed with small quantities of antiseptic solution. If necessary the operator's hands are again washed and gloves may be worn. The torn muscles are first sutured with catgut, approximating the lacerated edges as closely as possible. Too much tension is undesirable as the muscles are readily torn. The skin edges are then sutured together using nylon or silk interrupted or mattress sutures. Finally, the area is dusted with antibiotic or sulphonamide powder. The sutures should be left in position for ten days to two weeks. The wound need only be examined every second or third day unless there is evidence to warrant more frequent examination.

In some cases it may be advisable to use catgut sutures, which are absorbable, for the skin wounds. Such sutures are less strong but permit the bird to be released without delay.

In some small or deep infected wounds suturing is contra-indicated. Wounds do not readily become septic but if pus does develop it appears as a cheesy mass. This may have to be removed and the area swabbed with a mild antiseptic, such as cetrimide or gentian violet, or sprayed with a 10 per cent common salt solution. Daily attention to the area is then necessary and it will heal by second intention.

OTHER PHYSICAL INJURIES

It is not only trauma that will produce wounds and tissue damage. Wild birds are rarely affected either by burns or scalds but they may on occasion come into contact with corrosive liquids such as quicklime. In the majority of such cases death supervenes very quickly due to shock. However, if there is a reasonable chance of survival the bird should be treated for shock primarily and the corrosive materal washed off with a solution of bicarbonate of soda or a suitable antidote applied – vinegar at 50 per cent dilution, in the case of quicklime. The feathers protect the body to a great extent so the underlying skin is unlikely to be damaged. However, the legs, eyes and mouth may be quite severely affected. Tannic acid jelly may be applied daily to the legs and skin, the eyes and mouth bathed in bicarbonate of soda and antibiotic ointment applied. Affected birds must be kept warm and the floor of the cage should be covered in blotting paper or newspaper. Sawdust or peat should not be used since they tend to adhere to the wounds.

Occasionally, birds may also be burned following a fire, exposure to an electric current or, in captivity, a poorly positioned source of heat. Treatment should proceed as above.

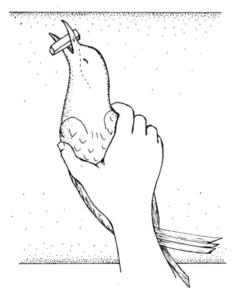

21 Artificial respiration is carried out by exerting gentle pressure on the thorax every 15–20 seconds. It is important that the bird's neck is extended and that the airways are kept clear; the use of a wedge to keep the beak open is advisable

Electrocution may, in addition to burning and/or killing a bird (see Plate 5) cause unconsciousness. Usually there is a history of contact with power lines or some other source of electricity. Treatment is palliative. If breathing has ceased artificial respiration should be carried out (see Fig 21) and oxygen, if available, can be administered.

Birds can drown if they climb into their water bowl and are unable to get out. The design of the container is very important. Although many wild birds will enjoy a bathe, drowning or chilling can again be a danger.

22 A bird with its feathers fluffed out to keep warm. Such an appearance in a casualty is suggestive of chilling but can also be a clinical feature of other diseases

A drop in body temperature can result in clinical signs of lethargy and depression, especially in young birds that are usually not capable of full thermo-regulation. If an adult bird gets both wet and cold a similar situation may result. Chilled birds should be gently warmed to a temperature of 30°C and must be carefully nursed. If frostbite has occurred exposed areas such as digits may appear red and swollen or (later) brown and wrinkled. Such changes are indicative of ischaemia (absence of a blood supply) and usually the affected areas will slough.[1] A veterinary surgeon may decide to amputate.

DAMAGE TO THE INTEGUMENT

Feather damage is common in wild bird casualties and may significantly influence whether or not the patient can be released. This and other factors affecting the plumage are discussed in Chapter 14.

If a claw is severely damaged it should either be cut off or removed surgically (by a veterinary surgeon). So long as the base remains it will regrow, though sometimes the new claw is rather deformed. The stump should be treated with gentian violet to prevent infection.

Cere damage is not uncommon and may be exacerbated if the bird is confined in a cage where it can fly at bars or wire netting. Local treatment of the area with a mild disinfectant or gentian violet is advisable.

If the beak is severely damaged the bird should be destroyed although such a decision will have to take into consideration the species involved. Fairly straightforward fractures can often be mended, and practically any method of immobilising the break may result in satisfactory healing. In small passerine birds the application of sticky tape, adhesive bandage or a strong glue may be sufficient. In larger patients plaster of Paris can be used or a piece of aluminium sheet cut to the size and shape of the beak. Alternatively the fractured ends can be wired together or, in certain cases, pinned. Perhaps the biggest problem is the feeding of the patient; many birds have to be force-fed (often by tube) or fed by hand, for two to four weeks until healing has taken place.

General attention to the beak is also important since overgrowth and abnormal development can occur even over a short period of captivity. Regular inspection is advisable and clipping of the beak, often coupled with manicuring using a sharp knife and nail file, may be necessary. However, before embarking on such procedures, one must be sure of the species in question; a few have an unusual appearance to the beak which might be mistaken for damage or unusual development (see Plate 6).

Mild abrasions of the skin are often seen in wild bird casualties. For example, the carpal area of the wing may become damaged if the bird is confined in too small a cage or if it uses the wing to compensate for a damaged leg. The wound should be treated as outlined earlier and every effort made to prevent further damage.

SKELETAL DAMAGE

Dislocations
These occur infrequently in birds; when they do they are usually of the elbow, tibiotarsal and metacarpo-phalangeal joints. In these cases the dislocation gives rise to loss of function, abnormal position of the limb and an unnatural movement of the joint. Every effort should be made to put the bones back into place, if necessary with the help of external fixation or internal wiring. Unfortunately, there is often a tendency for the dislocation to recur.

Fractures

A bone is fractured when it is either completely broken or cracked. Fractures are invariably caused by violence such as road traffic accidents, gunshot or the bird flying into stationary objects. Birds frequently attempt to fly through uncurtained windows, particularly when the latter are opposite each other and the birds can therefore see right through the room. Although this often results in skull damage and death, fractures of the wings can also occur. In addition, the wings can be fractured or dislocated by the action of the pectoral muscles if the bird, whilst struggling violently, is held without controlling the wings.

Fractures are referred to as simple when the skin is unbroken and compound when the fractured ends of the bone have penetrated the skin to the exterior. Complicated fractures are those which involve other tissues such as blood vessels, nerves, the lungs or spinal cord. Simple fractures can readily become complicated by injudicious handling. Comminuted means that the bone is broken in more than two parts at the fracture site, whereas a multiple fracture is said to be present when the bone is broken in more than one place. An impacted fracture is one in which the broken ends of the bone are driven into one another.

There is often pain and swelling at, or near, the site of a fracture and usually an unnatural amount of movement and loss of function. Deformity and shortening of the limb may be noted. Crepitus is often felt or heard as the broken ends are rubbed against each other. In old fractures, however, healing may already have occurred, often with resultant deformity (see Plates 7 and 21). The most common sites of fractures are the leg and wing bones.

In all cases involving fractures the bird must be confined closely for a reasonably long period. Diagnosis and treatment are aided if radio-

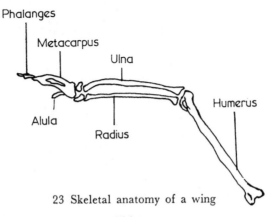

23 Skeletal anatomy of a wing

graphy is carried out, particularly since this will give some indication as to whether healing has already commenced (see Plate 8). Fractures may be treated either by external fixation (splinting or plastering), or by internal fixation (pinning, wiring, or plating the broken bone). General anaesthesia is essential in order to carry out the latter methods, but is also a great advantage when external splinting is attempted. The methods described later in this chapter are those recommended by the author. Other techniques also work extremely well.

It must be remembered that some fractures may not warrant treatment. For example, a fractured radius will be adequately splinted by the ulna and usually needs no further support. Old fractures, where callus is extensive, should usually be left alone; attempts to break down and reset the fracture are distressing to the bird and rarely successful.

Wing fractures

When the wing is at rest, folded against the body, the bones are usually in good apposition; this can be confirmed by radiography. As the bones are well supported by the body, all that is necessary is to fix them in this position and healing should occur. Three techniques based on this principle will be described.

One method is that first reported by Altman[2] and is depicted in Fig 24a and b. A strip of sticky tape is laid with the sticky side upmost along the back from the skull to beyond the tips of the flight feathers. Another piece is applied encircling the bird's body, including the wing, on a level just behind the wing butt, while a third piece encircles the flight feather tips and the tail. These two pieces are both applied sticky side down. The longitudinal strip is then doubled back on itself so preventing slipping of the chest band. The bird will have difficulty in maintaining its balance so it may be necessary to add more weight to the posterior band in order to achieve the best balance possible.

Alternatively the bird can be anaesthetised and the wing folded in the natural position. The humerus, radius and ulna and the metacarpals can then be sutured to the body wall, as recommended to the author by J. M. Hime. This method works extremely well in birds of the size of thrushes or larger.

Fractures of the phalanges may be dealt with in a similar manner by applying two sutures fixing the metacarpals to the radius and ulna with suture material placed on each side of the fracture site. The larger flight feathers are cut off to reduce the weight.

Another technique involves the use of intramedullary pins to fix the humerus and the ulna. The radius is very difficult to fix adequately but

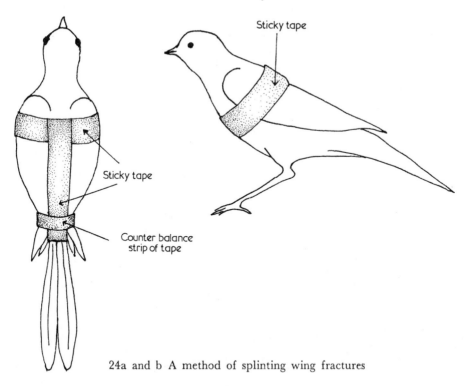

Sticky tape

Sticky tape

Counter balance
strip of tape

24a and b A method of splinting wing fractures

attempts can be made depending on the size of the bird. Small birds
up to the size of a blackbird may be pinned using Kirschner wires or
hypodermic needles of sufficient length and diameter as an internal
fixation pin. Avian bones are very brittle and the cavity is large; it is
necessary to use thinner pins than would be considered advisable in
mammals.

Leg fractures
In small birds the leg may be so badly damaged that the distal portion
hangs by skin or tendon alone. In such a case the appendage must
either be removed (cut off with scissors) or the bird will have to be
destroyed.

A number of different techniques can again be used to treat fractures
of the leg. When applying external splintage it is well to remember that
what goes on must be easy to remove without damaging the healed leg.
The larger birds are capable of accepting a plaster of Paris cast which
would be heavy and cumbersome for smaller birds, where a splint is
preferable.

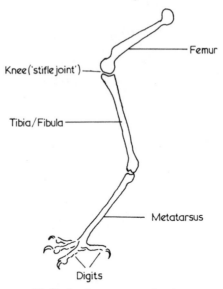

25 Skeletal anatomy of a leg

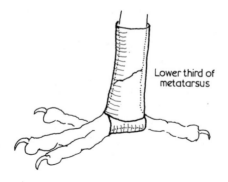

26 A method of plastering or splinting lower-leg fractures

Plaster of Paris casts are basically open weave bandages impregnated with plaster of Paris, and are made in different sizes. The material is thoroughly wetted and will dry rapidly, forming a rigid cast. When dealing with fractured legs it may be advisable to have the bird anaesthetised. The bones should be manipulated into apposition and the wetted bandage applied along the length of the limb including the joint above and below the fracture site. Two opposing slabs are applied and they are then moulded into the contours of the limb; any excess is cut off. Undue pressure must not be used when moulding the cast to the

114

leg, but it must fit snugly. Casts may be applied directly to the limb or applied over a layer of padding. The latter method makes the cast thicker but there is less likelihood of localised pressure necrosis. The cast must be as light as is consistent with complete rigidity. It should be examined within 24 hours of application to make sure that it is rigid and comfortable. The foot should not be cold and there should be no swelling. If either is evident the cast must be removed or cut in such a way that normal circulation is maintained.

Splints of any light rigid material can be used over a well-padded limb. These should be applied on opposite sides of the limb and held in place by sticky tape or bandage.

Limb fractures in small birds can be dealt with by using a feather quill of sufficient size split longitudinally. This can be opened and applied to the fractured leg over thin padding and held in place with strips of sticky tape made up of several thicknesses which are of sufficient size to cover the affected areas. An alternative to a feather quill is the plastic tube which houses a disposable hypodermic needle; these make excellent splints when cut longitudinally and are available (usually at no cost) from most veterinary practices.

The leg is positioned on one piece of sticky tape to which it will adhere. Another piece is then applied on the opposite side. When the

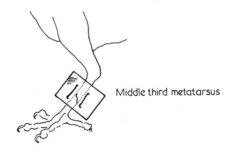

Middle third metatarsus

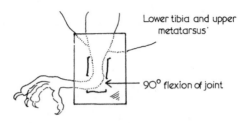

Lower tibia and upper metatarsus'

90° flexion of joint

27 Two methods of splinting leg fractures

115

two are pressed together they will enclose the limb. A flange is left in order to give more rigidity and the excess is cut away. Paper staples can be used to give extra strength. If the fracture is high in an area covered with feathers, it will be necessary to pluck the feathers to expose bare skin, otherwise the sticky tape will not stick to the limb. A fracture of the toes can normally be dealt with by using the neighbouring digit and binding the two digits together with strips of adhesive tape.

Internal fixation can also be used very satisfactorily in leg bones. Retrograde pinning is usually the method of choice although fractures can also be wired and plated. Such techniques must be carried out by a veterinary surgeon.

When an injury is so severe that healing is unlikely, the limb may be amputated. This is particularly acceptable in the case of a leg since many birds, especially passerines, survive very well with one foot or leg. Although walking birds are inconvenienced to some degree, if the foot alone is amputated a heavy callus and horn skin will develop quickly and allow the bird to walk on the stump. It may be possible to release a bird that has had a leg or foot removed but this is not so in the case of a wing. So, before amputating all, or part, of a wing, one must be certain that the bird can be offered a permanent home. Nevertheless, some patients do well following such surgery and may even breed in captivity.

The post-operative care of birds which have undergone treatment for fractures is most important and the role of the bird hospital cannot be over-emphasised. Attention must be paid to the welfare of the patient. Dressings should be checked to ensure that they are not too tight or rubbing the skin. Any evidence of infection, or of an intramedullary pin coming out prematurely, must be dealt with promptly. The bird must be encouraged to feed and, often most important of all, to take exercise. The latter will depend upon the case but in general it is true to say that prolonged immobilisation of a limb or joint is likely to prove deleterious; arthritis and ankylosis (stiffening) can result. For this reason a certain amount of physiotherapy may be advisable – ranging from the provision of a selection of perches (thus encouraging the bird to take exercise) to regular 'flying lessons'.

Arthritis
Arthritis is a not uncommon sequel to a fracture, especially if near a joint. It may also result from infection – for example, a penetrating wound or extension from a foot infection (see Chapter 10). An arthritic joint is usually stiff and cannot be flexed properly. In acute cases the

116

joint is swollen, warm and painful; chronic arthritis may be characterised by joint stiffness alone. Radiography will help in the diagnosis of both types.

Treatment of arthritis is rarely completely successful. The use of antibiotics (and, in some cases, corticosteroids) may result in a degree of recovery. In severe cases a limb may need to be amputated or the bird destroyed.

In all cases of severe injury it is essential to assess the chances of the bird's survival. Important considerations are whether it can be returned to the wild capable of fending for itself or, as mentioned above, whether suitable accommodation and care are available for its maintenance in captivity. It is unnecessarily cruel to attempt the impossible; in such cases the bird should be painlessly destroyed.

10 Infectious diseases
P. T. Redig

In providing medical care for wild birds, our attention becomes focussed on the problems affecting one bird at a time. This is vastly different from the way someone working in a poultry house approaches disease problems in a large flock. We do not have the option of killing several sick and dying birds in order to perform a thorough post-mortem examination together with bacteriological and virological investigations on several body organs. Often the history of the patient is unknown or only sketchy. The external signs of many diseases are non-specific, and to complicate matters further, most wild birds are very stoic, showing obvious signs of illness only when the disease is relatively advanced. The astute observer will note subtle changes beforehand. The recently captured bird will have all his defence mechanisms in full play, effectively masking any early signs of disease. Once disease is detected, some therapy must be instituted at the earliest possible moment. To delay while awaiting further evaluation or the isolation of specific pathogens may result in the loss of the bird. There are few diagnostic tools available to provide assistance in making clinical judgements. Such laboratory techniques as haematology and serum chemistry have been little developed even in poultry and almost not at all in wild birds. Serological (antibody) techniques are not readily available in most instances to aid in immediate diagnosis.

Thus it is apparent that a somewhat primitive condition exists in the art of diagnosing infectious diseases in individual wild birds. One is often compelled to take a gamble. Hopefully the research that is needed will be done in the near future; this may provide the answers needed to diagnose and treat disease in at least a few of the species of wild birds, particularly those that are endangered.

The approach used in this chapter attempts to do two things: first to describe what are felt to be some of the most likely encountered diseases and secondly, to provide a practical approach to the differential diagnosis and therapy of diseases in birds. Those drug dosages not given in the text are to be found either in Appendix 3 or in the publications in the reference section. The intention of this chapter is neither to

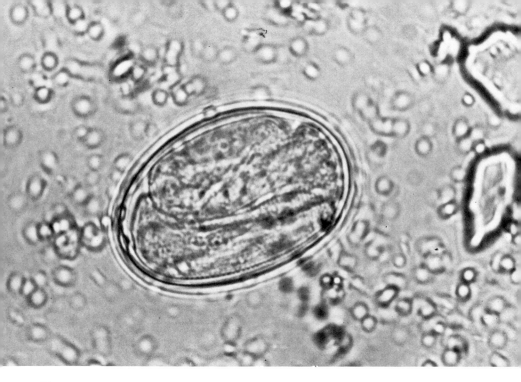

Plate 12a
A roundworm egg containing a developing larva: this species inhabits the air sacs and the eggs are first coughed up and then swallowed

Plate 12b
A larval worm emerges from a roundworm egg: the species is the same as above

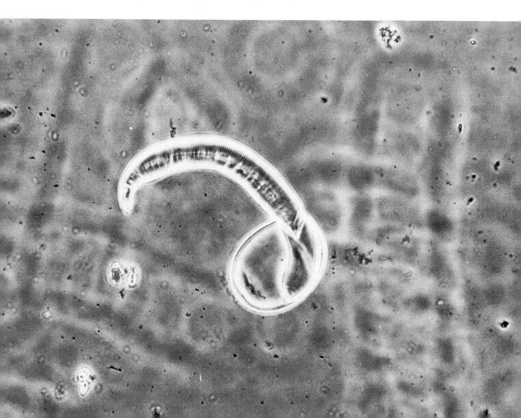

Plate 13
Oiled seabirds awaiting post-mortem examination. These birds appear to be only lightly oiled but have probably ingested considerable quantities

describe all the possible diseases that may be encountered in birds, nor to provide detailed descriptions of each disease discussed. Such material is very adequately covered elsewhere. It should be noted that much of the information in this chapter is likely to prove of practical value more to the veterinary surgeon dealing professionally with disease problems in wild birds than to the layman. Nevertheless, the latter may find it useful to refer to this chapter when discussing infectious diseases with his veterinary surgeon.

DESCRIPTION OF SPECIFIC CONDITIONS

Aspergillosis   Primarily a disease of the respiratory system, aspergillosis is caused by the fungus *Aspergillus fumigatus*. The disease is contracted by the inhalation of a large number of the infective spores from the environment. There is very little likelihood of the infection being transmitted from one bird to another.

Aspergillosis is the most common cause of death in captive birds. It is most likely to be seen in recently captured birds that are undergoing the stress of adjusting to captivity. Many birds harbour the organism within their body in a latent stage; disease occurs when the host's resistance is lowered by stress. Similarly, birds that have been injured or are infected with another disease frequently develop aspergillosis as a secondary infection.

Clinical signs associated with aspergillosis include dysnoeic (difficult) breathing, initially seen after mild exertion and developing over the course of a week to ten days into constant laboured, open-mouthed breathing. Accompanying this are loss of appetite, rapid weight loss and general listlessness.

Diagnosis is based on clinical signs and a history of recent stress and/or contact with an environment likely to be harbouring moulds. As is emphasised elsewhere in this book, accommodation for captive birds with straw or other organic litter in the vicinity is likely to be a source of infection. A wild bird with a broken wing forced to remain on the ground for an extended period of time is likewise a target for the *Aspergillus* spores that are often contained in organic materials on the ground.

A successful treatment for suspected cases of aspergillosis has not yet been developed. Work to date indicates that therapy must be vigorous and instituted early in the course of the disease. Agents that are likely to have therapeutic benefit include amphotericin B, pimaricin and 5-fluorocytosine. Therapy of aspergillosis must involve delivering antifungal drugs to both the lungs and to the air sacs. Therefore, simultaneous intravenous and aerosol therapy are indicated. Amphotericin B is given intravenously at 1mg/kg daily. Aerosol therapy is conducted by combining 1–2mg of amphotericin B and 100mg of chlortetracycline with 50ml of Alevaire. This is nebulised into a dark chamber in which the bird is resting over a one-hour period (see later). No controlled studies have been performed to determine how much time should be devoted to aerosol therapy, but 1–6 hours daily has been recommended. 5-fluorocytosine has promise as an effective treatment for aspergillosis and has the added advantage of oral administration (150mg/kg in four divided doses daily). Recent reports in the literature have shown compatibility between amphotericin and 5-fluorocytosine. Some authors recommend simultaneous administration.

The prognosis for treatment is guarded. Treatment must be instituted at the first suggestion if it is to be successful. Success where obvious clinical signs are apparent is virtually nil.

Tuberculosis   Reported in a wide range of species of birds.[1] Any one of three recognised types of tuberculosis organism (human, bovine and avian) is capable of producing disease in birds.

It is felt that the main route of infection is by ingestion of contaminated faecal material. Once ingested the organism spreads to the liver, lungs, spleen and other body organs. The course of the disease is usually one of protracted illness with infected birds showing unthriftiness. Appetite is generally good, but the birds lose weight rapidly. Other signs will reflect whichever organ or system is being colonised by the organism. Thus dyspnoea, lameness, jaundice and arthritis may be seen. The plumage becomes ruffled and lacks lustre. Infected wood pigeons are reported to have darker plumage due to feather atrophy and deposition of excess melanin. At post-mortem examination tubercles containing large numbers of acid-fast bacilli will be found in nearly all internal organs. Similar gross lesions may be seen in certain other conditions, for example pseudotuberculosis, and therefore microbiological and histological examination are important.

Accurate diagnosis of tuberculosis in a live individual is a difficult proposition. Intradermal tuberculin testing has been shown to be reliable in chickens, but not in turkeys. Pigeons, ducks and Japanese quail have been tested, but the procedure was found to be of limited value. Therefore, it can be concluded that the test would not be likely to be useful across the spectrum of wild birds.

Treatment of infected birds is not normally attempted. The disease is controlled by elimination of infected individuals and providing good hygiene in the housing facilities.

There is little evidence that avian tuberculosis is likely to be transmitted to man by infected birds; however, the possibility does exist. Suspected cases should be thoroughly examined to confirm the presence of avian bacilli and to find the source of infection.

Salmonellosis   In the United Kingdom, Macdonald and Cornelius[2] described epidemics of salmonellosis in house sparrows and greenfinches. With these last exceptions, *Salmonella* bacterial infections in wild birds are probably not a clinical problem of any significance. *Salmonella* isolates have been reported from small numbers of individuals over a wide range of species. The significance of the disease among wild birds lies in the potential source of infection for domestic poultry. The reported cases of epidemics of salmonellosis in wild birds involved gregarious type birds that were concentrated in one area for purposes of feeding or roosting.

In domestic poultry *Salmonella pullorum* and *Salmonella gallinarum* are the causative agents of pullorum disease (bacillary white diarrhoea) and fowl typhoid respectively. These two have rarely been reported in wild birds except for pheasant, pigeons and quail which are frequently managed under domestic poultry conditions. All other *Salmonella* infections, involving about a thousand serotypes, are lumped under the name of paratyphoid infections and these are of some concern in wild birds. *Salmonella typhimurium* is the most frequent isolate from wild birds.

Paratyphoid infections generally follow one of two courses. Among adult birds retained in captivity for some time the disease is an enteric one, producing weakness, emaciation and accompanied by diarrhoea. The other form is an acute septicaemia likely to be encountered in birds stressed by injury, malnutrition, or other ailments. In either case, the course of the disease is variable; it may terminate in immediate death or last one to several weeks. Recovered birds remain healthy carriers for long periods of time.

Diagnosis is most certainly accomplished by the recovery of *Salmonella* bacteria from faecal material. Isolation and identification of *Salmonella* spp must be carried out in a laboratory.

Several drugs have received attention for the treatment of paratyphoid infections including tetracyclines, chloramphenicol, streptomycin and the nitrofurans. The nitrofurans have proved to be the most effective. For the treatment of individual birds, furazolidone tablets are recommended. Water soluble nitrofurans may also be effectively used in the drinking water. However, successful treatment does not eliminate the organism and the recovered bird may remain a carrier.

All birds must be considered potential carriers of *Salmonella* bacteria : however, the gregarious types of bird are more likely to be carriers than other species. As with other enteric pathogens, hygiene is the best means of control. New birds being received for treatment should ideally be isolated from other patients until their *Salmonella* status has been determined. Bird handlers should be concerned about serving as mechanical vectors in transmitting the organisms from one bird to the next within the hospital and take precautionary measures to avoid this. Litter and cages should be adequately cleaned to prevent harbouring of the organisms. Vegetation may harbour the organisms for up to 28 months, protected soil for at least this long and hard surfaces (such as rocks and metal) somewhat less.

Paratyphoid infections are readily transmissible to man and bird handlers are again cautioned to exercise good hygienic practices in their work (see Appendix 6).

Arizona infections are also reported in wild birds. The disease strongly resembles paratyphoid infections in terms of history, transmission, host spectrum and treatment. There appears to be a notable effect on the nervous system with trembling, ataxia and blindness occurring in many cases.

Coliform infections   Infections caused by coliform bacteria, especially *Escherichia coli*, affecting the gastro-intestinal tract and the respiratory system of birds, are second only to aspergillosis in their occurrence and clinical importance. Such infections usually manifest themselves within the first two or three days after injury and/or capture. The most prevalent signs are those of gastro-intestinal upset, ranging from a simple refusal to eat to severe vomiting and diarrhoea. The respiratory form takes longer to develop and is usually manifested as an air sacculitis. Persistent vomiting is likely to accompany the air sacculitis along with dyspnoea and respiratory *râles*. Vomiting will be seen in more advanced cases, often immediately preceding death.

The gastro-intestinal form occurs as one of two syndromes : one involving the upper gastro-intestinal tract, crop, oesophagus and stomach, and the other involving the intestines. The former yields persistent vomiting or failure to turn the crop over, the latter a profuse watery diarrhoea.

E coli is the most frequently isolated organism although it must be remembered that in many species of bird it is a part of the 'normal' bacterial flora. In clinical cases it can be obtained in nearly pure culture from swabs taken from the oesophagus and stomach, cloaca, or from the faeces. In the face of disease signs described above, the recovery of B-haemolytic *E coli* should be regarded as diagnostic and therapy should be instituted immediately. Other organisms which may be encountered with much less frequency in these conditions are *Pseudomonas* sp, *Proteus* sp and *Klebsiella* sp.

Treatment of coliform infections consists of antibiotic therapy and good nursing care. Most cases respond to oral oxytetracycline therapy, and this is a good drug with which to institute therapy while antibiotic sensitivity of the isolates is being determined. Affected birds should be housed in an incubator or hospital cage where the temperature can be maintained constantly at around 30°C. Fluid replacement must be given. Many affected birds will drink large amounts of water; however, if signs are severe, additional fluid should be provided by stomach tube or subcutaneous injection.

Food should be provided in several small meals throughout the day. If solid food is not retained, the feeding of a concentrated nutrient supplement is indicated.

Because of the prevalence and severity of coliform infections in birds, prevention practices and early treatment of suspected cases must be employed. Among grain-eating birds, *E coli* is not a normal inhabitant of the gastrointestinal tract. Infection in these birds is most likely due to inadequate hygiene. In carnivorous birds, on the other hand, *E coli* is part of the normal gut flora. It appears that during times of stress, this 'normal' component of the gut flora may become pathogenic. This same stress may also increase the susceptibility to infection of those birds that do not normally carry the organism. Prevention is best accomplished by adequate cleaning of all holding facilities and equipment and keeping foodstuffs and water clean. Prophylactic therapy with oral broad spectrum antibiotics can be carried out for the first 3–5 days after admission but should be embarked upon only in exceptional cases, and then only under veterinary supervision. This practice will allow the bird an opportunity to begin recovering from its injuries and to adjust to the additional stresses of captivity (change in diet, unnatural surroundings, disturbance) without risking the chance of a coliform infection.

Staphylococcal infections   Infections due to staphylococci merit special consideration apart from other microbial organisms because of the frequency with which they occur and the severity of the pathology that is induced by them. There are essentially three syndromes of interest: post-trauma and post-surgical wound infections, septicaemias and synovitis, and bumblefoot. The organisms responsible for these syndromes are *Staphylococcus aureus* and, possibly, other species.

Staphylococcus spp are regular inhabitants of the skin and mucous membranes of all animals and are thus ready invaders of damaged tissue. Cooper and Needham[3] examined the prevalence of staphylococcal organisms on avian feet, comparing domestic poultry with birds of prey. *S aureus* was recovered from 4·7 per cent of the poultry and 10·8 per cent of the raptors sampled. *S epidermidis*, which is probably not usually a pathogen, was recovered from 80·9 per cent of poultry and 62·1 per cent of raptors.

The septicaemia/synovitis syndrome, though noteworthy among poultry flocks, occurs relatively infrequently among wild birds. The signs are swelling of the joints (particularly noticeable at the hock), lameness, and elevated body temperature. Diagnosis can be made by the recovery of the organisms from a lesion. For instance, material from a swollen hock can be aspirated with a needle and examined directly by microscope or cultured on blood agar. Treatment can be accomplished by the administration of high levels of antibiotics including penicillin, oxytetracycline, and chlortetracycline. Since a major predisposing cause to this condition is injury to the joint capsule and tendon sheaths, affected birds should not be kept in wire bottom cages but rather provided with a soft substrate on which to stand.

The presence of staphylococcal organisms as regular inhabitants of the skin gives them a great potential to infect wounds caused by trauma or surgery. In those instances where open fractures of pneumatised bones such as the humerus or femur occur, there is also provided a pathway for these skin-borne organisms to enter the respiratory system. Despite the potentialities associated with this problem, birds are relatively resistant to the development of such infections. Therefore, with a little care, such infections can be quite well prevented. Thorough cleaning and debridement of traumatic wounds, aseptic surgical techniques, and the use of sterile protective bandages over wounds are advised. Should an infection occur, the site should be opened, flushed with saline and drainage established. Systemic antibiotics should also be administered. It is necessary to cover the site with protective bandages and these should be changed at least every other day.

Probably the most frequent staphylococcal problem is infection of the foot pads which produces the condition known as bumblefoot. This occurs in a wide range of species although it tends to be most common in the larger species such as birds of prey and crows. The primary event in the development of this condition is a break in the epithelium of the

126

bottom of the foot which allows the entry of pathogenic bacteria. There are several factors that can cause this break in the epithelium. One is direct puncture by a thorn, nail, or by one of their own talons in the case of the raptors. Another is bruising of the foot which occurs among large birds confined in cages. Such birds tend to make very hard landings when moving from perch to perch. Finally, improperly shaped or uncomfortable perching surfaces often lead to the development of corns on the foot and toe pads. As the corn builds in thickness, pressure is applied to the deeper tissues of the foot resulting in damage. The corn loosens about the edges allowing the entry of bacteria which can rapidly and easily colonise the damaged tissues.

There are also several indirect factors that predispose birds to the development of bumblefoot. It is felt that diets deficient in vitamin A may compromise the integrity of the skin. Hygiene is important insofar as birds forced to sit on a perch contaminated by faeces are exposed to a larger number of pathogens. The nature of the perching surface can predispose to the development of this condition. Smooth wooden dowel perches often lead to corn development because there is not enough abrasiveness to produce normal sloughing of the epithelium. On the other hand, too rough a perch can cause damage to the skin. A similar situation can occur in water birds where a hard surface, such as concrete, can cause ulcerations of the feet which may become infected.

The lesions of bumblefoot (see Fig 28) in birds of prey have been classified by Halliwell[4] and this is a useful system of reference in other species. Four arbitrary syndromes are identified, as follows:

1 Enlarged metatarsal pad with infection and cellulitis (infection of tissues under the skin) of the entire pad; the most severe, sometimes accompanied by osteomyelitis (bone infection)
2 Enlarged metatarsal pad with a localised encapsulated lesion
3 Enlargement of one discrete area of the foot: corns; foreign bodies; or improper moulting of the foot epithelium
4 Enlargement of the distal extremities of the phalanx resulting from rupture of the flexor tendons at the ends of digits II, III, or IV

It is entirely possible that a bird may develop a combination of two or more types of bumblefoot. Further, without treatment, it is likely that the condition will develop from a less serious to a more serious type.

With these points in mind, the prevention of bumblefoot can be considered. Perching surfaces should be designed to match the foot of the particular bird being cared for. If possible several perches of various shape and texture should be provided. In the case of birds of prey it is generally a good idea to provide padding; leather, indoor or outdoor

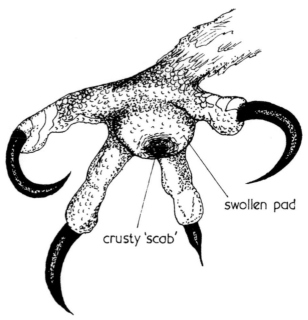

swollen pad

crusty 'scab'

28 Type I bumblefoot showing swollen and infected metatarsal pad

carpeting, and artificial turfs are satisfactory. Frequent examination of the foot for early detection of problems is important and it should be a general rule, with all species of wild bird, that the feet are inspected whenever the bird is caught, handled or restrained.

If treatment becomes necessary, immediate and intensive therapy is required. The entire foot should be scrubbed and necrotic material and keratinised deposits removed by curettage. One recommended therapeutic approach[4] is the local application of a mixture of dimethylsulphoxide (240ml), dexamethasone (4mg), and an effective antibiotic, daily for 2–3 weeks. Antibiotic sensitivity tests will help to ascertain which drug is most likely to prove effective. Another report[5] recently suggested that radiation therapy might be effective. The author has found that wrapping the toes around a large ball of gauze sponges, then dressing the whole foot with gauze and adhesive tape, accompanied by administration of effective systemic antibiotics, provides satisfactory resolution of the problem. If the condition results in the development of osteomyelitis, amputation of a digit may be required. If the entire foot is severely infected, it may be wiser to destroy the bird than to amputate since in some instances the remaining good foot will also develop severe problems.

MISCELLANEOUS BACTERIAL INFECTIONS

Erysipelas   A septicaemic disease of birds that is characterised by rapid onset and death, erysipelas is only infrequently encountered among wild birds, probably because the incidence is low and infected birds die very quickly. It may become a problem of serious proportions in a clinical setting or an aviary where the disease could spread very quickly from its initial source to healthy stock.

Erysipelas has been reported in a wide variety of domestic and wild birds. The cause, the bacterium *Erysipelothrix rhusiopathiae*, can produce disease in humans and pigs as well.

It is assumed that infection with this disease occurs either by ingestion of the organism or by wound infection. The organism may persist in soil or organic matter.

From a clinical standpoint, erysipelas is very serious. There are no specific signs associated with it. One sees a sick bird suffering from diarrhoea, listlessness and prostration. One may also note a cloudiness in the eye and detect a fever by the warmth of the feet and beak. The organism may be recovered by bacteriological culture of blood but death of the bird will probably occur before a determination on the culture is made. The organism is fairly susceptible to antibiotics and has often been treated in turkey flocks by a single injection of a long-acting penicillin. The diagnosis in a live bird will have to depend to a large extent on a history of recent exposure to situations where erysipelas could be encountered. The incubation period may be as short as two days. In the injured wild bird, where no history is available, such a diagnosis is nearly impossible. Again treatment with broad-spectrum antibiotics, good nursing care and close observation are the only options open until culture and antibiotic sensitivity tests can be made.

For the protection of all other birds in the aviary or clinic as well as the hospital personnel handling the birds, post-mortem diagnosis must be attempted in suspected cases. Care must be exercised as infection of humans can occur through cuts or abrasions in the skin. If a positive diagnosis of erysipelas is made, thorough cleaning and disposal of materials with which the bird was in contact is recommended. Administration of a long-acting penicillin to all birds is also advisable.

Listeriosis   The disease caused by *Listeria monocytogenes* is of rare occurrence, even among domestic poultry. Reports of the disease in wild birds are confined primarily to incidental findings upon post-mortem examination.

Avian cholera Like erysipelas, *Pasteurella* infections are typified by acute to peracute septicaemia, high morbidity and high mortality. Avian cholera has been recognised for nearly 200 years and reported in a wide range of wild birds. Waterfowl have historically been the most heavily affected with tens of thousands dying in the United States in outbreaks occurring at concentration points along the migration routes. Secondary transmission to scavenging and predatory birds accompanies these outbreaks and leads to further dissemination of the disease to surrounding areas.

The signs of the disease are non-specific. One is presented with a listless bird with no appetite. Differential diagnosis is virtually impossible. Death ensues so quickly after the onset of signs that bacteriological or serological techniques requiring even a few hours of time to provide results will be too late in guiding one clinically. However, a diagnosis can usually be made by obtaining a history and finding the point of origin. It is highly unlikely that only one case of fowl cholera is occurring. Among gregarious species several individuals can usually be found in all stages of disease from incubation to death. Moreover, scavenging or predatory birds that have been found anywhere near a concentration of waterfowl that are experiencing an outbreak of fowl cholera are also very possibly infected. Post-mortem examinations on dead birds will confirm the diagnosis.

The lesions seen post mortem vary with the acuteness of the disease, but are nonetheless characteristic of a septicaemia. Swelling and mottling of the liver, spleen and kidneys can be observed. Haemorrhage in the respiratory system also occurs. Copious quantities of purulent material frequently exude from the nares and pure cultures of a *Pasteurella* sp may be obtained from this material. The organisms survive well in dead and decomposed animals and are reported to be recoverable from the bone marrow of such specimens.

Transmission of the disease is thought to occur by ingestion or inhalation. Control is achieved by not creating conditions that cause excessive concentrations of birds in any one area. Some areas of the mid-western United States have a history of avian cholera epidemics. Control has been brought about by not maintaining the open water that attracted large numbers of birds there in the first place. In the clinical setting, hygiene is again the best way of preventing in-house epidemics.

Penicillin and chlortetracycline given intramuscularly have been reported to be effective in treating individual birds caught up in an outbreak of fowl cholera. Such birds should also be kept in isolation.

Ornithosis (psittacosis)   This disease, caused by *Chlamydia psittaci*, has been extensively studied since the late 1800s. The main impetus for this interest has been the capability of the organism to produce fatal pneumonia in humans, particularly those who have come in contact with birds. Over the years, a somewhat confusing picture has developed. At one time the causal organism was thought to be a virus; there is now evidence to indicate it is an intracellular parasite that is not classifiable as a virus, bacterium, or rickettsia. Initially parrots and other psittacine birds were thought to be the only avian hosts and hence the name psittacosis was adopted. Further study revealed that many non-psittacine species were also natural hosts and the name ornithosis came into use to describe those infections resulting in man from non-psittacine sources. Subsequently the organism was discovered to be very prevalent in poultry flocks in the USA and not only chickens, turkeys, ducks and geese but also a percentage of the people that handle these birds may show evidence of infection. In the UK ornithosis is rare.

The incidence and severity of clinical infections in birds vary widely with the susceptibility of the host and the virulence of the particular strain of *Chlamydia*. Among wild birds, the feral pigeon has been shown to have the highest incidence of infection, with young squabs being the most likely sector of the population showing overt clinical infection. The disease is subclinical or latent in most adult pigeons as well as other species of birds. Chlamydial infections have been demonstrated by serological tests or direct isolation in over 140 species of birds. The disease is of world-wide occurrence. Latent infections can become clinical in times of stress, injury, or simultaneous infection with another organism.

The route of infection is primarily through inhalation of aerosols containing the organism. Infected birds will shed large numbers of these organisms in nasal discharges and in the faeces. As these dry, dust aerosols are easily generated by movements of the bird and they can set the stage for infection of other birds or of human handlers. Plainly, control is best achieved by isolation, hygiene, good ventilation and, where practicable, use of face masks by workers.

The signs of the disease are again non-specific; diagnosis cannot be made clinically or by gross post-mortem examination but depends upon laboratory tests using tissue extracts from dead birds or cloacal washings of live birds. In addition, serological tests can be carried out on blood samples from live birds. The indications that would lead one to formulate a tentative diagnosis of ornithosis are signs of rapid onset, mucopurulent nasal discharge and conjunctivitis, anorexia (loss of appetite), diarrhoea that may be blood-tinged, and often death. The history is suggestive and attempts to confirm other diagnoses are unsuccessful.

The saving grace of this diagnostic dilemma is that the causal organism is highly susceptible to the tetracyclines and chloramphenicol. The literature provides several formulations for providing therapeutic levels of chlortetracycline in the drinking water or food of various species of birds. Intramuscular injections of these same drugs at a rate of 50mg/kg may be given to birds that are too ill to eat. Care must be taken to prevent the production of infected dust aerosols and the operator should wear a mask during the handling to prevent contracting the disease.

In summary, ornithosis is a disease that is quite widespread throughout all species of domestic and wild birds. The latter are particularly prone to be latent carriers. However, in the care of wild birds, its prevalence as a clinical problem is far below that of diseases such as aspergillosis and *E. coli* infections. Further, its susceptibility to broad spectrum antibiotics enhances the opportunities for successful therapy in the absence of a confirmed diagnosis.

VIRAL INFECTIONS

Viral infections of birds tend to be either very serious, with great likelihood of mortality, or clinically inapparent. A wide range of viruses is capable of infecting birds and many have a very narrow host range. Further, within any given host/parasite relationship there may be manifested a range of signs depending on the immune status of the host and the virulence of the viral strain.

Those virus infections that produce overwhelming disease and high mortality (such as Newcastle, duck plague, falcon herpesvirus) must be diagnosed if one is to protect other birds at risk. There is little hope for the affected bird, but thorough laboratory investigation including virus isolation is indicated if history, clinical signs and gross post-mortem examination suggest the possibility of infection. The milder viral infections (such as pox and respiratory viruses) are important for the role they play in compromising the host's overall ability to withstand the challenge of secondary bacterial invaders. Indeed, it is possible that many of the diseases of birds now thought to be caused by bacteria (for example, *E coli* infections) may have an underlying primary viral component that is as yet unrecognised. A sizeable number of well recognised viral diseases are seen in poultry; however, few of these are known to occur in wild birds, except under conditions where such birds may have contact with poultry.

The following discussion will provide descriptions of viral infections that either are highly infectious and present a serious threat to a population of birds or are in themselves only mild, but that predispose to secondary bacterial invasion. There are undoubtedly many others that could be discussed but the inability to make a clinical diagnosis rapidly and accurately and the lack of specific therapy for viral infections put them beyond the scope of this discussion.

Newcastle disease   Important because of its wide host range, its contagiousness and because it is often fatal, Newcastle disease is common in many parts of the world and attempts to control its spread have resulted in strict regulations on the international movements of birds. The disease is characterised by either gastro-intestinal or respiratory problems followed by the development of central nervous system dysfunction. There is no clear-cut way to diagnose this disease definitely other than serology and/or virus isolation.

The organism is transmitted in the excreta, exudates, eggs, and offal of infected birds. The virus is relatively resistant to environmental inactivation and has been reported to survive on down feathers as long as 123 days at 20–30°C. Carrier states have been demonstrated in various species of birds.

Pathological changes in infected birds are variable making it impossible to confirm a tentative diagnosis on the basis of gross post-mortem findings. Thus laboratory supplementation is required in the form of serological tests and virus isolation. Newcastle disease is not likely to be diagnosed in a single free-living, live individual unless one is specifically looking for it.

Several vaccines, the efficacy of which has not been completely tested in wild birds, are commercially available and can be used to vaccinate at-risk birds if there is a likelihood of Newcastle disease developing in a group of flocking birds. The efficacy of vaccination in the face of an outbreak is not known.

Duck plague   An acute herpesvirus infection of ducks, geese and swans, duck plague is a highly contagious disease and has been responsible for the death of a large number of waterfowl. However, it was not until 1967 that it was recognised in North America.

The organism appears highly specific for members of the family Anatidae. Most reports of the disease have come from domesticated waterfowl. Many species of wild waterfowl have been experimentally infected. It is felt that the paucity of information concerning the disease

133

among wild populations can be attributed to a lack of recognition rather than a low incidence.

Sudden high mortality in a flock is the first sign of disease. Adult birds will be found dying, yet in good condition. Affected birds will be depressed, unable to stand, have photophobia (dislike of bright light) and watery diarrhoea. They will exhibit tremors if forced to move. Mortality among overtly ill birds approaches 100 per cent.

The disease can often be tentatively diagnosed on the basis of gross post-mortem lesions. The principal damage is to the vascular system resulting in the presence of free blood in the body cavities. The reader is referred to the supplementary reading for a complete description of pathology in various species.

There is no therapeutic or palliative treatment for the disease. Control is effected by the removal of healthy birds from the affected area, which in a wild population of migrating waterfowl, would be extremely difficult. It would hardly be feasible to attempt depopulating at the site of infection and dispersal of infected birds would only result in further spread of the disease to previously uninfected areas. Therefore, management procedures should employ means which prevent excessive concentration of birds in one area. Chicken embryo-adapted vaccines are currently being tested.

Avian pox This disease is characterised by areas of epithelial hyperplasia and proliferation (visible as scabs) on the feet, beak, cere and mucous membranes of birds. In wild birds, the condition is usually easily recognisable, benign in nature, and self-limiting. A condition in captive birds referred to as canary pox is considered more serious as the infection is known to become septicaemic and produce signs of acute respiratory distress. Mortality is high. In wild birds, two forms are described. The first is a diphtheritic form in which moist lesions develop in the pharynx and upper respiratory tract. The other and more common form is the skin form in which warty lesions develop on the unfeathered parts of the body. Little is known about mortality in free-flying birds afflicted with pox infections.

The organism is spread directly by contact between infected and uninfected birds or indirectly via biting insects or contaminated objects. The disease is usually mild and self-limiting. There is no treatment; the greatest clinical concern is prevention of spread to other birds.

Herpesvirus infection of hawks and owls Herpesviruses have recently been demonstrated in North America and Europe as the causative agents in peracute liver and spleen infections of birds of prey. The lesions produced resemble similar syndromes in other species of birds such as pigeon herpesvirus, duck virus enteritis and Pacheco's parrot disease.

The disease is peracute and invariably fatal. The most prominent gross post-mortem findings are light tan necrotic foci in the liver. Experimental investigations have determined that the virus is fairly host specific; however, modes of transmission are completely unknown. There is no treatment.

Though few cases have been so far reported it is felt that herpesvirus infections could threaten birds held in close confinement for propagation and other research work.

DIAGNOSTIC AND THERAPEUTIC APPROACH TO DISEASES OF WILD BIRDS

The majority of wild birds presented for treatment will be showing non-specific signs of illness such as loss of appetite, listlessness and, frequently, emaciation. One should begin making a differential diagnosis by obtaining whatever history is possible. Information as to when and under what circumstances the bird was found, the presence of other diseased or dead birds, knowledge about poisoning possibilities and contact with domestic species of birds may provide the most positive clues for making a diagnosis. Information regarding how long ago the bird was found, what attempts have been made to feed it and any other attempted treatments will assist prognosis.

Following history taking, a quick and gentle physical examination should be made. If nothing significant has been located, the bird should be confined in a semi-darkened cage to settle down, and then observed from a distance. Particularly noteworthy is the frequency and character of breathing. In most healthy birds there should be no noticeable body movements associated with respiration; the contour feathers below the sternum should lie completely still. Deviation from this status is highly suggestive of respiratory system disease or abdominal pain.

In any bird the first indication of illness is unusual behaviour. Even very slight aberrations are significant. For instance, a freshly caught wild duck that is content to sit quietly in a cage rather than flail at the approach of a human is showing signs of serious illness.

Determination of the particular disease or body systems affected is a big problem and often makes a definitive diagnosis difficult. The diseases that must initially be considered in making a differential diagnosis are as follows:

135

1   Birds that have been hospitalised for a period of time and suddenly show initial signs of illness probably have aspergillosis. This is especially true if the onset is accompanied by rapid weight loss, but no other signs. Close observation in an undisturbed setting is likely to show an increased respiratory rate as well as varying degrees of abdominal breathing.

2   If more specific signs are shown by hospitalised birds, they will most likely be vomiting, diarrhoea, or failure to digest a crop of food. The most likely cause is an overgrowth of normal gut flora, particularly *E coli*. Anorexia often accompanies or even precedes these conditions.

3   A newly obtained wild bird presented with non-specific signs forces one to rely heavily on whatever history is available to make immediate clinical judgements.

4   Individual newly obtained wild birds showing specific signs may be differentially diagnosed as follows:

a   Signs of CNS (central nervous system) disturbance should include various bacterial and viral encephalitides, concussion and poisoning, with the latter two being prevalent in most situations.

b   Signs of respiratory distress should include aspergillosis, air sacculitis and/or pneumonia from a variety of bacteria and most likely some viruses. The former will not exhibit moist *râles* (detectable with a stethoscope), sneezing or coughing whereas the latter will usually have moist *râles* at the very least. Mechanical impingements on the trachea and bronchi and tuberculosis should also be considered in those cases showing severe dyspnoea.

c   Signs of gastro-intestinal disturbance, vomiting and diarrhoea, are primarily due to *E coli* infections. However, *Salmonella* spp. and the fungus *Candida albicans* should be considered. The latter was omitted from the previous discussion because of its rarity. It is detected usually by culturing the faeces; therapy is discussed later.

d   Signs of septicaemia include elevated body temperature, usually detected on the legs and beak, cloudiness of the eye, as well as anorexia, depression, and possibly altered respiratory characteristics. *E coli*, *Pasteurella multocida*, *Erysipelothrix rhusiopathiae* and viraemias associated with pox or systemic viruses (hepatitis or respiratory viruses) are likely candidates.

THERAPY

Once illness has been detected in a bird, treatment must be initiated immediately. As is obvious from the previous section, diagnoses are not likely to be very certain and confirmation of any tentative diagnoses before instituting therapy will usually take more time than can be afforded. The majority of diseases encountered in wild birds presently fall into one of two categories : either the disease can be treated with broad spectrum antibiotics (most bacteria) or, apart from nursing care, it cannot be treated at all (viruses and most fungi). One must determine which body system(s) is being affected by the disease and what is the most effective way of delivering therapeutic drugs to that site. Additionally, provision of good nursing care is very important.

In the absence of a specific diagnosis, the following regimen has been found effective by the author in treating and partially diagnosing diseases in wild birds. It should be noted that it utilises laboratory facilities which may not always be available elsewhere.

At the time of initial examination a blood sample is taken and from this the PCV (packed cell volume) and total protein are determined (see Chapter 6). A blood smear is also prepared. Cultures are taken of the pharynx, trachea (accomplished by thrusting a swab of appropriate size through the open glottis) and cloaca. Then a broad spectrum antibiotic such as a tetracycline is administered. Birds showing signs of gastro-intestinal disease should be given preparations designed for oral use using the high end of the dosage-range recommended for that particular drug. Generalised septicaemic signs should be treated by parenteral admini-stration of antibiotics. Intravenous and intramuscular injections of tetracyclines or chloramphenicol are effective. Respiratory infections should also be treated with intravenous or intramuscular injections of antibiotics.

Additionally, good results are obtained by providing nebulisation or intratracheal therapy. The former is accomplished by placing the bird in an enclosure and nebulising a solution of antibiotics and mucolytic agents. A recommended aerosol mixture consists of 50ml of Alevaire, a mucolytic agent, to which has been added 100mg of chlortetracycline, oxytetracycline, chloramphenicol succinate, or other suitable broad spec-trum antibiotic. This solution is administered at a flow rate that will provide an hour of therapy. The treatment should be performed at least twice daily. In suspected cases of aspergillosis, 1–2mg of amphotericin-B should be added to the above mixture. Since this drug is light-sensitive, therapy must be performed in the dark. A similar solution can be used for direct intratracheal therapy. Here the antibiotics are measured out in terms of body weight dosage, suspended in Alevaire, the volume of which is determined as a function of body weight and is 2ml/kg. A blunted 18-gauge needle is mounted on the syringe and thrust into the trachea when the glottis of the bird is at its widest point during inspiration. The solution is rapidly injected into the trachea. DMSO (dimethyl sulphoxide) can also be used as the vehicle in place of Alevaire. It is felt that DMSO's great penetrating capability may more effectively carry antibiotics into an affected area of the respiratory system. At present, the choice of therapeutic agents and methods of administration is dictated primarily by convenience and availability of equipment.

Antibiotic therapy must be vigorously supplemented with nursing care. Aspects to be given attention include nutrition, fluid replacement, warmth and freedom from excessive disturbance. At the time of initial examination and treatment, vitamins A, D, and C and B-complex should be provided by injection. On subsequent days B-complex should be readministered if the bird refuses to eat voluntarily. It is also advisable to force-feed at this time. Waiting a day to see if the bird will adjust and eat voluntarily may only deprive it of an additional 24 hours of nutrition. Diagnostic information will be gained by observing how the bird handles this first meal.

For clinical purposes, dehydration can be assumed to exist in all injured birds. Corrective measures are taken by the subcutaneous injection of normal saline or 5 per cent dextrose given at the rate of 4 per cent of normal body weight in 2–3 divided doses daily. This fluid is easily administered along the medial surfaces of the thighs with a 25- or 27-gauge needle. In a 1kg bird up to 15ml of fluid may be injected at one site. Finally the bird is placed in a darkened container where the temperature is maintained at a constant level (26–30°C) and food and water are provided.

If the first force-fed meal is retained and digested, one can allow the bird an opportunity to feed on its own, provided it is already in a fair state of nutrition. An emaciated bird should be supplemented with force-feeding to ensure adequate intake. If the animal refuses to eat, force-feeding must continue. If the meal is vomited or retained in the crop, tube feeding of a fluid diet must be implemented. A recommended mixture consists of the normal ration for the bird combined with 5 per cent dextrose and an appropriate amount of a protein hydrolysate preparation. This is all put in a blender and thoroughly mixed until its consistency is such that it can be administered via a syringe. As an example the mixture for a buzzard weighing 1,000g would consist of the whole bodies of 4–5 skinned laboratory mice (40g), 50ml of 5 per cent dextrose and 10ml of Nutri-cal paste. This is administered in 3–4 divided doses throughout the day, using a 50ml syringe to which is attached 12cm of polyethylene tubing. Adequacy of the technique in meeting the nutrient requirements is best monitored by weighing the bird daily.

138

After the first day of therapy, alterations in the regimen may be indicated on the basis of results obtained from bacterial culture and sensitivity as well as other diagnostic efforts.[6] However, in most cases, due to the sensitivity of many organisms to broad-spectrum antibiotics, the initial therapy will be continued. If the fungus *Candida albicans* is recovered from the cloaca or from caseous lesions in the mouth, therapy will have to be altered at this point to handle this organism. Antifungal therapy will be necessary.

Treatment of suspected systemic viral infections is handled similarly. The aim is to provide nursing care and prevent complications arising from secondary bacterial invasion.

The subject of infectious diseases in wild birds is a vast one and whole texts have been devoted to it. Insofar as wild bird casualties are concerned, it is probably of less importance than physical injuries, poisoning and oil pollution. Nevertheless, some birds submitted to a bird hospital are likely to be suffering from an infectious disease and others may succumb to one, often as a result of reduced resistance, during their time in captivity. In the relatively intensive environment of a bird hospital spread of pathogens can occur fairly easily and, as was emphasised in Chapter 7, preventive measures are necessary if this is to be avoided. However, much depends on an understanding of the infectious agents involved and it is hoped that the examples given in this chapter will help in the provision of adequate guidelines.

11 Parasites

J. E. Cooper

There are many species of parasite that can affect wild birds and these range from tiny single-celled protozoa to cestodes (tapeworms) which can be several centimetres in length.

Although parasites live in, or on, a bird, they are not necessarily associated with clinical disease. Parasites are found in apparently healthy free-living birds and this leads one to question under what circumstances they prove pathogenic. It seems probable that parasites cause disease when their numbers increase excessively or when the host's resistance is reduced by disease, stress or debility.

Very often these two factors operate concurrently and this is particularly true in the case of wild bird casualties. For example, an injured jackdaw may come into captivity. It is accommodated in a small cage and therefore soils its food; as a result ova or larvae are ingested and parasitic worms in its intestine increase in numbers. At the same time the jackdaw's ability to deal with parasites, and to combat their effect, is reduced by its injured state, by its poor nutritional condition and by the stress of captivity. The result in such circumstances can be clinical disease associated with parasites.

The control of bird parasites is an important subject and one that concerns all those who keep wild birds in captivity. However, it must be remembered that the answer is not simply therapy. Parasite numbers must be reduced by good hygiene so that life cycles are broken; if a cage is thoroughly cleaned every three days, for example, certain worm eggs and other parasites are removed before they can develop. Prior to this they will do no harm if ingested by the bird or one of its cagemates. Likewise, carriage of parasites from one cage to another can be reduced by carefully washing the hands and by other precautionary measures. Some parasites can be introduced into a cage with food; for example, a dead pigeon used as food for a kestrel may infect it with the protozoon *Trichomonas gallinae*. The use of an old nest for the rearing of a fledgling can result in the introduction of mites, ticks or fleas.

Life cycles of internal parasites vary from species to species and this must be considered when attempts are made to kill them. A generalised plan for the life-cycle of a nematode (roundworm) is as follows:

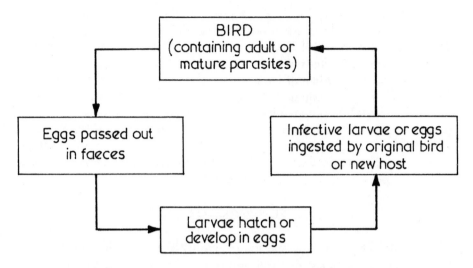

Some parasites can (and in some cases must) develop in other hosts before they return to a bird – trematodes (flukes) are a good example – and this can complicate the sort of life cycle depicted above. In general, the more complex the life cycle of the parasite, the less likely it is to cause problems in captive birds.

The treatment of parasites may be necessary for a number of reasons. If a bird is showing clinical disease, treatment may be imperative in order to ensure its survival. More often, the bird shows only mild clinical signs, such as loss of weight or condition, and, while treatment is still advantageous, it need not be immediate. Alternatively, a bird may show no clinical signs of disease but parasite control is necessary to prevent a build-up in the aviary or cage.

The main groups of parasites of birds are as follows:

Ectoparasites (external parasites): mites and ticks (Acarina)
lice (Mallophaga)
fleas (Siphonaptera)
louse flies (Hippoboscidae)
other flies (Diptera)

Endoparasites (internal parasites): roundworms (Nematoda)
tapeworms (Cestoda)
flukes (Trematoda)
spiny-headed worms (Acanthocephala)
single-celled organisms (Protozoa)

141

Each of these groups will be discussed in this chapter but details of the various species, their identification and life cycles will not be given. The emphasis will be on parasite control and prevention, with particular reference to captive wild birds. For those interested in bird parasites, the book *Fleas, Flukes and Cuckoos*[1] is unreservedly recommended while a number of other texts discuss diagnosis and treatment in captive birds.[2, 3] A final plea is that any parasites removed from or passed by birds be preserved in methylated spirit and submitted for identification to a suitable laboratory such as the Natural History Museum in London. Much remains to be learned about avian parasites and new species probably await description.

ECTOPARASITES

Mites and ticks Certain species of parasitic mite will attack birds. Usually they suck blood or tissue fluids, causing anaemia, irritation and restlessness. Mites of the genus *Knemidocoptes* particularly affect the feet and legs and produce swollen, deformed lesions[4] (see Plate 9). These and certain other species remain on the host but the red mite *(Dermanyssus gallinae)* is only a nocturnal visitor to the bird, spending the remainder of its time hiding in crevices of buildings. As such it can be difficult to control. Spraying of the accommodation with gamma benzene hexachloride has been recommended in order to control red mites in aviaries but should only be used with caution.

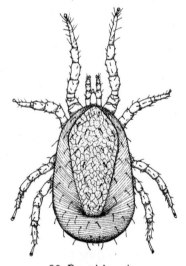

29 Parasitic mite

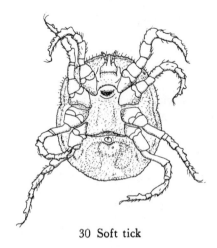

30 Soft tick

Treatment of mites on a bird should be carried out with an appropriate insecticide. Birds tend to be sensitive to such chemicals and therefore special care should be taken in their choice and use. Plant products, such as pyrethrum, are usually safe while a 10 per cent emulsion of benzyl benzoate has been recommended specifically for knemidocoptic mange.[2] A number of products are available for the treatment of cagebirds, their cages and nestboxes, and these can usually be employed safely for wild birds. Nevertheless, it is important that the manufacturers' instructions are followed. Trichlorphon, in an aqueous solution, has been advocated as a general parasiticide for birds of prey.[5]

Ticks differ only slightly anatomically from mites. They are large and very much more conspicuous, especially when the female is engorged with blood. Although heavy tick burdens may occur on birds from time to time, they are not common and those who handle birds regularly are likely only to see the occasional tick. Individual ticks usually cause no clinical signs but large numbers may result in anaemia and irritation or dermatitis (skin inflammation).

Ticks can usually be removed fairly easily, especially if ethyl or methyl alcohol (for example, methylated spirit) is first applied to the parasite's body. Care should be taken to ensure that the tick's mouthparts are not left in the skin since this can result in infection. Heavy infestations of ticks (or their immature stages) are best treated with insecticides, as described above for mites.

Lice Probably the most common ectoparasites seen on birds, it is important to remember that those found on avian hosts are all

143

biting lice – that is, they chew feathers and skin debris – and not sucking lice, which feed on blood. Louse burdens often increase when a bird is in poor condition. Affected birds may show poor plumage which lacks lustre and which is often rather 'moth-eaten' in appearance. The lice themselves may be seen on feathers, especially round the head or under the wings, and their characteristic eggs (nits) are laid in rows on the barbs of the feathers.

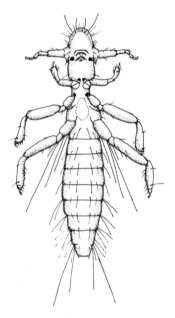

31 Biting louse

Large lice can be removed manually but usually the treatment of choice is administration of a suitable insecticide together with attempts to improve the general condition of the bird. Feathers heavily infested with nits can be cut off.

Fleas These are seen commonly on some species of wild birds and in others may be acquired from prey. They suck blood but in small numbers are unlikely to cause obvious harm to a bird. Control of fleas is less easy than other parasites since fleas breed *off* the host, that is, they drop their eggs which develop into larvae and pupae in a suitable locality (for example, a nest) and only the adult fleas return to the host to feed. Hygiene will help to break the life cycle and insecticides will go some way towards elimination of the adult fleas.

144

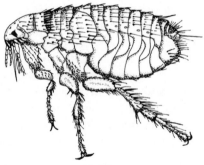

32 Flea

Louse flies These parasites are flies (Diptera) that have become highly specialised towards a parasitic way of life. They are rather flat with large feet which grip firmly on to the bird's feathers or skin. Like lice they tend to leave a bird when its body temperature had dropped, for example if it is shocked or during general anaesthesia.

Hippoboscids suck blood and may transmit organisms, including protozoan parasites. However, control is rarely necessary unless there are clinical signs of anaemia or irritation. The hippoboscids can sometimes be removed manually. Alternatively, insecticides may be used if their numbers are great.

Other flies Mosquitos and other biting flies may bite captive wild birds and probably play a role in the transmission of certain diseases, for

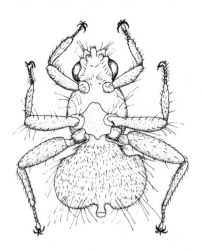

33 Hippoboscid

145

example pox. In addition they can cause localised swellings on the head and legs; these usually resolve spontaneously.

Certain species of fly may lay their eggs on wild birds, especially nestlings, and the larvae eat the bird's tissues. This is termed myiasis;[6] it is not commonly seen in captive wild birds but infected wounds may become maggot-infested and warrant treatment. If adult flies are seen in the vicinity of injured birds the latter should be examined carefully for evidence of maggot infestation. Often the wound smells unpleasant and the maggots may cause slight movement of infected tissues.

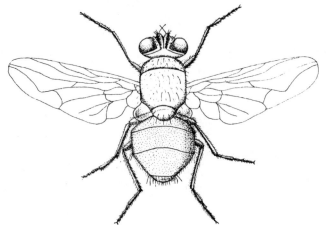

34 Blowfly: larvae of these flies can cause myiasis

Maggots can be removed manually, with forceps, or flushed out by spraying the affected area with a syringe-full of warm, slightly soapy, water. In severe cases a suitable insecticidal preparation may need to be used but, as was emphasised earlier, care must always be taken with such agents.

ENDOPARASITES

Roundworms These are perhaps the commonest parasites of wild birds and the ones that give rise to particular concern. There are many species of nematode, inhabiting areas as diverse as the intestinal tract, the trachea, the muscles and the blood (see Plate 10). They likewise vary in their effect on the host. Some suck blood while others do not. Some may obstruct the intestine if present in large numbers (see Plate 11b). Those that inhabit the intestinal and respiratory tracts are probably of most concern and are usually fairly readily diagnosed and treated. In many cases the eggs of the parasite are passed out in the faeces and

146

a microscopical examination of the latter will detect them (see Plates 11a and 12a). Even the eggs of those nematodes which affect the respiratory tract may be observed in the faeces since usually it is by coughing up and then swallowing the eggs that their life cycle is completed (see Plate 12b).

Treatment of nematodes is usually very effective provided the correct anthelmintic drug is given. Piperazine and thiabendazole are both safe and effective by mouth but nowadays many people prefer levamisole – by either the oral or injection route. Routine treatment is not usually recommended unless a nematode problem exists. Instead, long-term patients should have faecal samples checked for parasites every 4-6 weeks.It is more important to practise strict hygiene in order to break the life cycle. Faeces in particular must always be removed promptly so that the same or another bird cannot become infected.

Tapeworms These are generally less harmful to birds than are nematodes. They usually live in the intestinal tract where large numbers may cause poor condition, diarrhoea or other clinical signs. Diagnosis is by demonstrating the proglottides (segments) or eggs of the parasites in the faeces.

Treatment of birds infected with cestodes is possible using a number of drugs such as niclosamide and bunamidine hydrochloride. Hygiene is again important in control but it must be remembered that tapeworms need an intermediate host in their life cycle and therefore a bird will *not* become infected from its own or another bird's faeces. The ease with which transmission can occur depends upon the parasite, the intermediate host involved and the type of management. Certain invertebrate intermediate hosts may be present in aviaries containing soil or vegetation but are unlikely to occur indoors or in enclosures with cement or sand floors.

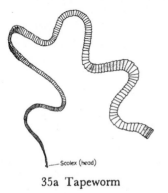

Scolex (head)

35a Tapeworm

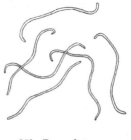

35b Roundworms

147

Flukes Various species of flukes are not uncommon inhabitants of the intestinal tract of many birds. However, usually they are not associated with clinical signs of disease. If disease does occur symptoms are likely to be diarrhoea and loss of weight. Fluke infestation is usually only detected at post-mortem examination or when eggs are found in a faecal sample.

The author does not recommend that flukes in birds be treated. Like tapeworms they need at least one intermediate host and transmission under conditions of captivity is therefore rare.

Spiny-headed worms Well recognised parasites of birds, these are particularly common in aquatic species – for example, *Polymorphus boschadis* in waterfowl. Most species use crustaceans as intermediate hosts and when these are eaten, the worm hatches and develops in the intestine of the bird. Damage can be caused to the mucosa (lining) of the gut and affected birds may show loss of weight and diarrhoea; they may also die. A diagnosis is often only made post mortem. Thiabendazole has been recommended for treatment but there is some doubt as to its efficacy. Prevention of infection, by denying birds access to crustaceans which may be intermediate hosts, is desirable.

Single-celled organisms Parasitic protozoa of a variety of species occur in the avian intestinal tract, in the blood and elsewhere. Many of them live as commensals; that is, they exist in an equilibrium with the bird and usually cause no disease. Under certain conditions, however, the balance may change and some protozoa can then prove pathogenic. In other cases the parasite is one that is generally pathogenic for a particular avian species; so interaction between host and parasite will almost certainly result in disease. An understanding of the host/parasite relationship is therefore important in assessing the significance of a particular parasite burden. It must be reiterated that the presence of parasites or their eggs is not necessarily synonymous with parasitic disease; a finch, for example, may be passing coccidial oocysts in its droppings but is not necessarily suffering from coccidiosis.

Clinical signs attributable to protozoa are variable and cannot be fully enumerated here. A definite diagnosis can be made only by demonstrating the parasite itself and therefore laboratory tests are required. Clinical signs that may be associated with intestinal protozoa include diarrhoea and/or caseous (cheesy) exudate in the mouth or throat. Blood parasites are common in a variety of wild birds but are unlikely to prove troublesome in captive ones; nevertheless, they are

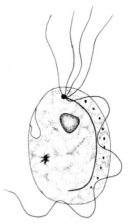

36 Flagellate protozoon

interesting parasites and if blood smears are taken from wild birds they should always be examined for evidence of protozoa.

Treatment of protozoal infections is possible with a wide range of drugs but the choice depends upon the species involved. The sulphonamides, such as sulphadimidine, are effective against coccidia while dimetridazole or metronidazole is the drug of choice for infections with flagellate organisms, such as *Trichomonas* spp. Hygiene is of great importance since the majority of protozoa are transmitted directly between birds.

As was mentioned earlier, it is probable that hitherto unrecognised parasites may be identified from wild birds in due course since relatively little work has been done on this (and other) aspects of their biology. For example, in the USA a recent paper described an epidemic disease in knots and about 150 of the birds were found sick or dead.[7] Detailed laboratory investigations, including the use of electron microscopy, showed the causal organism to be an unidentified protozoan parasite.[8]

In this chapter it has not proved possible to discuss the various parasites in detail. There are many hundreds of species with varying life cycles. The main points that have been emphasised are that parasite burdens do not necessarily mean disease, and, although drug treatment of parasites is possible, it must be accompanied by hygiene measures.

Parasites are, and will remain, a source of concern to those who treat wild birds. Under conditions of captivity many of them increase in numbers. However, by regular observation and screening of birds, by strict hygiene and by judicious use of drugs, they can be satisfactorily controlled.

12 Poisons

A. G. Greenwood

INTRODUCTION

Toxicology (the study of poisons and their effects) is one of the most complex and fascinating areas of medicine. The subject is complex because of the enormous number of substances now known to be poisonous to animals, which may be made available to them in their environment, either accidentally or deliberately. Indeed, on many occasions, substances the effects of which have not been studied at all may be released into the environment; the toxicologist is then faced with the task of discovering and proving that these substances have poisoned dead or sick animals. Once the connection has been established, attempts can be made to ascertain in what way the toxin has affected the animals, in an effort to find a treatment, and to establish a clinical pattern of symptoms that may help in the recognition of the next case of intoxication.

For these reasons this chapter will aim not only to illustrate the circumstances, clinical signs (symptoms) and treatments relevant to the important known poisons, but also to help establish in the reader's mind a pattern that will enable him to detect new cases of poisoning in wildlife, which are likely to crop up frequently in the future. It has always been and will be the vigilance of naturalists, veterinarians, and all those who observe and care for wildlife, that has helped to pinpoint a new toxic hazard in the environment.

The understanding of a case of poisoning and its successful diagnosis, treatment and control depend on many factors: on good detective work to point to the origin of the poison; on clinical medicine and diagnostic tests in life to understand the symptoms, and on good pathology and analysis after death to determine any chemical in the body which may have caused the fatality. The detective work is the most important – because it is the most likely to yield results, and because effective use of our other tools depends on having clues as to which direction to take. The many known poisonous substances produce a very limited range of clinical signs in life and of pathological lesions in death. Sometimes these are diagnostic, but most often they are not, so treatment can only be general and aimed at controlling the symptoms, without attacking the root cause of the disease. Furthermore, the analyst can only look for those poisons which are suggested to him – lack of time and money prevents a search for all poisons.

Poisons have been classified by chemical type, by the signs and lesions which they produce, or according to their action. But from the viewpoint of the man in the field, confronted with an outbreak in wildlife, the most helpful and logical classification of poisons will consider their origins.

In this chapter, poisons are divided into natural and man-made hazards. Natural hazards are those produced by plant or animal life, or normal chemicals and elements which may locally be present in abnormal concentrations. Man-made hazards include industrial pollutants and waste, pesticides directed at vertebrates, insects, micro-organisms or plants, and carelessly handled domestic or household materials. Obviously, in an individual case, the groupings may overlap – lead, for example, may be spread by industry or individuals, but it is most likely that an outbreak of poisoning can be connected with some known activity that fits into these categories – poisonous plants, a factory outflow into a river, rodent control, field spraying with insecticides and so on.

Diagnosis without circumstantial evidence is difficult. Clinical signs are generally vague, often apparent in the nervous system – fits, paralysis, coma – and disturbances of the alimentary tract – vomiting and diarrhoea – all of which are easily confused with symptoms of other bird diseases. Of course, the large numbers of birds frequently involved in a poisoning outbreak may help separate it from all but the most severe epidemic diseases.

Thus our approach to treatment will have to be in two phases. The first will be general and aimed at preventing further acquisition or absorption of the poison by the bird, and at neutralising any poison left in the gut or on the skin. The bird will also have to receive general supportive nursing care, until the second phase, when specific antagonists or antidotes are applied, which will often depend on the identification of the poison in the field. Thus, the detective work will to a large extent direct the medical treatment. Often, either detection will fail or there will be no specific antidote available, and so nursing care, which is well within the capabilities of any competent bird hospital, will be the crucial factor in recovery.

General nursing of birds is discussed in Chapter 7. Particularly important in poisonings are the provision of warmth, quiet and darkness with a minimum of stimulation. Replacement of fluid and heat are vital when a bird has been disabled and exposed to the elements for some time, and when it is suffering from diarrhoea and vomiting. Vitamin and antibiotic treatment may be necessary; fits may need controlling, in which case diazepam is by far the safest and most useful drug, particularly when the cause of the fits is not known. Poisonous substances on the skin or in the eyes must be washed off, using fresh water only, and external injury treated with appropriate ointments and dressings.

Most important is the removal of poisons from the crop, stomach and intestines to prevent further absorption. There are two approaches to this problem. The contents of the crop or stomach can be sucked or washed out using a stomach tube and small quantities of warm water (more fluids may simply wash the poison into the intestine and hasten absorption). A veterinary surgeon can easily train a layman to carry out this procedure safely in birds.

Alternatively, or preferably in addition, a general antidote can be administered by stomach tube which will absorb the poison and neutralise any direct effects on the stomach lining, and then flush it rapidly from the body. A useful formula for a safe antidote for use in all birds is two adsorbents, activated charcoal (10 grammes), and kaolin (5 grammes); an antacid, light magnesium oxide (5 grammes); and tannic acid (5 grammes). Water is added to make a total volume of 500ml; dosage is 2-20ml orally depending on the size of the bird.

Tannic acid, which will precipitate many metals and alkaloid poisons and prevent their absorption, can be given in an emergency as a very strong brew of cold tea! If there is some information as to the type of poison, other general antidotes may be useful – tincture of iodine will precipitate some metals; lime water will neutralise acids, dilute vinegar will neutralise alkalis; and a dilute solution of potassium permanganate will precipitate phosphorus compounds.

Further treatment should be directed towards the control of the secondary local effects of the poison, particularly damage to the intestine, which will allow leakage of valuable fluids, electrolytes and proteins into the gut, and penetration of bacteria into the body. More specific antidotes are discussed with the individual groups of poisons but their administration will always be by a veterinary surgeon.

NATURAL HAZARDS

Botulism

The major natural poisoning hazard which affects birds is botulism, a fatal nervous disease caused by the toxin of a bacterium *Clostridium botulinum*. This disease was previously known as Western

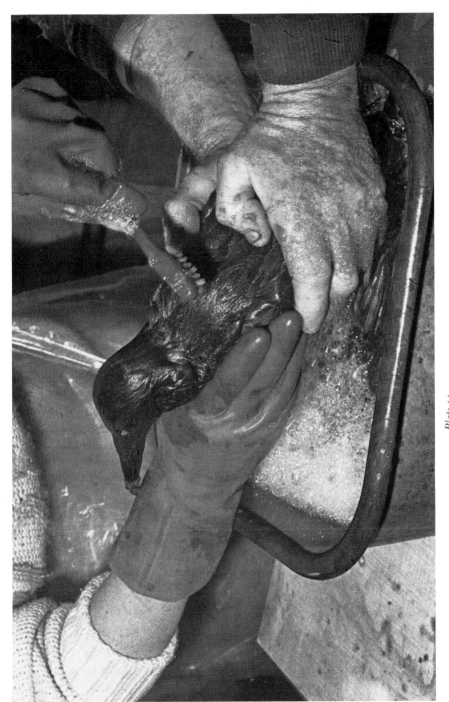

Plate 14
Cleaning an oiled bird

Plate 15
Guillemots in an outside pen prior to release

duck sickness, the term being used to describe mass mortalities of water-fowl in western USA, and recognised since the late nineteenth century. Such outbreaks still occur in North America and elsewhere around the world, but since 1930 the true cause has been appreciated.[1] Poisonings usually occur in summer and autumn when the bacterium, which normally lies dormant in the soil, multiplies rapidly in shallow, stagnant water above 15°C which usually contains much rotting vegetable matter. Surface-feeding ducks on ponds and shallow lakes, and particularly stagnant flood water, are chiefly affected, although other waterfowl, shorebirds, gulls and passerines may suffer. The organism does not infect the birds, but releases a toxin, the most powerful poison known, which is eaten by the birds either in vegetable matter, small aquatic inverte-brates, or in fly larvae feeding on carcasses.[2] Maggots used for feeding captive birds may be a source (see Chapter 8).

Botulism in birds is rare in the UK, but outbreaks were recorded in the hot summers of 1969 and 1971[3, 4] when several hundred birds died on shallow park lakes. These mortalities do not compare with the four or five million deaths in the USA in 1952, but still have involved a large proportion of the birds present on the water. Various strains of *Cl botulinum* are involved in poisoning man and other animals, but outbreaks in birds are usually associated with type C, and occasionally type E. By 1934, 69 species had been recorded as affected by the disease, and there was little variation in susceptibility. The turkey vulture, and possibly other vultures which are constantly exposed to rotting meat (an excellent medium for clostridial multiplication), can be shown to have a specific immunity to the disease.[5]

Clinical signs of botulism vary and probably depend on the amount and strength of the toxin absorbed. The poison exerts its effect at the junction of nerve and muscle, and produces flaccid paralysis of the legs, wings and neck. When the neck is affected, the head hangs downward as the bird is held in the hand. Other signs include immobilisation of the third eyelid, erratic pupillary movements, diarrhoea and a severe drop in body temperature. Many of these signs can be found in other diseases and poisonings, but the circumstances surrounding an outbreak involv-ing numbers of birds with signs of leg weakness and flaccid paralysis, and the absence of any twitching or nervous excitation, will lead to a presumptive diagnosis of botulism. This can be confirmed in life or by a post-mortem examination in a laboratory test involving the inoculation of mice. This test can be carried out by the major laboratories. Other-wise, post-mortem findings are limited to secondary damage, injury and enteritis.

155

In addition to gastric aspiration and provision of warmth and fluids, the chances of recovery may be helped by administration of specific antitoxins. Large numbers of birds have been saved in this way, but in the very large outbreaks efforts are probably best expended on control measures, such as drainage and flushing of affected ponds, removal of rotting organic matter, or even scaring or baiting the birds away from the danger area.

Algae, higher plants and fungi

Some outbreaks of botulism have been compounded by the presence in the water of poisonous blue-green algae, particularly *Anabaena* and *Nodularia* spp. These plants bloom heavily in shallow well lit waters in summer, giving a bluish tinge to the pond, and this effect may be heightened if the waters receive fertiliser runoff from agricultural land – the eutrophication effect. Not all species of algae are poisonous,[6] and some of those which affect test animals (mice) may not kill birds. Nevertheless outbreaks of algae poisoning have been reported in waterfowl in South Africa,[7] Canada[8] and the USA[9] and suspected in the UK. The clinical signs and circumstances of the disease are very similar to those of botulism in the laboratory. The care and treatment of affected birds can be only of a general nature, and control measures are likely to be of more benefit in terms of population.

Poisonings of this type do not occur at sea, but frequently severe outbreaks of disease in man, with considerable mortality, have been associated with the consumption of previously innocuous shellfish. Such disasters have mainly occurred north of latitude 30° in the Northern Hemisphere, and have coincided with an exceptional bloom of unicellular organisms, dinoflagellates, dense enough to colour the sea red – the so-called red tide. These dinoflagellates, of the genus *Gonyaulax* and others, produce a very powerful toxin, which is passed on when the organisms are filtered from the plankton by shellfish or other filter feeders. The toxin then renders the shellfish lethal.[10] Two seabird catastrophes have been associated with red tides, on the Pacific coast of the USA[11] and on the north-east coast of the UK.[12] The latter outbreak mainly involved shags in 1968 and it was suggested, on only circumstantial evidence, that these birds acquired the toxin through their fish and sand-eel diet. A flock of homing pigeons feeding on mussels on the beach was also affected. The toxin affects the neuromuscular junction, and causes death by respiratory paralysis. Thus a catastrophe with the characteristics of botulism, but occurring at sea in conjunction with cases of human paralytic shellfish poisoning, should be closely investigated to eliminate dinoflagellate poisoning. No antitoxin is available at present, and the toxin itself is difficult to detect in the laboratory, although the stomach contents of affected birds should be rapidly lethal to mice.

Poisoning by higher species of plants, a common source of disease in children and domestic animals,[13, 14] is not common in birds. In some cases, well known poisonous plants or fruits, such as hemlock or mountain ash, are not toxic to birds, but in general it is likely that birds instinctively avoid dangerous species. Poisonings of wild birds are on record, including *Crotolaria* seed poisoning,[15] and cyanide poisoning from eating almonds,[16] but such instances are few. Following the basic dictum that common conditions occur commonly, it would therefore be unwise to attribute a suspected outbreak to a poisonous plant present in the vicinity, unless the circumstantial evidence is overwhelming. Aspiration of seeds or vegetable matter from the crop is the most beneficial treatment, as absorption is slow. The possibility that some non-poisonous plant has been sprayed with a toxic chemical should not be overlooked. In suspected cases of true plant poisoning, the help of a competent plant toxicologist must be enlisted, as this area of toxicology is one of the most difficult.

On this basis, the familiar types of fungi – toadstools – are not likely to be implicated, but tiny species of mould, growing on stored animal feeding stuffs, have caused major outbreaks of disease in domestic animals and poultry. Aflatoxin, the specific toxin produced by the mould *Aspergillus flavus*, is responsible for severe liver damage and death in ducks and turkeys. Although there are no records of this in wild birds, the fungus and toxin are widespread, and flocks of birds often gain access to spoiled animal feeds. Various other moulds produce toxins, some on living plants, such as ergot (*Claviceps purpurea*) which parasitises cereals, and produces severe poisoning if eaten in quantity. Typical signs of ergotism in domestic birds are gangrene and dermatitis. All these types of fungi are available to birds, and might be eaten in error, so one should be on the look-out for such occurrences.

Other types of natural hazards, although they may be a threat to bird-life in some parts of the world, are of little importance in the UK. Venomous animals are almost absent, and although the occasional swan may be bitten by the occasional adder, the problem is not a common one. Similarly, high levels of naturally occurring toxic minerals are not a hazard in the UK, although in Morocco and Iceland particularly, fluorine and nitrates in natural rocks may cause significant poisoning in domestic stock and wildlife, through water contamination.[17]

MAN-MADE HAZARDS

Besides facing the many dangers which have existed in the natural world throughout the evolutionary period, wild birds, which have in part been moulded by these pressures and have evolved to live with them, now have to face a whole new range of threats produced by man. In a very short space of time, only about a hundred years, barely noticeable in terms of the history of birds, too much has changed too rapidly to allow any significant behavioural or physiological adaptations by which birds might protect themselves.

The effects of some man-made poisons are acute: birds are killed, sometimes in large numbers; the problem is recognised, and sometimes dealt with. But other poisons, the organochlorine insecticides for example, may have both acute and insidious effects and it is the latter which are difficult for us to recognise. Enough is known about this kind of poisoning for us to appreciate that it is better to be safe than sorry; we should take steps to prevent the accidental dispersal of any chemical substances beyond their initial target. Later there will be time to study what the unknown effects might have been, without having first reached a point of no return, where the environment is irretrievably contaminated for centuries. Birds act as sensors for this kind of pollution, often being affected before other creatures, but being well studied so that their disappearance is noticed very quickly. Clearly the bird hospital cannot play any significant part in solving this type of problem, except by noticing and recording important details about the birds that pass through, and by submitting bodies for analysis to any interested laboratories. It is in the identification of the acute case of poisoning and in the treatment of affected birds, that the naturalist can have influence.

In the overcrowded societies of Western Europe, industry lives hand-in-hand with nature. Birds are forced, and have learnt, to live close to industrial plants, and sometimes benefit from the large areas of secluded waste land and open water that are created. Many of these areas are used for waste disposal, and surrounding rivers and arable land may also be accidentally polluted by this waste, which is often toxic. At this stage much of the industrial contamination is limited by natural dilution, and never reaches beyond the surrounding area, but occasionally, particularly when the plant is near the sea, large areas of water may be affected, and if this coincides with large congregations of birds, the scene is set for a major disaster.

Small kills of wildlife in our rivers and fields occur very regularly, often accidentally, as a result of the disposal of industrial waste. There

158

are so many chemicals, organic and inorganic, that may be involved that it is impossible to mention more than a few in detail. Often the nature of the chemical may never be known, or it may not have been previously recorded. It requires much work and skilful diplomacy to locate the source and nature of the pollutant, but this is essential if any specific treatment is to be attempted. Occasionally an antidote will be known, or can be suggested, but general care will be the only course open in most of these cases, and it is surprising how often it will be successful. Problems can arise when large numbers of birds have to be handled, and the handling of small or individual cases should always be regarded as training for a large-scale disaster, when significant work can be done, particularly where the habitat of a rare species is struck.

Industrial contamination
Industrial materials or waste may reach the environment by direct discharge either into waterways or as fallout on to land, or by leakage and runoff from stores and tips. Water birds are the most likely to be affected by such pollution as water is the commonest route of dispersal, but other birds may be poisoned if they feed on arable land contaminated by fallout.

Toxic metals, of which there are many, are responsible for a large number of deaths in both domestic stock and wildlife. Lead probably accounts for the maximum total number of deaths in both groups annually,[17] despite our knowledge of its dangers. Wildlife has access to lead in those materials (paint, batteries etc) that poison many farm animals, but for wild birds the major sources of lead are from lead mines and smelting plants, and from lead shot. Lead mining in the UK is now very limited, but waterways passing through old mining areas, particularly if the water is soft and acid,[18] may contain very high concentrations of dissolved metal, and poisoning of waterfowl by this route has been recorded quite frequently in the North-West of the UK. Similarly, the soil around old lead workings and lead-smelting plants can contain very high levels of metal which are absorbed by the plant and insect life, and thence by birds, or their rodent prey. Even the lead content of the air and dust around major plants can be high enough to produce recognisable poisoning in local birds.[19] Whilst the effects of petrol, a source of atmospheric lead pollution from the 'anti-knock' additives, may be expected to affect only city birds, it should be realised that the grassy verges of motorways, rich hunting grounds for many predators, can be heavily contaminated.

159

These types of pollution account for the majority of the cases of lead poisoning in the UK[20] but in North America, where wildfowl are hunted on a massive scale, the main source is probably lead shot.[21, 22] A layer of lead pellets rapidly accumulates on the bottom and banks of lakes that are intensively hunted. Wildfowl pick up these shot in mistake for grit, and then retain them in their gizzards. As few as two pieces of shot have produced fatal lead poisoning in a dove, and many poisoned swans carry less than a dozen.[23] In general lead is poorly absorbed from the gut, but when it is held for long periods in the gizzard large quantities can accumulate in the body. The massive death toll of waterfowl has stimulated the search for a non-toxic shot, but at the time of writing, it is not commercially available.[24] The answer may lie with a lead shot that disintegrates into tiny fragments and is less likely to be picked up by birds.[25] Surprisingly, although birds are often found with lead shot embedded in their body, absorption from these sites is virtually nil, and shotgun wounds are probably not a cause of poisoning.[26]

The clinical signs of acute lead poisoning are not specific. Birds may be found dead, or may only suffer from severe diarrhoea and nervous signs. Chronic poisoning, the more common form, causes progressive emaciation, anaemia, weakness, and bright green droppings. The diagnosis can be confirmed by the demonstration of high lead levels in blood and droppings, and often shot can be seen in the gizzard on radiography. Examination of blood smears from waterfowl by fluorescent techniques has provided a quick and valuable method of diagnosis in the field. The post-mortem findings of impacted gizzard, perhaps containing lead, with green staining of the lining are suspicious, but for confirmation, it is usual to measure the lead levels of the liver, kidney and bones.[27, 28]

Treatment for poisoning is possible. Lead in the gizzard should be removed, surgically if necessary, as it will provide a continuing source. Calcium disodium versenate is a specific treatment which binds up the lead in the blood and hastens its excretion; but it has to be given by intravenous injection, and many repeated treatments may be required. Attempts to treat affected whistling swans by this means have not been entirely effective.[29]

In general, the discharge of metals other than lead is now strictly controlled, although it has caused serious pollution in the past. A number of metals are associated with specific industrial processes – mercury with wood-pulping, chromium with tanning, arsenic and zinc with smelting, copper with mining and nickel smelting – and although instances are known of their affecting wild birds, these are rare. A knowledge of the potentially toxic byproducts of local industry may give a clue to the cause of wildlife kills, should they occur in the area. Mercury pollution is at its most significant in the Baltic Sea, which receives the outflow from many paper mills, but mercury, arsenic and copper poisoning in the UK more usually result from the use of these metals in pesticides than in industrial processes. Copper poisoning of swans has been recorded after the birds had accumulated pieces of brass in their gizzards,[23] and this tendency of grain-eating birds to collect such materials should be remembered.

Certain types of industrial pollution which may affect birds require long periods to produce effects, and these effects are generally complex and insidious. For this reason it is unlikely that wild birds will be involved unless they are temporarily confined in the immediate area or because some food source attracts them repeatedly. Fluorine, as an effluent in dust and smoke from aluminium plants, brick works and potteries causes chronic poisoning in livestock confined to adjoining pasture, the main clinical sign being slow lameness as a result of bone damage.[17] Knowledge of affected fields has led farmers to avoid them except for short periods, but wildlife cannot recognise such contamination.

Another hazard, at present extremely rare but likely to become important in the near future, is radiation. Mild leaks of radioactivity from nuclear power stations would be dangerous only to birds that spent long periods in their vicinity. Although such leakage is rigidly controlled, disasters will probably occur sooner or later. It is to be expected that birds will be attracted to such plants, if only by the heat which will encourage roosting, and that cases of radiation poisoning will occur. Once again, the birds will probably act as environmental sensors, and recognition of the hazard may prevent a human disaster. The signs of radiation sickness are very variable, and depend on the dose and time of exposure.[17] The skin, intestine, lungs or bone marrow may be affected together or separately, and once again it will be the detective work that suggests the possibility, leading to a direct examination with a radiation counter. In some instances, it may be that a very subtle effect, such as an abnormally high incidence of tumours in a local bird population, will give the clue, and this may emerge only from a careful scrutiny of the bird hospital's records. The treatment of radiation poisoning can only be symptomatic.

Although a vast amount of potentially dangerous organic chemicals is used in industry, particularly the paint and plastics industries, relatively few individual outbreaks of poisoning among birds have yet been traced to this source. However, there are two major exceptions: crude oil and PCBs (polychlorinated biphenyls).

The contamination of the sea by oil has caused mass mortalities of birds since the 1930s, but it really became recognised as exerting a major influence on delicate seabird populations in the 1960s.[30, 31, 32] Most of the oil at sea is crude heavy tank washings, but accidents may release lighter and more refined fuel and diesel oils, which are more toxic. Similar light oils may get into streams and rivers by accident or by careless disposal. Occasionally a wild bird may become covered in oil or fuel as a result of its own carelessness or curiosity. The major effects of oil pollution are covered in Chapter 13 which fully describes cleaning methods; but it must not be forgotten that although heat loss and drowning from the physical effects of oil take the greatest toll of birds at sea, once birds have been brought in for treatment, we should be more concerned with the internal poisoning than with the external appearance of the feathers.[33] Some of the very light oils which produce the severest internal damage have external effects that are frequently overlooked, or interpreted as burns from other types of chemical.

Other oil and tar products used in industry can be highly toxic to birds. These are often used as preservatives, such as creosote and phenol, or in lubricating oils, paints and varnishes such as the chlorinated naphthalenes. The tar byproducts may be found in the effluent from gasworks, coke burners or any plant producing disinfectants and similar substances. Most are quite safe when used in their normal dilutions, but the raw materials are lethal. Clinical signs include external and internal corrosive burns, pulmonary oedema and asphyxia in acute cases, or liver damage in chronic poisoning. Convulsions are common. Treatment can be only along symptomatic lines. Alcohols are toxic in pure form, and anti-freeze (ethylene glycol) is particularly dangerous as it causes internal haemorrhage, liver damage, and paralysis. Even the diluted product, as in the water drained from car radiators, is dangerous to birds, which are quite sensitive to this compound.

Detergents and soaps are among the most frequent contaminants of streams and rivers. These are highly toxic to freshwater and marine life, particularly the emulsifiers which have been used to disperse oil slicks. However, their toxic effect on mammals and birds appears to be low and the evidence required to implicate them in acute poisonings must be strong. There is also evidence that after widespread sea spraying, birds showed deteriorations in behaviour and breeding although it is difficult to attribute such effects to the detergents alone.[34] It is more likely that they cause wetting of the plumage and skin inflammation,

162

and this also increases the absorption of some of the more toxic constituents of the oil, such as phenols.[35]

Certain chemicals of great importance to the plastic, paint, ink and pesticide manufacturing processes were recognised as important marine pollutants in 1968.[36] These chemicals, the polychlorinated biphenyls (PCBs), are closely related to the chlorinated hydrocarbon insecticides which they help to produce, and like those insecticides, have been implicated in reproductive failures and population declines of seabirds.[37, 38] Occasionally acute effects – lack of coordination and paralysis – have been seen in birds that have accumulated very high levels of PCBs through their food chain, particularly when high levels of DDT residues have been present as well; but such occurrences are rare. It is more likely that their toxicity is manifested by the slow insidious effects of long-term absorption, as these chemicals are extremely persistent in the environment.

Action to curb the spread of PCBs was gratifyingly rapid, and widespread legal controls had been introduced by 1972. Remarkably, it has been found that the levels of PCBs in surface water have declined very fast, probably because of sedimentation.[39] Although they are still present, they must be largely out of harm's way at the bottom of the sea. Nevertheless, it will be wise for us to continue to analyse residues in bird corpses for some years to come.

Pesticides
Man has always attempted to control pests, both plant and animal, which have threatened his health, agriculture or welfare, by selective poisoning. Ideally, the effect of these poisons has been directed towards the pest, and away from domestic plants and livestock, either by careful control of the siting of the poison, or by choosing a chemical with a rather limited effect. This process has nearly always failed in that harmless or beneficial species have suffered through carelessness or neglect, or through ignorance of the complete effects of the pesticide.[40]

From the point of view of wild birds, the most dangerous of the pesticides have been those directed against insects parasitising crops or domestic animals, and have included the chlorinated hydrocarbons (organochlorines), the carbamates, the organophosphates and their more recent form, the phosphorothionates. The effects of this group have been twofold: there have been mass mortalities associated with their early large-scale use, and slow insidious effects on the bird population associated with the environmental persistence of the organochlorines (DDT and its derivatives).[41, 42, 43]

163

These chemicals were introduced on a large scale in 1945, and in the 1950s severe bird casualties resulted from the spraying of *Brassica* crops with organophosphates (derived from wartime nerve gas experiments), and the dressing of wheat seed with organochlorines against bulbfly. This phenomenon reached a peak in 1960, when the newly formed BTO and RSPB Joint Committee on Toxic Chemicals logged 59 major incidents in the first six months of the year, including very large kills of woodpigeons, pheasants and rooks feeding on winter and spring-sown wheat. This led to the introduction in the UK in 1961 of a voluntary ban on the use of the more potent organochlorines aldrin, dieldrin and heptachlor on spring-sown wheat and a limitation of their use in autumn. The result of this ban was almost complete cessation of the mass deaths by 1963.[44]

Of this group of pesticides the organophosphates and carbamates have the lower toxicity for birds in the concentrations normally used, and are not persistent to any extent. The organochlorines, however, are broken down slowly in the environment and accumulate through food chains, so that, by 1963, after a decade of intensive use, long-term effects on bird populations began to be recognised. These particularly affected the birds of prey, which, being at the top of long food chains, received a high concentration of residues in their food, and could build up high tissue levels over a short period. A severe population decline of peregrines[45] in the UK was noticed, and golden eagles were affected through their consumption of dieldrin (used in sheep-dips) on sheep carcasses.[46] These population declines, which were seen in other countries,[47] appeared to result from low fertility, egg-breakage and poor hatchability correlated with high pesticide residues in parent birds and in their eggs.[48] After further restrictions in 1965-6, this rate of decline slowed, and by 1969 some reversal of the trend was reported. Despite indications that the worst effects of the organochlorines are now over, a 1974 study still demonstrated significant eggshell thinning in sparrowhawks in the UK. The relative stability of some raptor populations, such as the kestrel, emphasised that the main route for concentration of the poisons was through seed-eating birds, thus terminating chiefly in the bird-eating raptors. As seed dressings the organochlorines and organophosphates were often combined with organic mercurials as fungicides, and these too had similar long-term effects, particularly in Scandinavia where large quantities of mercury were used.[49] Occasional accidental seed-dressing poisonings still occur from time to time, particularly in waterfowl, and these may now be expected to be by a combination of organophosphates and organic mercurials.[50, 51]

164

The prolonged storage of DDT metabolites in bird fat led to higher than normal bird mortalities in hard winters, for when the hard-pressed birds drew on their fat reserves they released the chemicals into their bloodstream sufficiently rapidly to cause acute poisoning. It was found that birds tended to die, apparently of starvation, at weights at which they would previously have survived. It is this prolonged fat storage of the organochlorines, as well as their environmental persistence, that is responsible for their long-term effects.[42]

Although the mode of action of these groups of compounds differs, they all exert their main effect on the nervous system. The organochlorines, of which there is a vast range, vary greatly in their toxicity, lindane and dieldrin being more dangerous than DDT; they also vary in their persistence in the body, DDT being particularly easily taken up and stored for long periods. The clinical signs of organochlorine poisoning are those of intense stimulation of the nervous system, particularly with the more toxic forms. Birds poisoned with these exhibit convulsions alternating with prolonged muscle spasms, rendering the limbs rigid and trembling, in a similar manner to the organophosphates. The milder poisons, as in mammals, induce very short spasms, which appear as a fine tremor all over the body, occasionally breaking out into a full convulsion, particularly if the bird is stimulated by sound or touch. The third eyelid is drawn across the eye in a permanent spasm. In between fits the bird may be very quiet and depressed, and only tremble faintly. Milder cases show less characteristic signs, but all are attributable to nerve-muscle derangement. The symptoms, and especially the lethal levels in the diet, have been shown to vary between different species.[52, 53, 54]

The effects of prolonged low-level poisoning of birds have been well documented, and include reduced sperm production, poor eggshell formation and altered reproductive behaviour, all leading to reproductive failure. Regrettably there are no characteristic post-mortem findings in organochlorine poisoning, although birds may have depleted fat reserves, and a diagnosis must depend on the identification of significant levels of residues in fat, liver and brain. It is difficult to lay down accepted lethal levels and comparisons between species are very unreliable. Thus the diagnosis will often depend on a combination of circumstances, signs, tissue levels, and the absence of any other findings.

There is no specific antidote for organochlorines; however, it is often possible to take advantage of the chemistry of the poison to reduce its effects. If the bird can be kept alive long enough to build up its fat stores, then the poison will be removed from the blood and stored safely in the fat, hopefully to be excreted slowly over a period of years, if another starvation episode can be avoided. The feeding of high fat diets to poisoned birds in the hope of removing poison from the gut and of promoting the storage effect has been recommended, but there is a real danger that this will merely increase the absorption of further chemical, which is much more readily absorbed in a fatty base. Thus the administration of a simple adsorbent, such as kaolin, to remove poison from the gut is preferred.

Keeping the bird alive, whilst it is built-up by normal feeding, depends entirely on controlling the nervous signs. These can be minimised by eliminating all possible stimulation, placing the bird in a dark box, avoiding overheating as this is a side-effect of prolonged convulsions, and then directly controlling fits with diazepam or barbiturates. After an initial injected dose it may be possible to continue with a low level of drug in the food, often for several days. B vitamins in high doses will also be useful.

Although many acutely poisoned birds die, it is possible with perseverance to save some, but the intensive care necessary in these cases makes a large incident very difficult to manage. It is likely that small outbreaks dependent on careless disposal of organochlorine containers will be seen nowadays, rather than the massive kills of a few years ago.

The organophosphates, (parathion, malathion, dichlorvos and ruelene are well known examples) are extremely poisonous to birds, but because they are rapidly degraded in the environment incidents are usually limited to consumption of large quantities of dressed seed or carelessly discarded raw substances in containers. An unusual type of bird poisoning has occurred from dichlorvos granules which, when administered to horses for worming, have passed through unchanged, and then been picked up by birds scavenging around the midden. A considerable number of these compounds are used as parasiticides for farm animals, but on the whole they are the less toxic types. These poisons upset the normal transmission of information from nerve to muscle, leaving the muscle permanently contracted.

Some compounds are directly active, and others only after conversion in the body to the active principle. For some of the latter, it appears to be a basic metabolic difference that renders birds more susceptible than mammals. Clinical signs appear either rapidly or after a delay, depending upon which of the two types of compound is involved; symptoms are muscle twitching, violent limb contraction followed by weakness, and diarrhoea due to excessive gut motility. The pathological findings are entirely secondary to the symptoms and very variable; precise diagnosis in life or after death is very difficult although some residues may be found in the stomach.

The only effective treatment, apart from warmth and darkness, is direct use of another chemical – atropine – to remove the perpetual stimulation, and allow the muscle to relax. Regrettably this effect is only on the involuntary muscles of the gut, and actual reactivation of the body's own system is required for treatment of limb muscle spasms. In man and animals this is accomplished with a series of compounds related to 2-PAM, but little is known of their value in birds. The phosphorothionates (such as diazinon) are indirectly acting organophosphates, and the carbamates have a similar effect and mechanism of action.

The fungicides, applied to seeds in combination with the insecticides, are organic mercury compounds and thiram. Both also cause nervous signs, which are usually manifest as a limb weakness. Mercury is much more toxic in this form than as the pure metal, and little can be done for affected birds, although the administration of dimercaprol, effective against metallic mercury and arsenic, may help. Fortunately, diagnosis from tissue levels is possible, liver and kidney in particular, and there are clear lesions in kidney and brain on post-mortem examination. Mercury has also contributed to long-term breeding failure in wild birds, and its use is banned in many countries.

In general, the drastic reduction in the use of these types of pesticide should be borne in mind. The terrible disasters of the 1950s and 1960s have forced insecticides to the forefront of the problem of environmental pollution, but on a practical basis they are now probably less likely to be the cause of severe mortality than industrial wastes.

Herbicides
The quantity of chemicals sprayed on to the land to control unacceptable plants, by farmers, gardeners and local authorities, far outweighs the amount of insecticides used, but fortunately, the vast majority are not persistent, and are of low toxicity for wildlife.

Contact herbicides, which kill plants at the point of application, include sulphuric acid, sodium chlorate and the DNP derivatives.[17] All are little used nowadays, and are very unattractive to birds, but the DNP compounds are most important, being very persistent and readily absorbed through the skin. Poisoning with these compounds is characterised by yellow staining of skin and feathers for they are persistent dyes. The metabolism of affected birds is deranged, so that the body temperature rises, and there is prostration and coma. Rapid development of rigor mortis is reputedly a feature. The compound can be measured in the blood of a live bird, or in the organs post mortem, so precise diagnosis is possible. Treatment can be only symptomatic, with washing of the skin and stomach to remove any remaining poison. If sedation is necessary, care should be taken, as some sedatives may potentiate the action of the poison.

Other herbicides poison the plant by absorption into its system, and these include paraquat and the hormone phenoxy-acetate derivatives – 2,4,D, 2,4,5,T and dalapon. Paraquat has recently been responsible for some severe poisonings of pets and children, but is dangerous only in its concentrated form. The poison produces severe pulmonary oedema – fluid accumulation in the lungs – and the victim literally drowns. At present there is no treatment. The post-mortem diagnosis is characteristic. The hormonal weedkillers have received wide publicity due to their military use as defoliants, and great concern has been expressed about their effect on wildlife, but all the evidence suggests that they are non-toxic in the form in which they are applied. Poisoning of birds has been suspected in association with the spraying of dykes with dalapon.

Molluscicides

Only two types of poisons are in use against molluscs. Pastures are sprayed to control certain snails, which spread liver fluke disease in cattle, but copper sulphate has been replaced for this purpose by newer compounds which apparently are not a serious hazard for wildlife. However, metaldehyde which is used to kill slugs in fields and gardens (often mixed with oatmeal) is toxic, and has been responsible for much poisoning of domestic animals. Toxicity to wild birds varies greatly with the species, and is generally low, although ducks are particularly susceptible, and have been poisoned by eating affected slugs.[55] Clinical signs include incoordination and twisting of the neck; death, which is rare, results from respiratory failure. Damage to liver and brain are the main features; the non-specific treatment is to counteract respiratory depression with stimulants, and to protect the liver as far as possible by dietary means.

Rodenticides

A vast number of appallingly dangerous compounds have been used in the past for the control of vertebrate pests, mainly rodents. These are now mostly illegal or obsolete, and in the consideration of a case of poisoning associated with rodent control programmes, there are a limited number of possibilities to consider.

Strychnine, undoubtedly the worst of these poisons, is now largely limited to use for control of moles underground and so should not affect birds, but there is still some illicit use, particularly against crows, using poisoned chicken eggs as bait. Its effect is extremely rapid and directed at the spinal cord, producing intermittent convulsions with a characteristic arched back when the victim is stimulated in any way. These convulsions usually progress rapidly to death. Diagnosis can be made by examination of stomach contents. Treatment before the onset of convulsions is the administration by mouth of dilute potassium permanganate and tannic acid, to oxidise and precipitate the strychnine, but thereafter full anaesthesia and intensive care are required.

Arsenic compounds, such as arsenious oxides, have little use now, and are more likely to be encountered as weedkillers. These two produce paralysis, haemorrhagic diarrhoea and rapid death. Post-mortem examination reveals a characteristic inflammation of the stomach and gizzard, with separation of the gizzard lining by haemorrhage. Diagnosis is by analysis of stomach contents, liver and kidney. Treatment is limited to gastric lavage and intestinal protectives, although dimercaprol has some specific antidote effect.

The use of phosphorus and zinc phosphide is also limited. These poisons work rapidly to produce lethargy, coma, and death.[56] Analysis is valuable only on unopened carcasses, as the poisons act by liberating phosphine (a gas) in the gut; this escapes when the post-mortem examination is carried out. However, diagnosis may be suspected if the odour is present. There is no effective treatment for phosphorus poisonings. Fortunately, there is little record of birds being poisoned by strychnine, arsenic or phosphorus. Another extremely dangerous group of rodenticides is the fluoroacetates, to which birds appear to be relatively resistant. Similarly ANTU, which is directed only against the brown rat, has little effect on birds.[52]

The two major rodent poisons in use today are warfarin and alphachloralose. The former is mixed with oatmeal and spread for rats to eat over a period of several days. It therefore has a cumulative effect: the blood cannot clot and the animal bleeds to death. Diagnosis in mammals can be made from the appearance of haemorrhages and bloody diarrhoea, and treatment with injectable vitamin K is often effective. The poison can be detected in the gut contents and the liver after death. The main problem is to determine whether or not birds are susceptible to warfarin. Poultry are certainly resistant,[17] but there is considerable doubt and argument about other species. The author has seen definite cases only in parrots in zoos, which have shown sudden death with massive haemorrhages under the skin, in the muscles, and into the liver and lungs. It seems likely that some of our native species

169

may be equally at risk. The resistance that has built up in certain strains of rats has now led the manufacturers to add a highly concentrated form of vitamin D3, which results in a severe and rapidly fatal vitamin overdose. As D3 is absorbed and used by birds, unlike D2, we may expect that there will be a similar effect on them.

There is no doubt about the effect of the other main rodent poison – alphachloralose – on birds, as it has also been used for the control of bird pests.[57, 58] These are mainly pigeons and sparrows, but any bait aimed at pigeons is bound to be attractive to other species as well, and deaths among harmless species are not uncommon. The poison is a narcotic, and stupefies the bird rather than killing it outright, so that there is a possibility for harmless species to be rescued and revived. The main effect of stupefaction on birds and rodents is that their body temperature falls rapidly in a cold environment, and death from alpha-chloralose poisoning is due to hypothermia.[59] As a rodent poison, it is not effective when the ambient temperature is above 17°C, and so is used out-of-doors. Clinical signs in birds are those of depression and incoordination leading on to prostration and coma. Treatment consists of gastric lavage to remove any remaining bait, stimulants and oxygen and, most important, gently applied heat. The bird should be nursed in a very warm atmosphere, remembering that this will increase fluid losses. Unlike most poisons, a high proportion of recoveries may be expected. Birds of prey have been affected by eating other stupefied birds,[60] so it is clear that there is some persistence in the tissues, and the poisons can be detected in the thyroid and liver of victims by gas chromatography.

Domestic hazards
Occasional risks to wildlife can occur following the careless disposal of household or non-industrial materials, although this is inevitably on a much smaller scale than incidents following industrial accidents. Many possible substances, such as lead, oil, chemicals, disinfectants and paints, have been discussed in previous sections. Perhaps one of the most important and yet one of the simplest of such poisons is salt. Considerable loss of wild birds has been recorded following the salting of roads in winter,[61] and from the careless disposal of brine used in tanning and curing.[62]

It appears that in winter, when the ground is covered with snow, birds are driven to the roadside for supplies of grit and water from melted ice, and there they take in a lot of salt with precious little water. This severely affects the nervous system, causing circling and fits.

170

Plate 16
A calculus, composed of urates, removed from the cloaca of a bird. Such calculi can form if a bird is recumbent for a long period or does not excrete urates regularly

Plate 17
Pinched off feathers, an abnormality that occurs following stress. There is marked constriction of the base of both feathers

Plate 18
A histological section of a crop wall showing *Capillaria* worms embedded in the tissues. These parasites are a common cause of mouth lesions in some birds

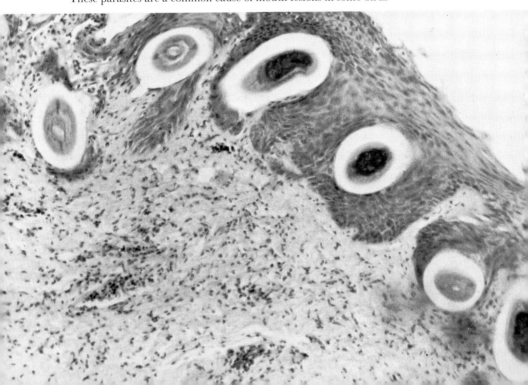

A diagnosis can be made by a simple analysis of crop and gut contents, and the pathology of the brain is typical. Treatment is rather difficult, as immediate consumption of large quantities of water may make the situation worse. General nursing and gradual rehydration can be recommended. Sedatives or anticonvulsants will probably be of little value.

Another interesting and unusual source of poisoning for man and animals from domestic materials, which may be used as a final example to illustrate the limitless possibilities, is non-stick cooking pans. These pans are coated with a polymerised plastic which is quite inert (as one might expect) under normal circumstances, but the fumes of which are extremely dangerous. When such pans are accidentally allowed to boil dry, and the coating is burnt, the fumes rapidly cause high fever and severe respiratory distress with pulmonary oedema – so called 'polymer fume fever syndrome'. These fumes have been immediately fatal to pet birds,[63] sometimes in conjunction with their owner, and as they may be released from most burning plastics, there may be a danger in the region of rubbish tips and plants where such materials are being burnt. There is an almost limitless range of potential poisons for wildlife in general use every day, and individual cases may be expected from the most unlikely sources.

CONCLUSION

Among all the causes of injury, disease and death in wild birds which have been enumerated in this book, poisons are perhaps the most common, the most evocative, and those about which we feel most guilty. For every single case of bird poisoning which falls outside the classification of natural hazards can be prevented by man. More care in the disposal of our waste products, and more care in the disposition of our selective poisons could prevent wildlife tragedies which are occurring daily. In the absence of such care, it will be the responsibility of naturalists and those interested in caring for sick wild birds and mammals to agitate for control. It is to be hoped that this chapter will enable them to assemble the necessary ammunition. In the meantime, the care and treatment of the individual victim is our concern, and, as has been emphasised repeatedly, success will depend to a great extent on an early identification of the source of the trouble. All the possible causes of wild bird poisoning cannot have been illustrated in this brief summary, but those that have should serve to give a general outline plan for future use.

13 Birds and oil pollution
J. Croxall

Oil pollution now occurs in every ocean in the world. As long as oil and oil products are essential commodities and are transported by, or through, sea it is clear that accidental oil pollution will continue on a large scale, whatever legislation is passed.

There is abundant evidence for the large-scale mortality of seabirds as a direct result of oil pollution. There is also considerable, perhaps mainly circumstantial, evidence that oil pollution may be a major factor in the continuing decline of most species of auk.[1] In spite of the impact made by spectacular incidents involving many thousands of birds – such as the 1967 Torrey Canyon disaster, when 10,000 birds were received by cleaning stations, and recent incidents in the Danish Waddenzee when over 30,000 birds perished[2] – the number of birds killed in identifiable incidents is probably very much less than the total killed by routine chronic oiling. The latter occurs throughout the year but is most marked between September and April.

Although the number of birds killed by both types of oil pollution may have declined since the late 1950s, the results of the winter surveys on beached birds conducted by the Royal Society for the Protection of Birds[3, 4, 5] illustrate the continuing magnitude of the problem. To take one example, over a single weekend in February 1973 coverage of 3,300km of European coastline produced a total of 3,651 dead birds, 1,500 being oiled. In the absence of any reported incidents this scale of mortality must be regarded as a typical result of chronic pollution and it seems likely that the estimate[1] of a million seabirds dying annually in the North Atlantic may be an appropriate order of magnitude.

Looking to the future it seems inevitable that the enormous intensification of oil production and transport activities in the North Sea will greatly increase the risk, both of recognisable oiling incidents -- especially involving the concentration of ducks wintering in the vicinity of coastal oil terminals – and also of chronic leakage and small scale spillage. For people living near the coast, and known to care for sick and injured birds, oiled seabirds is often one of the most common, and usually most difficult, problems encountered.

This chapter seeks to summarise the existing knowledge of appropriate treatments for oiled seabirds. Considerable research, on which many of the recommendations have been based, has been carried out by the

Research Unit on the Rehabilitation of Oiled Seabirds (RUROS) at the Department of Zoology, University of Newcastle-upon-Tyne, and many individuals, often with lengthy experience of oiled birds, have contributed much valuable information. However, there still remain large areas of ignorance and uncertainty concerning appropriate treatment; this chiefly reflects the present lack of detailed knowledge of avian physiology and pathology.

Although the birds mainly affected by oil pollution are those species – auks (Alcidae), divers (Gaviidae), grebes (Podicipidae), sea duck (Anatidae) and some gulls (Laridae) – that feed offshore (often near shipping lanes) oil discharge into estuaries, rivers and lakes is not infrequent and results in the oiling of many freshwater birds and waders. Auks and guillemots are most frequently oiled and hence the species for which the most reliable data exist. The information provided in the main part of this chapter refers basically to the guillemot. In most cases though, there are no interspecific differences in the treatment sufficient to require more than minor modification of the advice given. In the final section some information relating directly to other species is given where it is felt that additional advice would be helpful.

EFFECTS OF OIL ON BIRDS

Oil has an immediate external effect on birds by destroying the waterproofing of the plumage. This is rapidly followed by internal effects as the bird ingests oil in an attempt to preen the contaminant off the feathers. The consequences are somewhat different in each case, even though external oiling soon produces internal consequences, and can conveniently be considered separately.

Oil disrupts the regular precise arrangement of the fine structure of the feathers (see Chapter 3) and allows water to penetrate the plumage. Very heavily oiled birds may even drown;[6] usually the feather derangement is accompanied by loss of insulation (necessitating rapid use of energy resources to maintain body temperature) and considerable reduction in feeding efficiency. Atrophy of the pectoral muscles and severe emaciation develop very rapidly. The chilling and starvation induce clinical signs of physiological and organic stress, often also referred to as exhaustion or shock.

The most usual clinical signs and lesions produced by stress following oiling in birds are:

1 decline in white blood cell numbers, reducing resistance to infection;
2 disruption of general fluid and electrolyte balance leading to dehydration and metabolic disorders;
3 disturbance of endocrine balance, often associated with enlarged adrenal glands;
4 fatty degeneration of the liver which, among other things, reduces ability to break down toxins;
5 secondary kidney changes (often a consequence of 2) restricting elimination of waste products; and
6 necrosis and/or oedema in major organs.

It is not clear how far the last three lesions result from stress following chilling and starvation; neither are we sure what metabolic demands this places on the birds, or how far these may result from the toxic effects of ingested oil, or from the stress induced thereby. It is often difficult to be certain of the direct physiological and pathological consequences of oil ingestion, although experiments of feeding oil to birds by stomach tube[7] clearly avoid the complication of stress induced by chilling and starvation.

Ingested oil rapidly produces observable conditions in the alimentary canal and subsequently may clearly affect all the main organ systems of the body. The general findings below summarise the results of the investigations by Hartung and Hunt,[7] Snyder and colleagues[8] and various reports of post-mortem examinations[9, 10, 11] as well as the results of many general post-mortem examinations carried out by the RUROS (Croxall, in preparation).

Ingested oil rapidly causes inflammation of the mucosa and subsequently haemorrhage of the blood vessels of the gut lining as well as producing necrosis ('burns') and sloughing of areas of the epithelial mucosa and submucosa. An acute catarrhal or haemorrhagic enteritis usually develops quickly and with fatal results if not arrested.

Onset of kidney degeneration is also swift and acute clinical signs may develop within a few days of ingesting oil. Both proximal and distal tubular epithelia contain albuminoids and fat vacuoles with products of degeneration, indicative of toxic nephrosis.

Fatty infiltration and degeneration are also characteristic of dysfunction of the liver, which is often discoloured (pale brownish-yellow), due to presence of bile pigments, and sometimes friable. The liver parenchyma, which is occasionally dark green, due to retention of bile pigments, may also show lesions characteristic of coagulative necrosis.

Enlargement of the adrenal glands is not infrequent and changes resembling those of Selye's general adaptation syndrome in response to stress (see Chapter 14), as well as haemorrhage and necrosis, are sometimes noted.

The spleen is sometimes enlarged and darkened due to amyloid infiltration.

Lipid pneumonia, with intense lung inflammation, is not uncommon and is often associated with pulmonary oedema, producing fluid in the bronchi and parabronchi together with diffuse haemorrhage.

A major problem in evaluating oil toxicity is that there are large chemical differences in oil from different sources, as well as between the various refined fractions. Fuel oils exert a toxic effect mainly due to volatile aromatic (for example, benzene) and phenolic (for example, naphthenic acid) substances, suggesting that pollution from lighter oil fractions containing a greater proportion of volatile aromatics may be more deleterious than the heavier oils which externally appear more serious at first sight. Ingestion of emulsifying agents used in the dispersion of oil slicks is an additional hazard, though the less toxic emulsifiers currently recommended for use minimise this risk.

It should also be emphasised that, in addition to the direct effects of oil ingestion, detailed above, the resulting physiological stress renders birds far less resistant to the development of fungal and bacterial infections. Treatments for these conditions and for certain ailments often associated with seabirds in captivity are dealt with after the main section on the general treatment.

GENERAL TREATMENT

Clearly the major problem in rehabilitating oiled birds is to minimise the direct and indirect effects of external and internal oiling. Thus the reduction of stress and the rapid removal of oil from the digestive system of affected birds are the principal priorities in the early stages of general treatment and most recommendations in this chapter stem from these considerations.

The aim of this section is to present a fairly detailed scheme of appropriate treatment for oiled birds, which has been used with considerable success for auks. Although the treatment described has usually produced good results with other birds, experience with other species has been on a much smaller scale. Details of the treatment and fate of birds after particular oiling incidents are given by Clark and Croxall[12] and RUROS.[13, 14]

In many aspects of treatment a wide variety of techniques and medications has been used and this account does not attempt to provide a conspectus of them, although useful alternatives are indicated where appropriate. Knowledge of avian physiology and pathology is generally inadequate to predict the theoretical efficiency of medicinal and other treatment and there are seldom adequate data to evaluate their role in a practical sense.

Even with adequate facilities and adhering to the suggested scheme a variable level of success is to be expected. Much depends on the condition of individual birds when they come into the hands of people sufficiently experienced and knowledgeable to treat them. The length of time an oiled bird spends on the sea, the immediate treatment given once it is found and the time-lapse before it receives suitable subsequent treatment all drastically affect the bird's chance of survival. Even the best treatment administered late may be unable to redress earlier damage.

The treatment of oiled birds can conveniently be divided into three sections: capture and subsequent pre-cleaning treatment, cleaning and post-cleaning rehabilitation prior to release. Certain minimal facilities are essential, without which birds will probably not be fit for release for many months, if at all. The following are absolutely essential facilities in a cleaning centre:

1 an abundant supply of piped hot water;
2 a piped cold water supply with good pressure;
3 indoor shelter that can be heated, particularly in cold weather;
4 an outdoor pen with sand or concrete flooring (good turf is acceptable providing the pen can be moved to prevent muddy or fouled conditions developing);
5 continuous access from the pen to a pool of clean bathing water;
6 a reliable source of food (for example, fresh or frozen sprats or other small fish for most seabirds). This will almost certainly involve substantial frozen food storage facilities which are stocked when fish are locally available.

CAPTURE AND PRE-CLEANING TREATMENT

The priority here is to reduce stress to a minimum. This is achieved primarily by disturbing the bird as little as possible, keeping it warm, and preventing further oil ingestion while removing oil from the gut and rebuilding the bird's food reserves. The sooner birds receive care and attention after coming ashore the better their chance of survival.

Capture

Whether it is on the beach or floating in shallow water, the bird should always be approached from the seaward side. A wide net, attached to a pole, is often valuable. Chasing should be kept to an absolute minimum.

In the event of an oil slick from which the victims far outnumber the equipment and facilities available for dealing with them, it may be advantageous to select those birds that are likely to have the best chance of survival. To try and deal with all birds irrespective of condition would probably mean giving suboptimal attention and treatment to all and hence prejudice the survival chances of the healthier subjects.

Previous assessments have usually been made on the basis of the degree of external oiling. However, there are frequent cases where birds come ashore fairly lightly oiled mainly because they have preened oil from the plumage and ingested it (see Plate 13). There are also cases where very heavily oiled birds have been unable to preen much – presumably following a rapid, partly immobilising oiling – and hence the quantity of ingested oil is smaller; and the chance of survival correspondingly greater. A number of factors seem useful in assessing the overall condition of oiled auks and these are outlined below:

1 *Weight* Guillemots weighing less than 600g and razorbills weighing less than 425g have a very poor chance of survival, whether they are heavily oiled or not. In a large incident, birds with heavier weight will also die but birds with weights below those given can rarely be rehabilitated even with constant individual attention. Equivalent data for other species are not available and with these the degree of emaciation, as judged by the wastage of the breast muscles, will provide a fairly adequate guide to condition.

2 *Degree of oiling* Other things being equal, heavily oiled birds are likely to fare worse than lightly oiled ones. As noted above, care should be taken to distinguish birds that are fairly lightly oiled externally but have ingested large quantities of oil. Such birds are nearly always passing oil in the faeces and significant traces of oil can usually be seen in the mouth.

3 *Eyes* A glazed appearance of the eyes and/or an unusually slow movement of the nictitating membrane are usually associated with birds in poor condition.

4 *Back* In birds that are lying down a pronounced arching of the rump and lower part of the back is generally a sign of poor internal condition.

5 *Behaviour* The ability of oiled birds to stand up, and in particular to do so on the webs of the feet alone, is a good sign. Alertness

179

and general liveliness (aggression, attempts to escape from box, and such) usually indicate satisfactory condition.

Some experience is needed to recognise these conditions, but whenever possible all should be considered together before making an assessment. There is, however, a case for implementing the weight criterion before considering other factors.

IMMEDIATE TREATMENT

When caught the bird should be held so as to prevent its wings flapping. The bill should be wiped clean and the body enclosed in a cloth (ideally a poncho) pulled over the head, leaving the head and feet projecting. Tubular gauze is also useful for this. Such restraint helps to immobilise the bird and prevents preening and further oil ingestion, as well as keeping it warm. Thus wrapped, the bird should be placed in a cardboard box well lined with newspapers and/or rags (never straw). The flaps should be folded to keep the bird in the dark though sufficient holes must be left to ensure adequate ventilation.

Two or three birds of the same species may often conveniently be placed in the same box – providing it is of sufficient size – but it is preferable not to put a greater number together. Some species, such as razorbills and guillemots, may safely be boxed together but in most cases it is best not to mix species.

SUBSEQUENT TREATMENT

At the above stage birds are ready for moving to wherever experienced attention will be given. Care should be taken to ensure adequate ventilation during transportation. If this journey will take two hours or more an attempt should be made to feed the birds immediately.

Experience and research have shown that the feeding of whole fish to birds freshly brought in is usually distinctly disadvantageous. The skeleton and fin spines of such fish aggravate the epithelial inflammation, initiated by ingested oil, and massive haemorrhage frequently results. Strips (finger-sized for razorbill and guillemot) of uncooked filleted whitefish (such as plaice, cod, whiting, sole) are recommended. This avoids any unnecessary internal abrasion and the blandness of the diet helps remove oil from the gut.

Force-feeding is often necessary and this should be attempted with great care by the inexperienced. It is best if one person can hold the bird and open its bill while the other inserts the strips of fish, the bill then being held nearly upright and the throat gently stroked to reduce the chance of regurgitation. With practice a single person can conveniently manage by holding the bird under one arm to prevent the wings flapping, opening the bill with both hands and then keeping the mouth open with the fingers of one hand while inserting strips of fish with the other.

Birds should be kept on a white fish diet until oil is no longer passed with the faeces, by which time (normally 24–48 hours) most birds are usually in good enough condition to be cleaned. Up to this stage they should still be kept in boxes, with frequent changes of newspaper linings and ponchos.

Medication

Dosages and basic techniques for administering medicines are covered elsewhere in the book. Injections are not recommended by the author as they appear to cause excessive stress; gelatine capsules are normally used to give medicines to individual birds.

There is evidence that administration of a broad spectrum antibiotic and steroid base is helpful in controlling enteritis. Tetracyclines and neomycin appear to be effective antibiotics and dexamethasone a useful steroid.

There have also been reports[15] of successful use of milk of magnesia (magnesium hydroxide) as a mild emetic to clear oil from the gut but the additional stress involved may offset any advantage gained. It might be useful with strong birds that appear to have ingested large quantities of oil.

Treatment with these substances should be confined to a few days; prolonged medication is not desirable. However, if a course of antibiotics has been initiated, it must be completed since otherwise bacterial resistance may be encouraged.

Vitamin additives (particularly vitamins A and B) may also be of value in increasing the birds' resistance to infection. Suitable vitamin doses, multivitamin tablets and mineral supplements can be added to the diet at any stage or administered in capsules.

Cleaning

Birds are not normally cleaned until they are in a reasonable general condition and are no longer either passing oil in the faeces or being force-fed. It is occasionally desirable to make exceptions to this, particularly with badly oiled birds where considerable difficulty is experienced in preventing preening. An early preliminary clean to remove most of the oil may avoid continued oil ingestion in these cases. As a few birds do not remain fairly quiet when placed in a box and expend much energy trying to escape, it may also be preferable to clean these quickly and then allow them greater liberty to avoid a build-up of stress.

The cleaning technique recommended here was developed following considerable research into the nature of plumage waterproofing in birds, and the consequent understanding of the requirements of potential cleaning agents, by the Research Unit on the Rehabilitation of Oiled Seabirds (RUROS).

The characteristic waterproof plumage of seabirds is principally dependent on the water repellency of individual feathers and this is a function of structural and surface properties.[16, 17, 18] The role of preen gland secretion seems chiefly to help maintain the cohesive nature of the feather structure, enhance the contact angle between the feather and water and prevent dirt from easily penetrating the plumage. Not only contaminants, such as oil, but also residues of cleaning agents remaining after oil removal, disturb the fine structure of birds' feathers, thus reducing both resistance to water penetration and the directional water shedding properties of the individual feathers, and rendering the plumage permeable to water.

Clearly the basic requirements for a cleaning agent are that it should remove contaminating oil from the feathers with the minimum of damage to the plumage and that it should not remain as a residue on the feathers after the treatment. RUROS tested a very wide range of cleaning agents using a variety of experimental techniques.[13, 19, 20] A third practical consideration which also influenced this investigation was the need to ensure that the recommended techniques should be simple and the cleaning agents widely available. Only in this way could the efficient cleaning of oiled birds be practicable on a nationwide basis. This bears in mind that much of the cleaning of the casualties from chronic oil pollution is undertaken by individuals without substantial resources and that oiling incidents may often occur in isolated areas where it may be necessary to use inexperienced voluntary help.

It was for these reasons that one or two compounds, notably organic solvents, were not recommended as alternative methods, although the tests showed their performance to be as good as the chosen cleaning agents. The use of such solvents in cleaning oiled birds has been widely publicised.[15, 21] Although these solvents are not particularly easy to use, they are efficient at removing oil and seem to leave the plumage in good condition. However, there is a lack of critical evidence for the rate of re-attainment of waterproofing in birds thus treated; and the solvents are extremely expensive to use, even in the quantity necessary to clean only a very few birds – really they cannot be considered a practical proposition unless the costs of the cleaning operation are borne by the defaulting party.

The method recommended below results from RUROS research and was originally published in the UK as part of the booklet 'Recommended Treatment of Oiled Seabirds'.[22] If followed with meticulous attention to detail, it will usually leave birds with a clean, water-repellent plumage.

The treatment involves washing the birds with a warm solution of washing-up liquid. Many detergents will remove the oil, but most have other disadvantages. Washing-up liquids are by far the most satisfactory and four UK brands which have given consistently good results with oiled birds are Village, Co-op washing-up liquid (under various names), Winfield and Keynote. More expensive brands, whatever their merits for washing dishes, have not usually given consistent results with oiled birds and are not recommended.

The birds should be washed as follows :

1   Make up a 1 per cent solution of washing-up liquid in a tub or sink of hot water, that is approximately $\frac{1}{4}$pt in 3gal water, or 100ml in 10 l water. The solution should be hand-hot (40–45°C); that is, the highest temperature at which the hands can comfortably be held in the water.

  It is important to have the solution within the recommended temperature range and to use the recommended concentration of washing-up liquid in water. Do not use a stronger solution or the efficiency of the washing-up liquid at removing oil will be reduced.

2   Immerse the bird up to its neck in the cleaning solution and hold it immobile for ten seconds or so, to allow the fluid to penetrate the oily feathers.

3   Two people are usually needed to carry out the washing : one to hold the bird, the other to agitate the plumage in the solution. The oiled parts of the plumage should be rubbed and the feathers separated to allow the liquid to reach all the oil. The head and area around the eyes should be cleaned by the gentle use of a toothbrush, repeatedly dipping it in the solution (see Plate 14).

4   Transfer the bird to a fresh bath of washing-up liquid at the same concentration and temperature as before, and complete washing until all visible traces of oil are removed. If a bird is exceptionally heavily oiled, a third fresh wash is often necessary.

5   The bird must be very thoroughly rinsed with hand-hot water. A shower attachment linked to the hot and cold taps of a bath or

basin is best for this and the water should be jetted strongly into the plumage, working against the grain so that it penetrates to the skin. Continue spraying all parts of the plumage until the appearance of the bird changes from being utterly waterlogged to regaining some of its former fluffiness and the water begins to pearl off in drops. This condition should be achieved in all parts of the plumage.

Complete removal of the oil and sufficient rinsing to remove the final traces of washing-up liquid from the plumage are essential if the birds are to regain a water-repellent plumage. The cleaning process may take some time, but unless it is thorough an early release of the birds cannot be anticipated. Light oils (such as diesel fuel) are particularly difficult to remove and some birds may need two separate cleaning sessions to remove all the contaminant.

After rinsing, excess water should be mopped off with a clean cloth and the bird placed near a source of heat. If hot-air driers are used care should be taken to ensure that the bird cannot approach too closely and become scorched or suffer the cracking of exposed skin, particularly on the webs of the feet. To guard against this, the feet may be treated with a vegetable oil or moisturising cream before drying. Even when dry the bird should be kept quiet in a box for an hour or so before the post-cleaning phase of rehabilitation is begun.

POST-CLEANING REHABILITATION

When a bird has been cleaned it should be amply fed on a diet of whole small fish, usually sprats.

The aim of post-cleaning rehabilitation is to encourage the bird to a rapid re-attainment of plumage waterproofing so that an early release may be effected. Providing a bird has been thoroughly cleaned and rinsed the speed of re-waterproofing depends chiefly on the cleanliness of the surroundings (as faeces and other dirt act as plumage contaminants in exactly the same way as oil and cleaning agent residues) and on the incidence of preening.

The basic requirement is for an outdoor pen with continuous access to a pool of clean water. The pen floor must be clean; sand, concrete, or good turf (providing the development of mud can be prevented) are all acceptable. The pool water must be changed regularly but addition of salt to the water does not seem essential. A ramp should be provided to facilitate access to and from the pool. Some form of shelter, preferably with provision for a source of heat, is highly advisable. Birds coming into the pen for the first time should be kept warm in the shelter for the first night or two, or if this is not possible, brought indoors overnight. Thereafter heating should not be necessary unless the weather is particularly bad.

A close watch must be kept for signs of loss of condition in any bird; if such signs are detected, particularly in a bird that is not yet waterproof, the patient should not be left out at night until it improves again. If there is reason to suspect the persistence of internal digestive complications (for example, foetid and/or very discoloured faeces) the bird should be brought in and returned to a whitefish diet until the condition clears up.

It is vital to permit birds, and to encourage reluctant ones, to bathe frequently as this is accompanied and followed by preening, which completes the reorganisation of the fine structure of the feathers and is thus critical to the final reattainment of waterproofing. In some species, particularly auks, where there is strong social facilitation of behaviour, the proximity of a group of birds greatly encourages bathing and preening, as well as allowing mutual preening to occur. Considerable recent attention has been given to the effect of group size on social behaviour in both wild and captive guillemots[13, 14] and this has demonstrated quantitatively how levels of alarm are decreased and behaviour such as preening and courtship increased, with increasing group size (see Plate 15). It is hoped soon to make firm recommendations for the optimal group size, in relation to pen area, in which to keep rehabilitated auks. With auks the provision of an artificial cliff or raised ledge around part of the pool appears to have beneficial social consequence and may also stimulate increased bathing.

Many birds will be nearly waterproof within a day or so and the great majority within 7–10 days. A small proportion, particularly including birds in heavy moult and those the faeces of which indicate the existence of residual internal complaints, may take rather longer.

Before release can be considered the plumage must be completely waterproof after prolonged periods of bathing. Many birds may seem waterproof after a few moments bathing but may become quite waterlogged if they stay longer in the water. Great care must be taken not to release any bird that has not attained perfect ventral waterproofing.

If possible release should take place on a relatively unfrequented stretch of coast (or freshwater, depending on the species involved) and in fairly quiet weather conditions. Cleaned and rehabilitated birds should clearly not be released on a coast where oiled birds are still coming ashore.

Ideally a group of birds should be released together and their progress followed from the shore. If individuals have been released prematurely they will tend to come ashore fairly quickly and should be collected up for continued rehabilitation.

AILMENTS OF REHABILITATING SEABIRDS

Earlier in this chapter details of routine recommended medications for oiled birds were given. These were designed chiefly to arrest the development of ailments, such as enteritis and nephrosis, resulting directly or indirectly from oiling; and also to help birds maintain resistance to bacterial and fungal infections.

However, there are a number of ailments to which seabirds rehabilitating in captivity are particularly prone. This section attempts briefly to list some of these with their clinical signs and to indicate any treatments which may exist. A number are discussed in more general terms elsewhere in this book.

Aspergillosis Caused by the fungus *Aspergillus fumigatus*, aspergillosis results from inhalation of spores which can develop to cause lesions in the lungs and air sacs. Susceptible birds usually show signs of difficult (often rasping) breathing and death usually follows within a few days. Lack of coordination and acute diarrhoea are sometimes later symptoms. Although mouldy food and bedding (especially damp straw) can be sources of infection, the fungus is so widespread that it can often be isolated from apparently healthy birds. Although cleanliness and good sanitation help reduce the risk, it is clear that birds under conditions of stress have a lowered resistance to infection and a general inability to combat the development of the incipient disease. Hence deaths due to aspergillosis may reflect the consequences of stress associated with oiling rather than inadequate facilities or care.

Prophylaxis and treatment have not proved very successful although the antifungal agent nystatin may have some preventive qualities. It has also been claimed[23] that the inhalation by penguins of nystatin and chlortetracycline administered as aerosols has been effective in preventing aspergillosis (see also Chapter 10).

Birds in captivity that develop breathing difficulties should be isolated from the remainder in an attempt to prevent the spread of any potential infection although it is unlikely that aspergillosis is transmitted from bird to bird.

Arthritis   Lesions of the feet, webs and legs, symptomatic of infective arthritis, are not uncommon in seabirds (particularly auks and seaduck) in captivity. The leg joints progressively stiffen, the webbing of the feet becomes contracted and coliform and staphylococcal bacteria can usually be isolated from the purulent exudate of the joint capsule.

Decubitous ulcers (that is, bed sores or pressure sores) are not uncommon at the site of the phalangeal joints on the underside of the webs. In some cases drying of the tarsi and webs, with resulting cracks in the skin, may be responsible and birds whose feet show a tendency to become excessively dry and/or hot should be treated with a moisturising cream. In many cases the conditions seem to develop as a result of unaccustomed constant pressure on the tarsal and phalangeal joints as the bird stands on an unyielding floor. It may be significant that birds kept on turf rarely develop arthritic joints and there are indications that a covering of thin foam rubber in indoor pens can help minimise the occurrence of the complaint.

Even if detected in the early stages pressure sores are difficult to alleviate although the use of dressings to relieve the pressure has had a little success.

Cloacal impaction   Massive distention of the cloaca, which is filled with firm greyish-white faeces and accumulated urates, is occasionally reported in rehabilitating birds, particularly grebes and divers, although it has also been noted in gannets, razorbills and guillemots. The condition is not easy to diagnose but the distended cloaca can often be palpated manually. Treatment should be undertaken by a veterinary surgeon (see Plate 16).

Ensuring regular defaecation in grebes and divers, by lifting the birds up once or twice daily and, if necessary, placing their tailparts in a tub of water, may be one way of avoiding the development of cloacal impaction in these species.

Eye irritation   Inflammation of the cornea and/or conjunctiva is sometimes reported. Direct irritation from oil may often be responsible though prolonged periods out of water probably also contribute. Application of antibiotic-corticosteroid ointments seems a satisfactory solution.

Thiamine toxicosis   Naviaux[15] recognised the first known occurrence of this disease affecting wildfowl. The enzyme thiaminase occurs in certain fish (for example, smelt, carp, chub, white bass, turbot) and if these are

187

eaten, thiamine (vitamin B1) which is important in the neural metabolism of birds, can be broken down resulting in polyneuritis and rapid death.

Clinical signs are loss of appetite and marked constriction of the pupils with convulsions just prior to death (which may result in three days). Thiamine can be administered individually or as part of the routine vitamin dietary supplement, or in soluble form with the drinking water. It is doubtful if the condition is at all widespread and it is unlikely to be a problem in captivity unless a large element in the diet consists of fish containing thiaminase.

Parasites Acanthocephalan, nematode and cestode parasites are quite frequently found in the gut of birds on post-mortem examination but fatal hyperparasitism is very rare. Routine administration of anthelmintics is not recommended (because of inducing additional stress) unless the bird is clearly heavily infected, as judged by the state of its faeces or regurgitated food (see also Chapter 11).

Other ailments A wide variety of bacterial and fungal diseases has been isolated from rehabilitating birds that have died in captivity. It is seldom clear to what extent these diseases have contributed to the cause of death. Administration of antibiotics, indicated in the section as general treatment, may prove helpful in some cases but overall reduction of stress is probably the best form of prevention.

TREATMENT OF INDIVIDUAL SPECIES

Most of the foregoing account has related to the treatment of auks, particularly guillemots and razorbills. Much of the advice, except when noted to the contrary, can be fairly easily adapted to suit the needs of other species, for example the quantity and kind of food. The cleaning process also should remain essentially the same, though for some of the larger species it may be convenient to keep the bill closed, with a thick elastic band (taking care not to obstruct the nostrils), during the cleaning operation.

It seems useful to summarise the rather small amount of additional information that has been found particularly relevant to the treatment of other species.

Divers (Gaviidae) and grebes (Podicipidae) All species pose a difficult rehabilation problem, chiefly because the position of the feet so far to the rear of the body makes them clumsy on land and unable to stand with the ventral body surface out of contact with the ground. As a result fouling of the ventral areas is very difficult to prevent and re-attainment of waterproofing correspondingly slow. Particularly meticulous cleaning may help and it appears best to keep these birds either on their own or in very uncrowded facilities, to minimise the chances of contamination.

Divers and grebes seem liable to dehydration in captivity. Before cleaning, the head should be immersed in a tub of water and the bird allowed to drink at least twice a day. Earlier the importance of ensuring regular defaecation was noted. Birds of both families are particularly susceptible to respiratory diseases.

Petrels and shearwaters (Procellariidae)   The fulmar is the most likely member of the family to be found oiled. In the wild, fulmars seem to prefer oil-rich fishy foods; sardines and herring soaked in cod-liver oil have been fed to rehabilitating individuals with some success.

Gannets (Sulidae) and cormorants/shags (Phalacrocoracidae)   Apart from their large size, these species do not seem to present any particular problems of rehabilitation. Success rates, especially with gannets, are usually good. Initial force-feeding is not for the inexperienced but can be conveniently accomplished singlehanded by grasping the bill and then exerting firm upward and backward lifting pressure on the upper jaw until the gape is sufficiently open to insert fish. The mouth must be closed to allow swallowing. Release of gannets in particular should take place from a slight elevation, and preferably into the wind, to help the bird become airborne.

Swans, geese and ducks (Anatidae)   Swans, geese and freshwater duck are not normally difficult to rehabilitate; seaduck frequently present additional problems.

Swans are usually transported in canvas sacks, tied to prevent wing and foot movement, with the head and neck projecting through a hole. It is often difficult to clean swans thoroughly but fortunately, if left with access to a pool or water spray, they preen extensively and do not usually take longer than three weeks to regain full waterproofing. Usual foods include soaked mash, grain and bread often mixed with pondweed, grass or other chopped vegetable material. After this stage swans and geese will usually be self-sufficient, grazing in a grassy field. Swans are sometimes susceptible to pneumonia (signs include darkening of the bill and wavering of the head) and injections of a broad-spectrum antibiotic

189

and a corticosteroid have been recommended for this.

Freshwater duck are usually little trouble in captivity and the type of food suggested for swans is usually quite adequate for them as well.

The species of seaduck most frequently oiled (eider, scoter, scaup and goldeneye) rarely have to be force-fed and, in spite of the proportion of molluscs in the wild diet, can normally be started on chopped pieces of white fish and then transferred to a diet of whole sprats in the same way as auks. Sometimes eiders seem prone to swollen joints and drying out of the feet should be avoided. They also have a tendency to develop pressure sores around the breastbone and, if possible, a thin foam rubber substrate, covered with newspaper, should be provided for them to lie on. Scoter often seem very reluctant to enter water and at first may need to be placed in the pool and prevented from leaving until they have spent several minutes swimming.

Gulls and terns (Laridae)   Terns rarely seem to become oiled; gulls are usually badly oiled when they are unable to evade capture and it is a common sight to see a number of partly oiled gulls in most large wild flocks. Gulls, including the kittiwake, are amongst the easiest birds to rehabilitate, and tolerant of a wide range of diet though normally finding the usual routine of white fish, and later sprats, perfectly acceptable. Small and large species should not be mixed but it is not usually necessary to keep each species separate. Small gulls can safely be mixed with auks and duck though this should not be done with the larger species, especially if they are taking up space that could better be used by other, more endangered, species.

Oystercatcher (Haematopodidae), plovers (Charadriidae) and other waders (Scolopacidae)   Force-feeding waders is not easy but narrow strips of white fish are probably suitable food during the critical stages. Small waders will often take soaked chick crumbs to which minced meat and fish can be added. Most waders, especially the larger ones, will take mealworms and maggots and many are known to live in captivity on mashes of mixed insectivore food such as Sluis pâté, to which other items can be added.

The information in this chapter, although imperfect and incomplete in many respects, should enable people with adequate facilities to have reasonable success in rehabilitating oiled birds.

The final success rate at the Research Unit on the Rehabilitation of Oiled Seabirds was about 60 per cent of all birds brought in, which included quite a number that were inadequately treated elsewhere and also birds that had been several days without any treatment whatsoever. However, it should be clear that, in the event of a large-scale oiling incident, involving thousands of birds, individual people and small groups would be quite unable to cope. Ideal requirements of advance planning for the occurrence of such incidents in the United States have been set out by Naviaux[15] and Stanton.[24]

Operations on such a scale are unlikely to be fully practicable in the UK but serious attempts are being made by the RSPB, RSPCA, the Scottish Society for Prevention of Cruelty to Animals and RUROS to establish at least two permanent rehabilitation centres to which oiled birds from large incidents could be taken for treatment. These would be situated in critical areas (near Edinburgh to serve the large wintering areas of the Firths of Forth and Tay; and near Taunton to serve south-west England) and would provide facilities sufficient to cope with 1,000–2,000 birds at a time.

It is hoped that the planning stages for these projected developments will be completed soon so that their construction may begin. Now that our knowledge of treatment procedure is adequate to rehabilitate a substantial proportion of affected birds it would be particularly regrettable if a lack of adequate facilities meant that it was impossible to improve drastically on the aftermath of the Torrey Canyon disaster, when less than 1 per cent of birds were finally rehabilitated.

14 Miscellaneous diseases

J. E. Cooper

In the foregoing chapters the main groups of diseases were discussed : those due to injuries, infections, parasites and poisons. These, however, are not the only causes of disease and in this chapter some other conditions are discussed. The list is not exhaustive but particular emphasis has been laid upon conditions that are considered important in the context of wild bird casualties. Managemental problems, such as overgrown claws and beaks, are not discussed in detail. They are important in captive wild birds but can usually be dealt with by laymen using standard avicultural techniques.

It is not only trauma that will cause damage. Birds can suffer also from the effects of burning and overheating, freezing and chilling, electrocution and irradiation. In captivity such conditions are usually attributable to management factors and can often be readily remedied. Some aspects are discussed in Chapter 9.

Diagnosis usually poses no problems since the clinical history is likely to be known. In addition there may be characteristic clinical signs; for example, the bird that is overheated will pant and its wings will hang loosely. The bird that is suffering from mild chilling may appear depressed and cold to the touch while in cases of freezing (frostbite) the affected part of the body is initially pale and cold and later red, swollen and painful. Treatment is less easy since such physical factors can often produce severe injury. Euthanasia may be necessary in some cases. In the case of overheating the bird should be slowly cooled and fluids administered. The chilled bird should be warmed gradually to 30°C and encouraged to feed while local lesions associated with either cold or heat must be treated topically. Amputation of necrotic digits may be necessary.

FEATHER ABNORMALITIES

The important role of the feathers in birds is emphasised in Chapter 3. If wild birds are to be released the plumage should be as near perfect as possible. Often it has been damaged as a result of an injury or becomes so during the course of treatment. As was stressed earlier, most wild

192

birds moult once a year, usually after the breeding season. It follows that severely damaged feathers may not be replaced for several months and this may result in the bird having to be retained in captivity long after its injury or disease has resolved. Care of the plumage is therefore most important.

Bent or frayed feathers can be soaked in warm (not hot) water to straighten and clean them. However, severely damaged feathers are best removed. Plucking them out (if necessary under light anaesthesia) may result in their regrowing but it must be stressed that much depends upon the species of bird involved. A moult can be stimulated by the administration of the hormone thyroxine but care must be taken in the use of this drug. This and other aspects of feather growth and developments are discussed in the book by Voitkevich[1] and this authoritative publication is recommended to all those concerned with the care of wild birds.

An alternative way of dealing with broken feathers is to mend them by 'imping' on a piece of feather. This technique, which has been practised by falconers for centuries, appears not to have been adopted widely by aviculturists. In the case of wild birds it could prove extremely valuable, allowing casualties to be released (or, at least, to start flying again) before the next moult. The technique of imping will not be described here; reference should be made to falconry books.[2]

Many other conditions may affect feathers. Parasites, such as biting lice, can cause a dry plumage with a 'moth-eaten' appearance. Stresses, such as reduced food intake, during feather growth or moulting can cause lines of weakness, termed hunger traces, fret marks or fault bars (see Chapter 3). A condition termed pinching off may also occur following stress; it is characterised by a marked constriction of the feathers which fall out prematurely (see Plate 17). Generally, poor plumage may be a manifestation of a number of diseases. In most of these cases there is little that can be done in the form of therapy. The feather is a dead structure and no amount of dietary supplements or injections will influence its appearance. However, the provision of a better diet will help ensure that the next set of feathers will be strong and healthy. Birds should be fed well during the moult; the addition of a vitamin/mineral supplement is often advisable. Stressors, such as disturbance, must also be reduced to a minimum at this time.

Abnormal moulting patterns are not uncommon in wild birds kept for considerable periods of captivity. The clinical picture varies – sometimes there is no moult, on other occasions the bird drops feathers continuously. Temperature may play a part in these syndromes, a higher temperature tending to encourage moulting, a lower one retarding it. Changing the temperature may, therefore, prove beneficial. Thyroxine can also be used, as mentioned earlier. Often, however, the picture is complex and there is as yet insufficient information on the subject for the author to be able to offer sound advice. This is an example of an area where avicultural experience, especially that involving aviary-bred close-ringed birds in the UK, is likely to prove useful to those working with casualties.

Other aspects of feather damage are discussed elsewhere in the book — for example, that caused by oiling in Chapter 13.

NUTRITIONAL DISEASES

Although the subject of feeding birds is amply covered in Chapter 8, nutritional diseases must be mentioned.

Birds should receive a diet of the right quantity and quality. It is possible to overfeed a bird in captivity and this is undesirable since it can result in obesity and pathological lesions, such as atheroma (narrow ing and hardening) of the blood vessels and fatty changes in the liver. Excess protein in the diet will result in overgrowth of claws and, in some cases, visceral and articular gout.[3] However, underfeeding is more common, especially when wild birds are reluctant to feed in captivity or when a suitable diet is difficult to obtain. One of the first signs of reduced food intake is the passing of green bile-stained faeces. Later the bird shows an obvious reduction in condition and in the terminal stages will become weak or, in some cases, develop nervous signs. It is useful to weigh captive birds regularly as this will serve as a guide to their condition. If sufficient food is being eaten and yet weight is being lost, the bird may be suffering from a disease, such as parasitism.

The quality of a bird's diet is a most important factor. Unfortunately we still know little about the nutrient requirements of birds, with the exception of domestic poultry and some encouraging work in recent years on cage birds.[4] In the case of captive wild birds one can usually only extrapolate from such data. It seems likely that requirements of vitamins, minerals and certain other nutrients may be increased under conditions of stress and a sick or injured bird will undoubtedly need extra quantities for healing and regeneration of tissues. Certainly, in practical terms, the addition of a vitamin/mineral supplement will often produce a clinical improvement in birds that have previously fared poorly. Some non-specific conditions, including skin diseases and poor feathering, also appear to improve with vitamin supplementation.

Hyperkeratinisation (thickening of the skin and associated scabbing) is commonly seen on the feet and cere of captive wild birds and this will often respond to vitamin A by injection; the use of a mineral oil topically, to help soften and remove the scabs, will also assist recovery. However, it is impossible at this stage to do more than speculate as to whether the condition is a straightforward vitamin A deficiency.

Under other circumstances certain deficiencies are well recognised in birds, including those of vitamin A, vitamin B1 (thiamine), vitamin D and vitamin E. Vitamin B1 deficiency is discussed in Chapter 13; it can occur when carnivorous birds (including gulls and waders) are fed on diets high in fish. Some fish contain a thiaminase, which breaks down thiamine, and a deficiency can result. A vitamin D3 deficient diet can cause true rickets in birds while steatitis (yellow fat disease) and white muscle disease have been reported in birds and are believed to be due to a lack of vitamin E.[3]

Supplementation of the diet with vitamins/minerals, while probably often advantageous, must be done with caution. Excessive amounts of vitamins, especially vitamins A and D, can cause ill effects. The author's approach is not to use such supplements more often than three times a week unless a specific deficiency has been diagnosed.

A disease that is well recognised in the larger birds, especially those that are meat eaters such as birds of prey and crows, is osteodystrophy. The condition is commonly called rickets but this is a misnomer since it is due not to a vitamin D deficiency but to an imbalance of calcium/ phosphorus in the diet. The ideal dietary ratio of these minerals is 1.5 : 1.0 but in most meats they are in the region of 1 : 30. Unless such diets are appropriately supplemented, a relative calcium deficiency occurs; the bird is unable to manufacture a proper skeleton and spontaneous fractures and bowing of long bones occur. Finally the blood calcium level falls and the bird dies.

The condition is readily recognisable by its clinical features; radiographs show poorly calcified bones and the lesions described above. Birds that are severely affected should be killed on humanitarian grounds but earlier cases can be given a calcium supplement or, preferably, a balanced diet. If meat is being fed it should be accompanied by bones (which contain the optimum calcium/phosphorus ratio) or have sterilised bonemeal added. This condition has been described in detail in a number of publications.[5, 6] It may occur also occasionally in non-carnivorous birds; again calcium supplementation is needed and the addition of milk to the water will help provide this.

Both constipation and diarrhoea can occur in wild birds and although

195

the latter in particular is usually associated with infectious disease or injury, other factors may be involved. Constipation, which is usually manifested by the bird straining or showing abdominal distress, can be relieved with liquid paraffin or cod-liver oil. Diarrhoea can be controlled with a kaolin suspension. These drugs are given by mouth.

METABOLIC DISEASES

These are often closely linked with nutritional diseases. A metabolic disease is not caused by an infection or by trauma but is due to some derangement of the normal metabolic processes of the body. In the case of osteodystrophy the disease is essentially a metabolic one (a secondary hyperparathyroidism) but the initial cause is a poor diet.

Relatively little is known about other metabolic diseases of wild birds. Thyroid and other endocrine disorders are recognised in cage-birds[7] and probably occur in other species. Some of the feather conditions so commonly encountered in captive wild birds may well have a metabolic origin, since, as was mentioned earlier, the whole process of feather development and moulting is a complex one involving (amongst other things) the hormone thyroxine produced by the thyroid.

Hypoglycaemia, a lowering of the blood sugar levels, almost certainly occurs in wild birds. It is probably the cause of the terminal fits that occur in birds that are starved or otherwise in poor condition. Other causes of nervous diseases are mentioned later.

Gout occurs commonly in captive birds but its cause is not fully understood. In visceral gout, urates (excretory products) are deposited on the internal organs, especially the heart, liver and intestines. In articular gout, the deposits are in the joints (see Plate 19). There are no characteristic clinical signs of the former but the latter is usually associated with incoordination and lameness or inability to fly. Diagnostic tests were discussed by Hasholt[8] who also recommended treatment by dietary alteration, drugs and (in part) local therapy.

Metabolic factors are possibly also involved when birds fail to breed in captivity since the reproductive cycle is a complex one involving many hormones and a 'feedback' mechanism. However, nutrition and behaviour probably also play an important role in such cases.

Stress and shock can be conveniently listed under metabolic diseases. Both are terms which are widely misused and misunderstood and frequently they are considered synonymous. Even in scientific circles the definition of stress is debatable but it is now generally accepted that Selye's concept is a suitable one for birds as well as for mammals. A useful paper on stress in birds is that by von Faber[9] who listed many stressors in poultry, amongst them excess heat and cold and disease. These and others can produce the 'General Adaptation Syndrome' with changes in the adrenal and other glands designed to counteract the stressors. If the bird is unable to cope with the stressors a stage of exhaustion is reached and the bird finally dies of stress. However, usually the picture is complicated by other factors such as intercurrent disease. Stress probably plays an important part in wild bird populations. For example, research on wood pigeons has shown that a definite social hierarchy exists.[10] Subordinate birds have a lower bodyweight and reduced prospects of survival compared with dominant birds. In addition, there are characteristic changes in the adrenal glands of subordinate birds. This and other work help support the suggestion that some wild bird casualties in which no definitive diagnosis can be made may be suffering from stress. Even if this is not the original problem, it is possible that stressors in captivity may exacerbate underlying problems and make successful treatment difficult.

It is difficult to be certain, in clinical terms, of the features of a bird suffering from stress but some indications are probably a failure to thrive, poor plumage, nervousness and susceptibility to secondary disorders such as foot infections (see Fig 28). Recently injured (or captured) wild birds may die within 10–14 days with no specific clinical signs and at post-mortem examination no diagnosis can be made. Such deaths are commonly attributed to stress and stressors may well be involved.

Treatment of the stressed bird should be aimed at reducing the number of the stressors – and this should also be the basis of prevention. Some examples are given in Chapter 20. Any wild bird casualty should be protected from unnecessary disturbance and such ruses as provision of cover (vegetation or pieces of bark) or covering much of the cage with cloth or paper may help the bird to acclimatise to captivity. Other stressors known to be significant in poultry include reduced food or water intake, infections and fatigue; it goes without saying that every effort should be made to minimise these. Much depends upon the species involved; the more difficult ones, which require very specialised conditions, are more prone to succumb to non-specific diseases which probably are associated with stress.

In the Foreword Joy Adamson speaks of the 'scientifically shunned word "loved" ', but her work and that of countless other people involved with wild mammals and birds testifies to the value of personal care and affection in work with casualties. The scientific basis of such success is the individual attention given to each patient so that, for example, it is encouraged to feed and drink and there is prompt attention to minor discomforts and disabilities. Such diligence, coupled with great patience, probably reduces stressors to a minimum and, very often, tips the balance in favour of recovery rather than death.

The administration of certain medicines may also help to reduce stress, usually by countering infection or increasing the bird's ability to resist adverse conditions. Examples are antibiotics – which should not, in the author's opinion, be used unless there is evidence of infection – and such dietary additives as vitamins. The latter, if used sparingly, will do no harm and can be given to birds that fail to thrive and show general non-specific signs which may be attributable to stress.

It is clear that little is known of the role of stress in wild birds and the bird hospital could prove a useful location for the study of the syndrome. Far more work is needed on this subject and great care should be taken not to use the term stress too loosely; its misuse can lead to confusion and may even hamper research in this field.

Shock is rather easier to describe, though it too is often wrongly diagnosed. True shock is a physiological process characterised by a drop in blood pressure and a reduction in blood flow to the peripheral parts of the body. As a result the bird's extremities become cold and pale and the patient is usually listless. The most common cause in wild birds is where there has been severe damage, especially if blood loss has occurred. This is discussed in Chapter 9. Treatment is by increasing the circulating blood volume by the administration of saline, or glucose saline, solution as outlined in Chapters 7 and 9. The bird should be gradually warmed, over a period of 2–3 hours, to a temperature of 32°C at which it should then be maintained.

Birds may also die unexpectedly for other reasons; often, however, shock is given as the cause of death. The aetiology of these deaths is largely unknown but in some cases sudden haemorrhage may be responsible, presumably following a rapid increase in blood pressure, while vagal nerve inhibition, causing heartblock, is an as yet unproved possibility. More of these cases should be submitted for detailed pathological examination.

NERVOUS DISEASES

Nervous conditions are not uncommon in wild birds and those affecting the central nervous system (CNS) are a cause for particular concern. Affected birds may have fits[6] or show severe incoordination, such as inability to stand or fly. In some cases (usually following traumatic injury) the bird's head may be held at an angle or even upside-down. Following traumatic injury a bird may show any of the features mentioned above or may be concussed (see later).

There are probably many causes of fits in birds. Poisons are an important consideration (see Chapter 12). Hypoglycaemia, due to a drop in condition, was mentioned earlier. Low blood calcium levels, also discussed earlier, is another possible factor. Vitamin B1 deficiency is described in Chapter 13 and it too can result in fits and other CNS signs. Control of fits consists of nursing (keeping the bird warm, in the dark) and the administration of a drug such as diazepam to quieten the patient. Specific treatment should be carried out if the cause of the fits is known but often an empirical approach is necessary. Vitamin B1, glucose and calcium can all be given but such therapy must be accompanied by symptomatic treatment and nursing as mentioned earlier.

37 A bird with brain damage; in this case the head is held upside-down

Traumatic injuries to the central nervous system are commonly fatal; for example, when birds fly into a glass window they usually die as a result of skull and brain damage. In some cases, however, they merely concuss themselves; the bird may be unconscious, or on its feet but dazed in appearance. Many such cases recover spontaneously, usually within 2–3 hours, if kept warm and quiet. Some cases of wing or leg paralysis are due to spinal cord injury, often associated with a fracture of the vertebral column. The author's experience of these has been restricted to post-mortem material.

Conditions involving peripheral nerves are commonly seen in wild birds. Trauma is the commonest cause and this is discussed in Chapter 5. Nerve damage is usually manifested by limb paralysis or dysfunction, often coupled with a loss of sensation of some areas. A particularly common example in wild birds is characterised by an inability to extend the digits; as a result the foot closes and the bird tends to 'knuckle over' as it walks. Nerve damage to the wing is also regularly seen – the wing hangs loosely and there is no evidence of skeletal damage on palpation or radiography. There is no specific therapy for such conditions other than supportive treatment (for example, protecting a paralysed foot from abrasion on a rough floor) and recovery, if it is going to occur, should take place within four weeks. Some cases of apparent nervous damage may be associated with dietary deficiencies and administration of B vitamins, preferably by injection, is a useful precaution in all such cases.

DISEASES OF THE SPECIAL SENSES

Traumatic injuries to the eyes are commonly encountered in wild bird casualties. The extent of the damage varies from mild corneal damage to complete collapse or luxation of the eye. Ocular conditions should be treated by a veterinary surgeon since a careful clinical examination is important and removal of the eye or other sophisticated surgical techniques may be necessary. Corneal ulceration is often painful to the bird and may fail to resolve with standard treatment; a useful technique is to suture the eyelids together for 2–3 weeks.

Blindness is not always easy to diagnose in birds. Again veterinary advice is advisable. Total blindness will commit a bird to captivity and, probably, hand-feeding for the remainder of its life; it may be more humane to destroy the bird. Partial sight, on the other hand, need not be so much a handicap although these birds should not, in general, be released.

200

Deafness is encountered from time to time; again it may be difficult to diagnose. There is no specific treatment; sometimes the sense of hearing improves with time. Birds survive well in captivity if wholly or partly deaf but should not be released. Ear infections may be manifested by purulent discharge from an ear or ears (often there is dampness of the overlying feathers) and/or inability to hold the head straight. Antibiotics can be used in treatment but in some cases there is irreversible damage and it is better to destroy the bird humanely. Occasionally birds show a clinical improvement but the head remains partly on one side, indicating permanent damage to the balancing mechanism of the inner ear. There is no objection to retaining such birds in captivity but they should not be released.

BEHAVIOURAL (PSYCHOLOGICAL) DISORDERS

These problems have already been mentioned briefly in Chapter 4 and will be referred to again, in the context of aviary and cage construction, in Chapter 20. Behavioural abnormalities not only influence the immediate care of a wild bird casualty; they can also affect a bird's subsequent life and its ability to fend for itself in the wild. Imprinting is an example; young birds reared by human beings may encounter problems in selecting a mate and in some cases fail to do so.

Some species of bird fare poorly in captivity and although such cases are usually labelled 'shocked', it is probable that behavioural disturbances, associated with a strange environment and diet, are the immediate cause. As was emphasised earlier, birds are basically creatures of instinct and therefore a sudden change of environment or routine can have severe effects on behaviour. An orphaned young bird, for example, will gape for food but will not usually take it for itself. In some cases it may be necessary to stimulate the gaping response by appropriate visual or audible stimuli; if this is not done the bird will die. There is also individual variation between birds and this is particularly important in the context of treatment. For example, some cases with relatively minor injuries show little 'will to live' and usually succumb; others, however, are extremely tough and the prognosis is good from the outset.

Other behavioural diseases may develop as habits or vices in captivity. These may be associated with boredom. Some species and individuals will pluck their own or their cagemates' feathers; similarly some will regularly remove dressings and pull out sutures. Others may show stereotyped behaviour in their cage, constantly repeating the same actions, even to the extent of severely damaging themselves. It should

201

not be forgotten, however, that some vices, especially feather pecking, may be due to, or associated with, parasites or dietary disease. In seeking a diagnosis all possible factors must be considered and clinical and laboratory examinations used to the full.

Control of behavioural diseases is not easy. Basically every effort should be made to provide an environment akin to that in the wild. Some species live better in groups, others in pairs and some singly. The sex ratio is important in certain species; two of the same sex may fight whereas a pair may not. Ample room and adequate stimulation are particularly essential and the bird that regularly shows a vice is best rehoused and given either more attention or distraction in the form of company, a varied diet and even playthings.

GENETIC DISEASES

There is very little information on genetic diseases of wild birds. Under free-living conditions the bird with a deleterious genetic factor would probably die very soon. In captivity, however, the situation is different. The more severe genetic problems are the gross abnormalities, such as duplication of limbs, and birds suffering in this way should be killed. Less obvious problems may also exist. New colour forms may appear as a result of mutation or because inbreeding brings together two recessive genes which were previously hidden.

The genetics of breeding cannot be discussed in detail. Those involved in the captive breeding of wild birds should remember that care must be taken in selecting breeding pairs, especially if there is any possibility of the offspring being released to the wild. A trait which is an advantage under captive conditions, such as tameness, could prove fatal in the wild! A tame bird does not necessarily produce tame offspring but it is best to assume that such traits are heritable and to plan the breeding programme appropriately. Other pitfalls of captive breeding include the problems inherent in inbreeding – particularly the reduction in fertility and the emergence of deleterious genes – and the undesirability of hybridisation, especially between species but also, probably, between races of the same species.

NEOPLASTIC DISEASES

Neoplastic diseases are more commonly referred to as cancers or tumours. It is probable that some are due to viruses but they will be included in this chapter. They are only rarely seen in free-living birds,[11] probably because they are primarily diseases of older animals, but they may occur more often in birds in captivity, especially budgerigars.[12] One neoplasm, a papilloma, has frequently been reported in chaffinches[13] and a virus has been isolated from the lesions.[14] Affected birds show cauliflower-like growths on the feet which are an encumbrance and may prevent walking or perching. Partial removal of the lesions is possible using surgical techniques, including thermocautery and cryo-surgery, but the swelling may reappear and secondary complications are not uncommon.

Other neoplasms may not be visible externally. For example, a tumour of an ovary will initially produce internal lesions and it is usually only in the later stages that such clinical signs as abdominal distension and leg paralysis are seen. Some neoplasms are benign, a proportion are locally invasive, while others spread from one organ to another via the bloodstream or lymphatic system. Such factors will influence whether or not therapy is feasible. Improved surgical techniques developed in cagebirds make the prognosis for such cases somewhat better than it was a few years ago.

Although neoplasms are rare in wild birds, this is a field in which the person working with casualties might make a positive contribution to knowledge. Any sick or dead bird with a swelling, particularly if it is long-standing, should be submitted for laboratory investigation, since the lesion may be a neoplasm. However, not all neoplasms produce swellings – there are also tumours of the blood and other tissues – and a diagnosis of these may be made at a routine post-mortem examination. There is currently great interest in cancer of all vertebrates and it is important that potentially useful avian material is not wasted.

EXTERNAL LESIONS

Other swellings occur in wild birds and although often termed tumours, these are usually not neoplastic. A detailed veterinary examination, including laboratory tests, is often necessary to make a definitive diagnosis. Among causes of body and limb swellings are fractures, dis-locations, haematomas, abscesses and tuberculosis lesions. Feather cysts occur occasionally in passerine species and are similar to those seen in cagebirds; they can be removed surgically. Well defined nodular swellings around the head are not uncommon in birds that have had an upper respiratory infection, especially sinusitis. The lesions contain caseous pus and are a type of abscess. They can usually be removed surgically. Subcutaneous distension with air – so-called emphysema – is commonly seen in wild bird casualties. It is often attributable to traumatic damage, usually involving an air sac, but occasionally gas producing bacteria may be responsible. Emphysema will resolve spontaneously over a 2–3 week period but it is sometimes necessary to take remedial action if (for example) the swelling is causing difficulty in eating or breathing. In such a case air can be removed using a sterile needle and syringe; the procedure can be repeated if necessary.

Subcutaneous oedema is characterised by the presence of fluid under the skin. Usually it is localised. A number of factors may be responsible, among them traumatic injury, local inflammation and circulatory disturbances. As a general rule no treatment is necessary and the oedema will resolve but occasionally drainage with a syringe and needle is necessary.

Lesions inside the mouth are not uncommon in wild bird casualties and can be a source of considerable concern since not only are they difficult to examine and treat, but also they may make it difficult for the bird to feed and breathe. Often such lesions are caseous but on occasions they are smooth and firm. Sometimes an ulcer is present. There are many possible causes for such conditions, some of which are discussed elsewhere in the book. Important examples are fungus infections, trichomoniasis and *Capillaria* worm lesions (see Plate 18). Swabs of the lesion should be taken for laboratory examination *before* treatment is started; even a smear on a microscope slide may reveal the presence of parasites or fungi. Thereafter specific treatment can be given. Sometimes, however, a definitive diagnosis cannot be made and treatment must be palliative. Dead material should be removed and the affected area sprayed with a mild disinfectant, such as cetrimide, or painted with gentian violet. A vitamin A supplement may aid healing. In some cases surgical excision of the lesion, by a veterinary surgeon, is advisable.

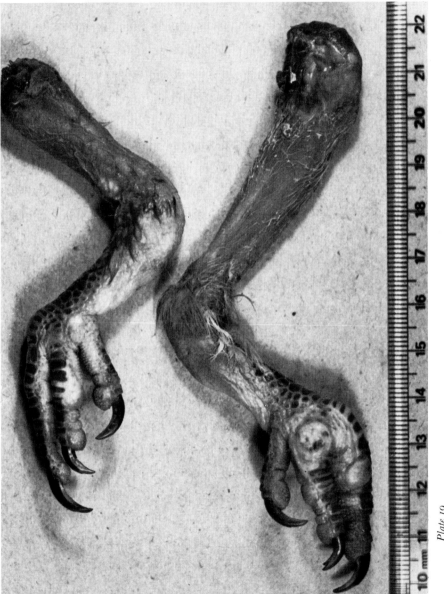

Plate 19
Legs of pigeon showing swollen lesions of visceral gout: this condition is due to an accumulation of urates

Plate 20
A swan which has been wrapped and fully immobilised in strong plastic sheeting

15 Anaesthesia and euthanasia
J. A. Dall and J. E. Cooper

ANAESTHESIA

The welfare of an injured bird should be paramount and one aspect of it is the prevention of unnecessary pain. There are no analgesics (pain killers) of particular value in the general care of birds: one relies upon good nursing to reduce pain on a day-to-day basis. If surgery is necessary, an anaesthetic should be given as a rule. Birds appear less prone to pain than mammals but this should not be used as an excuse for failing to employ an anaesthetic agent. There are, of course, exceptions; for example, the shattered foot on a robin which is often best removed while the bird is conscious with one snip of a pair of scissors. In other cases also, a veterinary surgeon may decide that an anaesthetic is likely to prove more distressing to the bird than any minor surgical procedure.

The administration of all anaesthetics is attended by some risk, so anaesthesia should only be carried out by a qualified veterinary surgeon. This is particularly important in birds as considerable experience is required to assess both the dose and the depth of anaesthesia. The layman will not usually be expected to administer an anaesthetic but in a busy bird hospital he or she will often have to assist and it is important to have basic knowledge of the terminology and methods used. Pre- and post-operative care, which are most important in the treatment of birds, will often also be the responsibility of the bird hospital organiser.

There are important physiological differences between birds and mammals and these can influence the efficacy and safety of avian anaesthesia.[1] In the case of wild birds the difficulties are exacerbated by the poor health of the patient, and it is usually advisable not to embark upon anaesthesia and surgery in the first 36–48 hours. During this time attention should be paid to treating shock and improving the general condition of the patient.

Despite these provisos, a wide range of anaesthetic agents is available for use in birds and great advances have been made in the past ten years. In this chapter attention will be drawn to some of the techniques and agents available but reference will be made to only a selection of the literature. For further information the reader is referred to the publications listed at the end of this book; a particularly concise and useful review article is that by Stunkard and Miller.[2]

Local anaesthesia (local analgesia)

Local anaesthesia is used to produce insensitivity of a localised area. The standard local analgesics for mammals can be dangerous in birds and must be employed with caution, preferably only in the larger species. If lignocaine is to be used it should be diluted 1 : 10 with normal saline; this will reduce the risk of overdosing. In all cases the smallest effective dose must be administered.

Alternatively, a surface-cooling agent, such as ethyl chloride, may be used to freeze an area of the body. This can prove useful when investigating or manipulating lesions of the feet and other superficial areas.

The main disadvantage of local analgesia is that the bird must be restrained during surgery; however, it can be used for simple short procedures, especially in birds which would be poor risks for general anaesthesia.

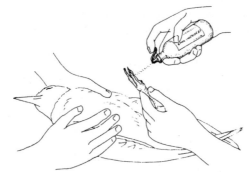

38 Applying a local analgesic spray to the foot of a gull

General anaesthesia

General anaesthetics can be administered by inhalation, orally or by injection.

Inhalation anaesthetics commonly used in avian species include halothane, ether, methoxyflurane, cyclopropane and trichlorethylene. It must be a matter of individual choice as to which is used as all can, in experienced hands, produce effective anaesthesia. When using an anaesthetic machine it may be useful to add nitrous oxide to the oxygen : this is valuable because of its analgesic properties.

Using the volatile agents, both induction and recovery are usually rapid in birds and the change in depth of anaesthesia occurs quickly. Great care must therefore be taken not to overdose. Methoxyflurane is particularly safe because of its low potency and relatively long period of induction.

Inhalation agents may be administered by face mask, by intubation or in an anaesthetic chamber. Both face masks and endotracheal tubes can be improvised using a variety of pieces of equipment that are commonly found in a veterinary practice. For example, the barrels of disposable syringes make useful face masks and drip tubing ideal endotracheal tubes. When an anaesthetic machine is used, the oxygen flow should be adequate to produce the correct concentration; a relatively high rate of flow will allow the depth of anaesthesia to be altered rapidly. An anaesthetic chamber can be useful for small birds and its construction is mentioned later. Ideally it should be attached to an anaesthetic machine so that the appropriate agents can be pumped through but it can also be used with a wad of cotton wool impregnated with halothane or methoxyflurane.

A novel way of administering inhalation anaesthetics involves passing the agents directly into the interclavicular air sac by means of a needle.[3] This has been used successfully in a number of species and provides an effective means of resuscitation, but it is primarily of academic interest at present.

The administration of anaesthetic agents by mouth is not to be recommended. The varying susceptibility both of species and individuals makes this an unreliable and potentially hazardous operation. Certain sedative and tranquillising agents can be administered by the oral route but these too are best given by injection.

Parenteral administration is satisfactory in the majority of cases. However, it must be remembered that the depth of anaesthesia cannot be reduced once the drug is injected. The dose is calculated on a body-weight basis according to the manufacturers' instructions. A lower dose should be used for shocked or debilitated birds and for poor risk cases. A useful procedure is to use an injectable agent to induce light anaesthesia or sedation and to deepen anaesthesia with an inhalation agent.

It is essential to weigh a bird accurately before administering an anaesthetic by injection. Small birds are best weighed in a cloth or canvas bag using a spring balance and these useful items should be available in any bird hospital. Larger birds can be placed on kitchen or bathroom scales.

A tuberculin (1ml) syringe is usually satisfactory for the administration of injectable agents to small birds. It may be necessary to use dilutions of 1 : 10 of certain agents or, for example in the case of ketamine, to take advantage of the less concentrated solutions available.

Intravenous injections can be given in the jugular vein of the neck or in the brachial vein where it crosses the radius and ulna on the underside of the wing. The feathers are slightly plucked and alcohol applied; the vein is raised by digital pressure. The veins of all birds are fragile so the needle should be small. A suitable gauge for a pigeon is 23 but for smaller birds gauge 26 or 27 should be used.

The intravenous route should not be used in birds weighing less than 100g. In small birds restraint is difficult so there is a tendency to damage the vein which is, in any case, difficult to manipulate. Intramuscular injections are then generally preferred.

For intramuscular agents the pectoral or thigh muscles are normally used. The calculated dose is injected into the muscle mass. The site is prepared with a swab of alcohol or other antiseptic to dampen the feathers and expose the skin. The technique of injection was described in an earlier chapter but it is worth emphasising that the plunger should be withdrawn slightly to ascertain that it has not entered a blood vessel. The dose is then given slowly. The volume deposited at any one site should not be excessive and if necessary the dose may be given in several places. When the thigh muscles are used the dose is delivered directly into the centre of the largest muscle mass thus avoiding the bone and nerves.

Intraperitoneal injections are difficult to carry out satisfactorily in birds as it is not easy to avoid the abdominal air sacs. Occasionally they are used to administer an anaesthetic. The correct site is midway between the sternum and cloaca, slightly to one side of the midline.

Subcutaneous injections may prove unsatisfactory as absorption is slow and uneven. If they are to be used, suitable sites are the side of the neck, the skin over the legs or the web of the wings.

A number of parenteral agents can be used in birds. Pentobarbitone sodium may be administered intravenously, intramuscularly or intraperitoneally. Induction time is approximately five minutes when given by the intramuscular route but only a few seconds by intravenous injection. The duration of useful anaesthesia is about one hour. This method is fairly successful in large birds[4, 5] but pentobarbitone, like other barbiturates, has the disadvantage of being a respiratory depressant and a poor analgesic.

A combination of pentobarbitone sodium, chloral hydrate and magnesium sulphate known as Equithesin can be used intramuscularly and is particularly popular in the USA.[6] Induction time is approximately ten minutes and the duration of anaesthesia approximately one hour.

Ketamine hydrochloride is both safe and effective when given intra-muscularly[7] and has been used by the authors in a variety of wild birds in the UK. In the USA it has been recommended by the intravenous route in birds of prey.[8] Induction time is rapid by both routes and the duration and depth of anaesthesia depend on the dose rate and the susceptibility of the patient. Maintenance or deepening of anaesthesia with an inhalation agent may be desirable.

Metomidate has been used intramuscularly in a variety of birds and has proved very satisfactory.[9]

The steroid anaesthetic CT 1341 has been used successfully both intramuscularly and intravenously. It has proved particularly useful by the latter route for short-term anaesthesia for radiography and for induction prior to inhalation anaesthesia.[10]

Many complications may occur during, or after, the anaesthesia of a bird. Casualties are particularly prone to apnoea (cessation of respiration) mainly because of their poor physical condition. If breathing does not resume, the bird's mucous membranes become blue and death will quickly supervene. The patient should be placed on its front and no more anaesthetic given. Often respiration will recommence spontaneously within 30–60 seconds. If this does not occur, oxygen should be given by face mask or the bird exposed to fresh air. Artificial respiration (gentle pressure on the sides of the chest every 20 seconds) may accelerate revival. Alternatively a piece of thin tubing on the end of a syringe can be slipped down the trachea and a small volume of air pumped backwards and forwards using the plunger.

Other emergencies will not be discussed here. The important features of care during and after anaesthesia are observation of respiration and general nursing. The bird must be kept warm and fluids may need to be given. Sudden movements of the bird's limbs or body must be avoided.

EUTHANASIA

Euthanasia is derived from the Greek word for death; in English it is used to refer to humane killing. A useful booklet on the subject is published by the Universities Federation for Animal Welfare.[11]

The destruction of sick or injured wild birds is an unpleasant but important subject. Many birds that are found should be killed on humanitarian grounds; there is no glory in keeping alive a bird that is suffering and that stands little or no chance of survival. Indeed, it could be argued that to kill a bird humanely is, in itself, an important and commendable act. The problem is that all too often a bird is *not* killed humanely.

There are a number of factors that influence the decision to kill a bird rather than to attempt to treat it. First and foremost, a bird should not suffer excessive pain or discomfort. Assessment of what is 'excessive' is difficult and tends to vary from person to person; if in doubt a veterinary surgeon should be consulted. The species of bird may also affect the decision; a broken wing in a pest, such as a wood pigeon, may be considered an indication for euthanasia but a comparable injury in an endangered species, such as a bittern, might justify an attempt at surgical correction. Birds suffering from infectious disease may be killed in order to prevent spread to other birds or to humans; in certain cases, such an action may be necessary in order to make a full post-mortem diagnosis, which will assist treatment of other birds. Finally, attention must be paid to the practical aspects of treating an injured bird. It might be quite feasible to treat such an individual successfully but who is going to tend it and who is going to pay for the drugs involved? If the answer to these questions is doubtful, then it might be wiser (and kinder) to destroy the bird. Likewise, treatment may result in a live bird but one that cannot ever be released; someone will have to care for it, possibly for years. The decision to kill a bird is rarely easy but often it shows a realistic and unsentimental approach to the problem.

There are two main methods of killing birds:
1   physical – using physical force such as a blow to the head; and
2   chemical – using a drug which can be inhaled (for example, ether) or injected (for example, barbiturate).

The aim in euthanasia is to cause the least possible suffering to the bird. Unfortunately the subject is an emotive one and as a result the method chosen is often based on subjective, rather than objective, factors. For example, many people prefer to kill a bird with anaesthetic ether rather than break its neck, but there is no doubt that the latter is far quicker, and less upsetting to the bird. Partly because of this conflict and partly because of his experience and access to drugs, a veterinary surgeon should be consulted whenever possible.

Various physical methods are available for killing birds and if carried out properly they are extremely rapid and humane. Small birds can be hurled at a wall or the pavement from about two metres; this will kill them instantly. It is probably less upsetting to the person involved if the bird is first placed inside a strong paper or plastic bag. Larger birds can have their heads hit hard against a wall or a rock; again it is vital that this is done with all one's force and not half-heartedly. Alternatively the head can be struck with a metal object or chopped off with an axe but these methods are less reliable and usually very messy. Birds can also be killed by shooting with a shotgun and large birds, such as herons, can have their necks dislocated or broken, as is carried out for poultry. They should never be drowned and electrocution, while recommended by some writers for larger birds, may prove difficult to perform humanely and safely.

If chemical methods are used, obtaining the appropriate drugs may pose a problem since most of those used are only available on prescription; such methods are therefore best carried out in consultation with a veterinary surgeon or at an established wild bird hospital. Small quantities of ether or chloroform, both of which are volatile liquids, can usually be obtained from a chemist and these are reasonably satisfactory for the euthanasia of small birds such as finches. However, the use of such agents still necessitates some care. The aim is for the bird to inhale sufficient of the anaesthetic to kill it but the following points must be remembered :

1   The bird should not come into direct physical contact with the anaesthetic. If it does, the anaesthetic will irritate its eyes and skin and the bird will suffer considerable discomfort.

2   The bird should gradually become anaesthetised and not die of asphyxia as a result of being plunged into a container full of anaesthetic. In order to achieve this, air should initially be allowed to enter the anaesthetic chamber until the bird becomes unconscious; the air can then be excluded.

3   A number of inhalation anaesthetics are inflammable or explosive; an example is ether. Care should be taken when handling such agents and they must not be used in the presence of a flame, excess heat or electrical appliances.

Non-inflammable volatile liquids include halothane and methoxyflurane and these, if available, are preferable to ether.

A number of gases can also be used to kill birds, a good example being carbon dioxide. This has the advantage of being non-irritant and non-inflammable (though some gases, such as carbon monoxide, differ in this respect). Again it is important that point 2 above is observed.

Whichever inhalation agent is chosen, an anaesthetic chamber should be used. A metal or glass container is recommended since plastic tends to be destroyed by certain anaesthetics. The size will vary but for small passerine birds 25 x 20 x 20cm is suitable. The euthanasia agent can either be pumped through from an anaesthetic machine or be applied to a wad of cotton wool which is safely enclosed in a small wire basket on the floor of the chamber.

The other group of chemical agents that can be used for euthanasia are the injectable anaesthetics. The most potent are probably the barbiturates but these are particularly dangerous and may be difficult to obtain. Other suitable agents for euthanasia include overdoses of ketamine and metomidate. These and the barbiturates can be given by any route but the most rapid results are obtained by intravenous or intracardiac administration. Such techniques need experience, however, and in most cases intraperitoneal injection is recommended (see Fig 39). If an injection fails to kill a bird completely it may then be despatched by a blow on the head as described earlier.

The layman may be uncertain when death has occurred, especially since a certain amount of movement may be noted after death. Indicators of death are absence of respiration, absence of heart beat, and failure to respond to pressure or a pinprick on the head or feet. Only when all three are observed should the bird be assumed dead. Under no circumstances should disposal of a body be carried out until a check has been made to ensure that the bird has been killed. A useful rule. is to wait until rigor mortis has been noted. Disposal should then be by burning or deep burial. Every effort should be made to ensure that carcasses are removed promptly since they may, if infected, spread disease. Whenever possible a post-mortem examination should be carried out.

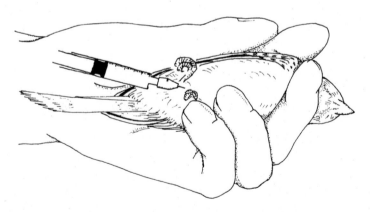

39 Euthanasia by intraperitoneal injection

16 Birds of prey

M. H. Williams

Birds of prey (raptors) are not infrequently found sick or injured and tend to attract particular interest from the public. As a result they are commonly presented as casualties. Many species are either rare or not frequently seen in the wild and therefore every effort should be made to ensure that they receive optimum treatment and, wherever possible, are released.[1]

The birds of prey comprise two orders, the Falconiformes and Strigiformes. Roughly, the former are diurnal species such as falcons, hawks and eagles, and the latter nocturnal species such as owls. Both groups are characterised by sharp beaks and talons that are adapted to a carnivorous way of life. As a result these birds may pose particular problems in terms of handling, feeding and management. However, it must also be borne in mind that falconiform birds have been kept for many centuries for falconry so there is a considerable amount of data on their management. Although some of this is anecdotal much of it can be used to advantage by the person tending a sick or injured raptor. For example, the use of leather jesses and a certain amount of training may be advisable when rehabilitating a bird of prey to the wild. Practical advice on these and other aspects can usually be sought from an experienced falconer. However, this is not to suggest that a casualty should be thought of as a potential falconer's bird : as is emphasised in Chapter 2, the law states that a bird must be returned to the wild unless unable to fend for itself.

In this chapter the author assumes that the reader either finds or is presented with a bird of prey which, for some reason or other, cannot fly away. What does he do with it? And, having established what is the matter with it, how does he care for it, in the hope that it may eventually be released to the wild?

If one is not in a place where the bird can be given a thorough examination, the first thing is to immobilise it in order to prevent any further injury. A coat or towel should be wrapped tightly round the bird to prevent it from moving its wings and yet allow it enough room to breathe. Part of the coat or towel can be used to cover the bird's head; if the bird is unable to see, this will stop it struggling too much.

The patient must now be taken somewhere where careful examination can be made. This examination should be thorough but if the bird is severely shocked, or in a weak condition, it may be wiser to carry out a fairly superficial preliminary examination and to delay detailed investigation until the bird's condition has improved. When examining a raptor it helps if one person is available to hold the bird, while another thoroughly examines the body and each limb. Gloves need not be used but they are often valuable; those manufactured for motor cycling are ideal. The handling of a sick or injured bird of prey is not always easy since many will tend to strike with their talons and/or bite. Some species, such as the buzzard and certain owls, may lie down when cornered and allow a limited amount of manipulation; however, one must be aware that the bird may suddenly wake up and either attempt to escape or wreak vengeance on its handler! Whenever a raptor is being held it is important to ensure that the hands are clasped firmly around the wings, so that the bird cannot flap. Pressing the patient gently on to a cushion, or a piece of sacking, will facilitate examination, especially if the bird grasps the material with its feet; this will usually permit the wings to be extended and examined one at a time. The use of subdued lighting is also a valuable ruse, as mentioned earlier. Diurnal raptors will not move in the dark and even a reduction in light intensity will help quieten a bird. For the same reason a falconer's hood, or a

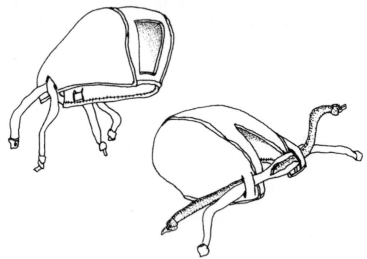

40 A falconer's hood can prove useful in the restraint of a sick or injured bird of prey

216

piece of canvas or cloth to cover the head, can prove very useful in examination.

In the case of injuries one must look for such things as cuts, abrasion wounds, missing feathers, blood stains on feathers – often the sole sign of gun wounds, particularly if only the odd pellet or particle of shot has entered the bird – and, of course, broken limbs.

Initial treatment should be aimed at preventing, or treating, shock. In particular the bird should be disturbed as little as possible. A cardboard box in the airing cupboard is useful but one must make sure that there are air holes in the box, A useful tip here is to place the holes near the *bottom* of the box; this will significantly reduce the amount of disturbance to the bird since it will be unable to see out.

Wounds may become, or already be, infected, and in such cases must be cleaned. A broad-spectrum disinfectant such as cetrimide is useful for this and should be used as a solution in warm water. Having been cleaned, the wound can be dressed with a suitable antibiotic or sulphonamide dusting powder. If the wound is badly infected a course of antibiotics orally or by injection may be required and a veterinary surgeon will be able to advise on this. If the bird is both injured and in a state of shock, glucose saline is very useful to counteract the condition. This can be administered intravenously or subcutaneously and here again veterinary assistance will be needed.

Having examined the bird, one may come to the conclusion that it is suffering from a fractured wing or leg; these are common injuries to raptors. If circumstances permit, the limb should be X-rayed to establish the nature and extent of the fracture, with a view to repair. There are many techniques for fixing fractures but in the author's view intramedullary pinning is usually the best method for fractured long bones. If, for one reason or another, this is not possible then a splint can be applied but before this is done one must make sure that the broken ends of bone are in close apposition and, at the same time, as near as possible to the original longitudinal axis of the bone. Light anaesthesia may be helpful in reducing pain and achieving satisfactory fixation. The material for the splint itself is usually a matter of personal choice, but it must be light, rigid and applied in such a way as not to restrict the circulation of the affected limb. The author finds Zimmer Splint quite useful, for it is made of a light metal alloy with a foam backing, and can be cut and bent to whatever shape one requires.

In the case of wing fractures in smaller birds, the author frequently does not use a splint, but just straps the wing up, using sticky brown paper. This is useful for two reasons: first, because it is easy to apply, and second, because it is very easy to remove by soaking with warm water, which does not damage the bird's plumage. The wing should be placed in its normal position and the paper applied around the second (carpus) joint and the primary feathers. It must be remembered that this will not suffice for larger birds, as they will be strong enough to remove it. In their case, a leather strap with a slit cut down the middle, leaving one end longer than the other, can be used. The wing is placed in its normal position, the second joint is placed through the slit and the two ends are tied together, thus keeping the wing in the flexed position.

Having progressed this far, and treated the bird's injuries, what points should one remember when looking after the bird prior to its release? There are three main considerations; housing, feeding and attention to specific diseases.

HOUSING

The main objective is to keep the bird in a place that is warm, dry, free from draughts and (preferably) with access to sunlight for some part of the day. The least suitable place for the bird is a damp outhouse in which may be old mouldy hay and straw; aspergillosis may be the outcome, as discussed elsewhere.

One of the main problems in accommodating a bird of prey is to do it in such a way as to prevent the bird crashing about too much and therefore breaking a lot of vital feathers, particularly those of the wing and tail that are so essential to flight. For this reason the author does not like any form of cage that has wire netting on it; the bird flies at it, can readily hang on it with its talons, and therefore can easily damage cere, wing and tail feathers. A preferable type of cage is the box-type, with the door barred in order to let light in. It must be sufficiently high to allow the bird to stand up in comfort on a perch and wide enough for it to stretch its wings. The total size must not be sufficient to give the bird too much room in which to crash about if frightened. The door must be barred with vertical slats, circular in cross-section: narrow bamboo pea sticks cut to appropriate lengths are very useful for this as, being vertical, they do not permit the bird to obtain any grip should it fly at them. Making the cage fairly confined is particularly important if the bird has a broken limb, since minimum disturbance is essential.

FEEDING

Whenever possible, the bird's natural food should be supplied. Birds killed on the roads are, if fresh, a useful source but should not be used exclusively since pesticide poisoning can result from eating wild birds.[2] Young mice and rats can be used for owls and kestrels; these are less likely to be a source of infection if obtained from a laboratory rather than the wild. Day-old chicks are also a useful food source and convenient if one happens to have a hatchery nearby. If none of these sources is available shin beef is probably the best and most easily obtained alternative food. It should be stressed that if the bird is being fed on unnatural food such as beef (or chicks, to a lesser extent), a vitamin/mineral supplement must be added, this being particularly important in the case of young birds. Some examples of such supplements are given in Appendix 3.

Birds of prey are particularly prone to osteodystrophy due to inadequate calcium and the feeding of meat alone can quickly result in this condition, again especially in young birds.[3] The bird's bones become decalcified and spontaneous fractures develop. Although a vitamin/mineral supplement may help adjust the balance it is often wiser to use sterilised bonemeal which can be sprinkled on the meat.

Another important point which must be remembered is that, if the bird is being fed a lot of shin beef, some roughage must be added or put on the food. This is in order to allow the bird's digestive system to function normally and so to form a pellet – or 'casting' – which is regurgitated; chicken feathers or rabbit fur (from the butcher) are useful here or, if one is desperate, paper tissues !

Water should be mentioned. If one puts water in for a healthy bird of prey, the only thing it is likely to do is to bathe in it! A healthy bird very seldom drinks water as such, for it gets all its moisture requirements from its food. If the bird is seen to be drinking water regularly, it is a sure sign that the bird is sick. Having said this, most birds of prey (with the possible exception of owls) are enthusiastic bathers and a supply of water allows them to keep their plumage clean and in good condition. Sick birds should be encouraged to increase their fluid intake since they are often dehydrated to a greater or lesser extent. The food can be moistened in water (or, preferably, glucose saline) or placed in a waterbowl.

DISEASE

If the bird is injured, the time it is likely to spend in captivity depends on the severity of its injuries. A fractured wing will take longer to heal than a flesh wound. In the case of infectious and parasitic diseases, diagnosis and treatment may prove difficult and with this in mind, the recognition and treatment of some of these will now be discussed.

The diseases to be described are those that are particularly common in birds of prey. More general aspects of avian disease are dealt with elsewhere in this book. The two most common classes of diseases are probably those affecting the digestive and respiratory systems, often associated with incorrect housing and diet while in captivity.

Diseases of the digestive system can manifest themselves in several ways. Examples are regurgitation of the crop contents soon after the intake of food or regurgitation of an abnormal casting, that is, one that is moist, sometimes foul-smelling and soft in consistency. Such clinical signs often indicate inflammation and/or infection of the crop. Treatment should be undertaken by giving small amounts of choice food at more frequent intervals than normal – that is, three to four times daily. To the food should be added small amounts of Forgastrin and ampicillin both of which are in powder form, and can be obtained from a veterinary surgeon.

Enteritis is another common disease of the digestive system. It is usually characterised by poor appetite, watery droppings (often tinged with green), and soiling of the feathers around the vent. The condition often appears to be associated with bacteria and treatment with oral antibiotics is usually successful, coupled, if necessary, with nursing and fluid replacement. All the clinical signs described above can be caused also by roundworm infestation. If this is suspected a sample of the faeces sent to a laboratory for testing will usually soon verify whether or not there is a heavy worm burden. Piperazine, thiabendazole and tetramisole are useful anthelmintics for treating birds of prey; tetramisole should be given on an empty crop.

Diseases of the respiratory system are common in birds of prey. Organisms of the *Mycoplasma* group may cause trouble although this has yet to be proved. Some birds may show nasal discharge, sometimes swelling of the eyelids and difficulty in breathing. They may lose their appetite. Treatment with tylosin orally or by injection effects rapid recovery in most cases. If the bird is in severe respiratory distress this can mean either pneumonia or aspergillosis.

Pneumonia can often be treated successfully with antibiotics such as oxytetracycline or ampicillin and a veterinary surgeon will be able to advise on this. Aspergillosis, which produces similar clinical signs, is caused by a fungal infection of the lungs and air sacs. It is probably responsible for the death of more captive birds of prey than any other single disease condition, particularly because, at the moment, there appears to be no drug with which to treat it effectively (see Chapter 13). It is often associated with housing the bird in conditions that are damp and dusty, which is why particular emphasis was laid upon correct housing earlier in this chapter.

Birds of prey can also be affected by a condition called gapes. The condition is caused by nematode worms (usually *Syngamus trachea*) that live in the trachea; it is characterised by respiratory distress, the bird usually breathing with its mouth open – hence the name. In severe infestations worms can often be seen by opening the beak and observing the glottis (opening to the trachea) at the back of the mouth : the worms are red and thread-like. Laboratory examination of the faeces will usually confirm the presence of eggs. Both thiabendazole and tetramisole are effective methods of treatment.

Mention should also be made of a condition known traditionally to falconers as 'frounce', which can be contracted by feeding contaminated food, especially pigeons. Early clinical signs are usually a desire to eat food but difficulty in swallowing it. If the beak is opened, cheese-like deposits will be found on the lining of the mouth and there may be spread of the lesions down the oesophagus and trachea. The condition is caused by *Trichomonas gallinae*, a flagellate protozoan parasite (see Chapter 11) which is a common inhabitant of pigeons. Although it may produce disease (usually referred to as canker) the pigeon is often unaffected clinically. For this reason, if pigeons are used as a source of food, the head and crop should be removed first. Treatment of affected birds of prey can be carried out using oral dimetridazole or metronidazole.

Foot infections, known as bumblefoot, are especially common in captive birds of prey and are discussed in detail in Chapter 10. It is important to take measures to prevent their occurring in casualty birds. A useful precaution is to clip the claws of incoming birds of prey since an overgrown talon can easily pierce the sole and introduce infection. If a foot infection is suspected, because of clinical features of a swollen, warm or painful foot, veterinary advice should be sought.

A few words should be said about toxic chemicals, which are frequently a cause of death in birds of prey since they are at the top of the food chain. Although there has been a decline in cases in the UK, mass

221

mortalities have been reported recently in birds of prey exposed to agricultural chemicals in certain countries – for example, in Israel.[4] Intentional poisoning of raptors also occurs and one recent report in the UK quotes 109 cases of deliberate poisoning over a six-year period including 66 buzzards, 10 golden eagles, 3 red kites and a goshawk.[5] Unfortunately, as is emphasised in Chapter 12, chemical poisoning is often very difficult to diagnose in the living subject; post-mortem examination and laboratory tests are usually the only methods of obtaining an accurate diagnosis. Added to this is the fact that, for the vast majority of chemicals, there is no specific antidote. Supportive treatment is all that can be recommended. In the author's experience of toxic chemicals in birds of prey in the UK, birds are usually presented 'more dead than alive', yet bear no sign of specific disease or injury. Death usually supervenes. Post-mortem examination and laboratory analysis have then confirmed toxic chemical residues in the carcass. It is important that any bird of prey that is found dead or dies shortly after coming into captivity is submitted for toxicological investigation and also, if facilities permit, full pathological examination.

Plate 21
A casualty barn owl with a wing injury that has failed to heal successfully. The bird's left wing is held at an angle and the primary feathers are drooping

Plate 22
A four-day-old guillemot chick which was hatched in captivity from an egg laid by a victim of oil pollution. This bird is normal

Plate 23
A black-tailed godwit, admitted to a bird hospital in cold weather, is dried on arrival. Newly admitted birds are often chilled and wet

17 Crows

P. R. Richards

In this chapter the members of the UK crow family (Corvidae) are described and their care is discussed. The species include the raven, carrion and hooded crow, rook, jackdaw, magpie, jay and chough. In other parts of the world there are many other species, but generally they are similar to their UK cousins, and have the same requirements.

Crows are all large birds, tough and hardy, and omnivorous in their feeding habits. Because they will sometimes take the eggs and young of other birds they are considered to be vermin by the shooting fraternity, and consequently injured crows (by which the author means all members of the family) often come into the hands of those who will undertake the care of sick birds.

Crows have a large vocabulary of sounds and can be taught to mimic human speech; they are all intelligent and inquisitive birds and make amusing pets. Although it may be illegal, many young crows are taken from their nests to be so raised. Some end up in unsuitable hands and these birds may ultimately require special care.

ACCOMMODATION AND CARE

Adult birds, because of their size, require a large cage or aviary with suitable perches, and partial cover to protect them from heavy rain. All crows like to have a daily bathe and an upturned dustbin lid is an ideal bath. The water will need changing daily; it quickly becomes foul because many crows like to dunk their food before they swallow it. Most crows are rather destructive and can easily break their way out of a fragile or insecure cage. Wire netting and stout wooden posts are better than plastic netting. The author's crow aviaries have an earth floor covered by straw. The straw is easily changed when dirty, and the birds enjoy exploring it for insects; they also use it for hiding their surplus food. A hard concrete floor in a featureless cage is cruel for birds that are as active and inquisitive as crows. If this is all that can be provided, a piece of rotting wood should be supplied for the bird to break up in order to relieve its boredom. Some birds of prey will sit contentedly all day in one spot when not hunting, but crows are inquisitive and busy birds that require a more stimulating environment.

The young crow is confined to its nest for the first four weeks of its life. It requires brooding by its parents for the first two weeks until feathers have grown on its back and head, and it can keep itself warm. An artificial nest can be provided by forming a newspaper cup in a flowerpot. A 10–15cm pot will suffice for a jackdaw or jay, and a 30cm pot for a carrion crow or rook. A little straw or hay which the young bird can grip with its feet should be placed in the bottom of the 'nest', and the pot placed inside a carton or box lined with paper or polystyrene to keep it warm. The paper and hay will need changing every 1–2 days, depending on how foul it becomes.

If the young birds require additional heat this can be provided by hanging a 40-watt electric lightbulb about 70cm over the 'nest'. If the baby bird is too cold it keeps its neck well into its body while at rest to minimise heat loss. If it is too hot is extends its neck and raises the feathers on its back to expose as much bare skin as possible, and it may open its beak to pant at the same time. Obviously the height of the bulb over the nest should be adjusted to the correct temperature.

Young nestling birds in good health have a simple and effective method of nest sanitation. They only defaecate after they have been fed. A moment or two after feeding, they will shuffle about in their nest and raise their vent in the air, to produce a neat packet of excreta enclosed in a jelly-like mucus. The parent birds collect this and either drop it some way away or swallow it, thereby keeping the nest clean. As soon as the baby birds are mobile in the nest they direct their vent over the edge of the nest and defaecate well clear of it. In poor health the faeces may be loose and not enclosed in mucus and the nest rapidly becomes soiled. Small birds will retain their overnight faeces until they are fed and the first dropping passed in the morning is almost as big as the egg from which they were hatched. The artificial nest will suffice for the first month or so but by this time the young crows will be almost fully grown and will spend a lot of time hopping about the nest, and exercising their wings by flapping them vigorously.

Should the young birds fall out of the nest at this time they should be replaced. Once they can perch steadily on a stick and, instead of squatting down in the nest as soon as they are replaced, hop off again, they are ready to leave the nest. Alternative accommodation is now required, although they probably will want to spend the night on the nest for the next 2–3 days.

When the author's young crows are spending all day perching he removes them to another cage. The cage is about a metre square; the bird can still be fed easily and the cage is easily kept clean. Young crows still require a lot of food after leaving the nest for they are not really fully grown for another month or so. All this food causes a lot of mess and it is important to keep the birds clean. After they have left the nest it is vital to provide perches well clear of the floor of the cage so that the birds do not soil themselves.

Young crows can fly as soon as they leave the nest and, being wild birds with wild instincts, they are easily frightened. A tame confiding nestling can easily be turned into a wild flapping creature if inadvertently frightened. Birds in a small cage cannot flap about or flee too far away if they are scared and their confidence can easily be restored. Feeding young crows in a small enclosure is no problem, for they require feeding by their parents or substitute parents for several weeks after they have left the nest. If they are placed in a large aviary while they still need feeding and become frightened, even when they are very hungry, fear may override hunger and the birds will be denied food at a time when they are still growing, with disastrous results. The creatures will beg for food but may not have the courage to come up to their human fosterparents to be fed.

A small cage can alleviate this problem, for although the birds might try to escape, all parts of the cage are accessible. As soon as the birds beg for food they can be easily fed and the relationship is restored at once; they soon settle down and become relaxed again.

For the first two weeks after leaving the nest the young birds spend much of their time resting. After three weeks they become more active and will begin to explore their environment. They should then be transferred to a larger cage where their natural interests can be stimulated, for at this time they will begin to pick up food for themselves and, if plenty of their favourite diet is available, they will soon learn to feed themselves. If they are not given the opportunity to search for and pick up food at this stage it may be months before they can adequately feed themselves.

Young crows are fully grown by this time and can fly strongly; however, even if one is tempted, it is quite wrong to release birds back to the wild at this stage. They are still very dependent on their parents and will not know how to search for food by themselves. A young crow released at this stage will starve to death in 2–3 days. The author does not release young crows until they have completed their moult at the end of the summer, when they are 5–6 months old. At this age they are fully grown, strong, and capable both of finding their own food and of standing up to competition from other crows. Younger birds are not able to cope with all the problems of existence in the wild, especially the difficulties of finding their own food and of bullying by established members of their own species.

Very tame birds are not really suitable for release as they are soon recaptured by other people. Injured birds also fare badly. Birds with damaged wing feathers should be kept until they have moulted completely; this may mean a delay of up to twelve months before they can fly strongly again.

FEEDING

Crows are omnivorous birds and require a large amount of protein if they are to remain in good health. All too often captive specimens in zoos are fed on a diet better suited to a goat and the result is a miserable bird, with dull lifeless plumage.

A basic diet, which the author uses for his birds, is as follows: table scraps, bread, insects, potatoes, poultry pellets (the best available being turkey-rearing pellets which have a high percentage of protein) and meat. Meat is expensive but most butchers make a 'dog sausage' out of the offal and other scraps, which is fairly cheap and consumed enthusiastically by all the author's birds. Proprietary brands of tinned dog and cat meat are also very useful but, again, rather expensive. The dead unwanted chicks from a hatchery are an excellent source of food but may be difficult to obtain. Egg mixed with bread is enjoyed by most birds. Some poultry farms will sell cracked eggs cheaply and these also are suitable; there is no need to remove the shell as this will also be eaten and is a useful source of calcium and roughage. Groundnuts are always enjoyed but are expensive.

The author gives his birds some wheat every day but this is not always eaten. Wild crows always seem to have corn in their crops if examined after they are shot; however, it appears that this is eaten very much as a second choice. Live insects and other invertebrates are consumed voraciously by all crows, but it is difficult to supply their total natural requirements. Clean white maggots can be bought from shops that sell fishing tackle and mealworms are available from some petshops but the price of both of these has increased enormously recently. The author endeavours to give his birds a few of each every day to keep them in good health.

Fruit, especially if it is rather over-ripe, is enjoyed as are fresh peas and beans. Table left-overs, such as chicken carcasses, cake crumbs and pieces of bacon rind are popular and there is probably enough in the way of table scraps from the average family to feed one crow.

228

Such left-overs will provide a balanced, high protein diet if supplemented with a few maggots and a little minced meat from time to time.

Young nestling crows are fed entirely by their parents for, as was mentioned earlier, they are incapable of feeding themselves at all until they have left the nest and are reasonably active and independent. In the crow family incubation of the eggs and brooding of the chicks is carried out by the female bird alone. Food collection for the young and for the female while she is incubating is done by the male until the young birds are half-grown and can be safely left unguarded.

When the young birds first hatch, their eyelids are closed and they are blind; if hungry, they respond to the sound of their parents' call and to vibration of the nest by lifting up their heads and opening their enormous beaks so that food can be placed inside. After their eyes have opened they will respond also to the sight of their parents but it is still to the sound of their parents' call that they respond most strongly.

In an artificial situation young birds can be made to beg for food by mimicking the parents' call. Most crows utter a soft deep note when offering food to their young but the call varies from species to species and the red-billed blue magpie, for example, whistles to stimulate its young. The author has found that hungry young birds will beg at practically any sound and will quickly associate with the voice of their feeder the sensation of having their hunger satisfied.

Young birds are best fed little and often and, ideally, every time they beg for food. The author believes that it is impossible to overfeed a fledgling bird but it is all too easy to underfeed, causing malnutrition and permanently stunted growth. Young birds require very much more protein than adults do, and their food should contain at least 50 per cent. While the birds are very small they will need the food finely minced so that they can swallow it. One should not be afraid to offer them a small piece of eggshell, bone or other roughage, because birds of the crow family, in common with many others, are able to reject undigested particles of food later, as pellets.

The author believes that one of the best available foods for young birds is scrambled egg. In the wild, insects are collected in large amounts and young birds in the first few weeks are fed on them almost exclusively, so caterpillars and grubs of all kinds are useful food for youngsters. Young birds cannot drink but, nevertheless, require water, so food given to them should be well moistened. Occasionally one even sees a wild rook dunking a beakful of food in a pond or brook before flying up to its nest to feed its young.

As the young grow they do not have to be fed so frequently but every 2–3 hours is still desirable if healthy growth is to be maintained. It is especially important to feed the young birds last thing in the evening so that they can sleep with a crop full of food. They can conveniently be fed by artificial light after dark when they would normally be asleep and later in the mornings than they would be by their natural parents.

Young birds grow at an enormous rate and if in the first week of life a bird does not get adequate food for 48 hours it can literally starve to death overnight. A bird has a very small body mass but maintains a high body temperature; its energy requirements are very large, so that it should be kept warm to minimise heat and energy loss while it is growing. Adult birds also consume a large amount of energy and if food of the right kind is unavailable, even a healthy adult bird will decline and starve to death very quickly. It is not easy to treat or cure a sick bird and the best approach to any ailment is prevention.

DESCRIPTION AND CARE

The raven   This is the largest crow in the UK; it is not common and is found only in mountainous areas and on certain sea cliffs. It feeds largely on smaller birds and mammals, insects and carrion. It has a large appetite and the term ravenous is an exact description. In captivity it requires more protein than other crows and one raven will readily devour half a rabbit or the equivalent amount of other meat.

The raven is a very strong bird and its large beak can give a nasty bite; it needs a large strong enclosure as it will easily catch and kill other birds. One of the author's ravens quickly caught and killed a rook that inadvertently managed to get into its enclosure. If the raven cannot fly it can be kept in an enclosed garden but it must be remembered that it could injure small cats and dogs or peck children.

Releasing ravens back to the wild is difficult for it is essential to release the birds into the right habitat. Ordinary arable farmland does not provide sufficient carrion to support a raven these days and a raven is such a large and conspicuous bird that, unless very wild and wary, it would probably quickly be shot by an over-zealous gamekeeper.

The rook   This is the commonest crow in the UK, and, because it breeds in colonies in close association with man, the best known. Young rooks of all ages commonly fall out of their nests in the top of the trees, especially at the stage when they are exercising their wings but cannot fly. Adult rooks are often shot by sportsmen and others who misguidedly think that rooks are dangerous to crops or game, so that rooks of all ages frequently come into the hands of those who care for sick or injured birds.

Rooks feed on the larger soil invertebrates such as worms, grubs and caterpillars. They also will take carrion, small mammals and birds and a certain amount of vegetable matter. In captivity they will thrive on a mixed diet, provided it contains a reasonable amount of protein. The author's rooks feed on bread soaked with raw egg, meat, turkey pellets and a few maggots. Rooks are pleasant birds, reasonably gentle and very gregarious. They can be kept in a flock without fighting and are happier together. They will breed freely in captivity if they are fed well.

Young rooks should be released in the autumn after their summer moult in an environment where they can find adequate food. If released in the summer they may stray into the territory of carrion crows which, being larger, can kill a youngster especially if it is weakened by hunger.

The carrion crow and hooded crow These birds are similar to small ravens and their dietary needs are similar. They are large strong birds that will attack and kill smaller crows such as jackdaws and magpies. Youngsters become very tame and make rather nice pets. In spite of their strength they become very gentle and do not attempt to peck or injure their owners. Young crows are not found as often as are young rooks, but adult crows are frequently shot as vermin and so come into the hands of those who will look after them.

The jackdaw This is our smallest black crow, being about the size of a domestic pigeon. It nests in holes in trees, cliffs and buildings, sometimes in small colonies. Jackdaws make delightful pets when they are young and this, regretfully, encourages people to take them from the nest. Unfortunately they are not always so tame and gentle when they grow up and may become spiteful and aggressive. If this happens they become a nuisance and often come into care because of the potential danger they can be.

Jackdaws feed on insects and a small amount of fruit and vegetable matter. They thrive on a diet of turkey pellets, groundnuts, a few maggots and some bread. They are not as fond of meat as are carrion crows and rooks. The author finds that male jackdaws become very aggressive in the breeding season but their beaks are small and can do little damage. Jackdaws will catch and kill smaller birds, such as robins and dunnocks, that get into their enclosures.

231

The magpie This is about the same size as the jackdaw but looks larger because of its long tail. Magpies nest in small trees and bushes, and build a large conspicuous nest. A large number of young magpies are taken from the nest to be reared as pets. They become very tame and make friendly pets while they are young; however, a number also become aggressive and will fearlessly attack people or larger animals that intrude on to their territory. Adult magpies are often considered to be vermin and are shot as pests in many areas.

Magpies are more carnivorous than jackdaws and require more meat in their diet. A diet similar to that for the carrion crow will provide adequate nourishment.

The jay This is a beautiful woodland bird which again is persecuted since it takes the eggs and young of other birds. Young jays are taken by children as pets but, as their nests are harder to find than those of the magpie or jackdaw, far fewer are hand-reared each year. Young jays make delightful pets, and the adult birds are much more gentle than magpies or jackdaws. The author has never known one become fierce or aggressive.

Jays are more vegetarian than other crows and, although they eat a lot of insects and will take meat, they seem to prefer nuts and acorns. The author feeds his jays on groundnuts, acorns, bread, meat, turkey pellets and maggots. They seem to prefer the maggots after pupation whereas the other crows are definitely more interested in larvae. Like other corvids jays are excellent mimics, probably the best of all.

The chough This is a very rare crow found in mountainous areas and some remote sea cliffs. It is halfway between a rook and a jackdaw in size, black in colour with a long, delicately curved, bright red bill. Its requirements would appear to be similar to those of the rook with regard to diet but it prefers smaller pieces of meat and more insects. The alpine chough has been kept successfully and bred on several occasions by Philip Wayre of the Norfolk Wildlife Park, who feeds them on a diet of turkey pellets and maggots.

Exotic and foreign crows A number of exotic crows, usually brightly coloured magpies and jays, are imported by dealers into the UK from time to time. Occasionally they escape and may be found as casualties. Although they are rather different in appearance they can usually be recognised as members of the crow family and they will thrive on a diet similar to that of their British cousins.

18 Waterbirds

P. N. Humphreys

This chapter will include all birds whose natural habitat is water, whether fresh or marine. They have their own special problems. It is important to remember that most need a very specialised habitat and diet, so casualties must be correctly identified before one plans housing or feeding. Also, many of them are likely to inhabit wild areas and the very presence of people or animals near them may give rise to considerable additional distress. Finally, after a period in captivity, some species become very tame and are then almost impossible to return to the wild as they come to rely on human beings for food and friendship, which is unfortunately not always reciprocated.

Handling
It is important to know how to handle bird casualties without damage to either the birds or oneself and this subject has already been touched upon in earlier chapters. One must consider how a bird is likely to try and defend itself. Seabirds have strong beaks which may jab or tear; a large bird like a gannet can inflict quite nasty injuries. It is therefore essential to secure the beak before trying to carry out any examinations. This is really a two-man job. While one person distracts the bird in front, the second can grab it just behind the head and thereby control the bill while the first person binds the beak shut with suitable tape or plaster. In the case of birds with very thin sharp bills, such as divers and grebes, a cork impaled on the end saves a lot of worry! The beak must, of course, be unencumbered once treatment has been finished. Coots and moorhens, as well as biting, scratch severely with their feet, and it is best to wrap such birds in sacking when carrying them from one place to another.

When handling any bird it is important always to keep control of the wings and not allow any flapping which may damage the bird and interfere with one's efforts to look after it. The author knows of one lady who placed an injured swan beside her on the passenger seat of her car, without securing its wings. As she was driving in heavy traffic the swan suddenly decided to try and take off, thereby causing some very anxious moments! The staff of the Wildfowl Trust at Slimbridge have devised a very neat idea for containing swans by means of strong

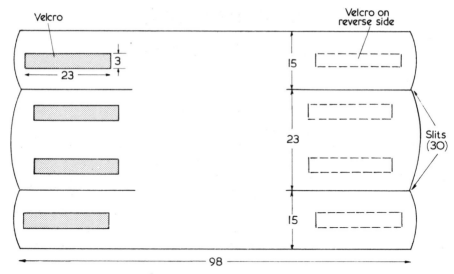

41a Construction of plastic sheeting wrap

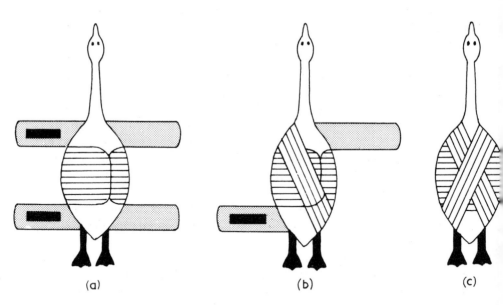

(a)   (b)   (c)

41b Application of the wrap

plastic sheeting secured by Velcro strips which can be easily released[1] (see Plate 20 and Figs 41a and b).

There are two points to remember when handling herons. One is to avoid getting the beak within range of the face as these birds not infrequently attempt to stab at one's eyes, and the other is always to allow them to travel in a standing position. If they are down for any length of time they may become paralysed in the legs; this also applies to other long-legged birds such as flamingos and cranes.[2]

CARE OF INJURED WATERBIRDS

The first things an injured bird needs are rest and warmth. An injured wild bird will probably be in a state of shock when found and handling is liable to make matters much worse. Therefore, it must be given time to adjust to the situation and recover some of its normal functions before attempts are made to diagnose or treat injuries. The best thing is to place the bird in a box on some newspaper or wood shavings (never hay or straw), supply some water in a firmly positioned dish into which the bird cannot climb or fall and put the box in a very warm place (30°C) with a dim light, such as an airing cupboard, for 24 hours. At the end of that time the bird can be offered some food, and the water can be renewed; it should then be left entirely alone for another 24 hours. By this time, a bird that has a chance of recovery will be ready to feed and will be less risky to handle. Many people make the mistake of trying to repair fractures and other injuries when the bird is first found and this is often the last straw to a bird in a state of shock.

The food offered must be suitable for the species concerned. Swans and geese will take lettuce, cabbage and short grass; all the dabbling ducks will take grain and bread, especially if it is given in a container of water. Many diving ducks, grebes, divers, gulls, herons and guillemots prefer fish in some form. Sprats or herrings cut into thin strips are most likely to be available; again they should be offered a few at a time in water. Some birds, such as shags, razorbills and gannets, will apparently not recognise fish presented in this way; very often one has to force-feed them the first few times until they learn to associate fish with food. Commercial fish-fingers are better than nothing if no other fish can be obtained easily and one lady known to the author reared a young kingfisher on this unlikely diet. After a bird has been force-fed it should be immediately left alone for 1–2 hours; any further excitement is liable to make it regurgitate the meal. It is important to realise that birds have very individual temperaments, even within the same species; some birds will very quickly learn to feed themselves and adapt to captivity while others have to be fed by hand for weeks.

After 48 hours, once the bird starts to recover, it should be given an opportunity to bathe. A dish of suitable size can be introduced or the bird placed in a bath or sink half full of water. Most waterbirds will immediately splash and preen themselves and become soaking wet; they should then be taken out and placed on a towel in a warm box in order to dry thoroughly. No more than five minutes should be allowed for the first bath, and this can gradually be increased as the bird becomes stronger. These baths are essential for water birds since not only will the plumage lose its water-repellency if bathing is denied, but some species will only defaecate in water and may otherwise acquire an impacted condition of the cloaca. However, bathing must be carefully regulated and the bird allowed to dry itself thoroughly.

Drinking water must be provided at all times; tap water is satisfactory for most birds but salt water or sea water may be helpful for marine species such as scoters, fulmars and shearwaters; when shocked, such birds lose a lot of salt via their nasal secretions and this needs to be replaced.

TREATMENT

Wild birds that are picked up are likely to be either suffering from injuries or else weakened by illness to the point where they can no longer fly. In either case the preliminary handling should be the same – warmth, quiet and rest. It may be a wise plan, if a bird is received in a hospital, to administer an initial dose of a broad-spectrum antibiotic; this can serve both as a prophylactic in injured birds and to assist in overcoming pathogenic bacteria in diseased patients. It is often believed that injections cause shock in severely ill birds and it is probably best to administer most sorts of drugs to waterfowl by means of a flexible plastic tube. This can be passed into the proventriculus via the oesophagus. The other end is attached to a 5 or 10ml syringe and an accurate dose can be administered without risk of choking the bird. After a little practice it is easy to pass such a tube down any bird's throat. Tablets can likewise be pushed down with the tip of the finger.

The dose of the drug should be related to the size of the bird; a table of drug dosages is given in Appendix 3. It should be noted that many of these doses are rather greater than those recommended for mammals of equivalent weight. This is because, in practice, it is found that larger quantities are necessary if they are to be effective; this may be related to the bird's higher metabolic rate. Since it is not envisaged that any of these treatments is going to be needed for more than 4–5 consecutive days, a cumulative effect is unlikely. Most of the formulations supplied for the poultry industry are not suitable for bird hospitals as they are packed for use in large numbers of birds rather than just a few or individual cases.

The question of diagnosis of disease in waterbirds is not easy and should be left to a veterinary surgeon who may wish to take blood or faecal samples to help him reach a conclusion. However, it may be pertinent to mention a few of the diseases which, in the absence of any injury, can cause clinical signs of weakness. Some of these are discussed in more detail in other chapters.

Salmonellosis, caused by bacteria belonging to the genus *Salmonella*, is not uncommon.[3] Clinical signs are usually those of increased faecal production and general lethargy. The disease is potentially dangerous because of the risk to human beings and, in general, it is probably wise to kill affected birds.

Pneumonia is associated with various organisms but is often due to *Pasteurella* spp. It. is commonly diagnosed in birds wrecked after a storm or periods of intense cold : rapid breathing is the main clinical sign. Antibiotics are usually effective.

Aspergillosis is caused by the fungus *Aspergillus fumigatus* which may multiply in the lungs, bronchi or airsacs. An affected bird loses weight and has gasping respiration. The disease is often diagnosed in birds of the open sea (such as scoters, eiders and guillemots) that have been in captivity for some time. Treatment is very difficult but amphotericin B inhaled by the bird in a closed box is said to be of benefit. The disease can be prevented by excluding all sources of mould (for example, hay and straw) and also by supplying sea water since the saline nasal secretion is known to inhibit the growth of *Aspergillus*.

Gizzard worms can cause illness and death in wildfowl, especially young swans and dabbling ducks. A diagnosis can be made if worm eggs are detected in the faeces. Treatment of one species of worm (*Amidostomum* sp) is effective by administration of tetramisole by stomach tube. The other gizzard worm (*Acuaria* sp) is almost impossible to treat because it produces fibrous lesions in the gizzard wall and these do not respond to drugs.

Lead poisoning is usually caused by picking up and swallowing items such as lead shot and fishing weights (see Chapter 12). Significant clinical signs are loss of weight and green staining around the cloaca; there is often an increased appetite leading to impaction of the gizzard. Diagnosis can be made by radiography, which will detect the lead. Swans and ducks are most commonly affected, other species only rarely.

Birds will poison themselves also by picking at such items as loose pieces of wire netting; it is essential to examine the netting of each hospital run regularly to see that it is in good repair.

Traumatic injuries should also be mentioned. The two main causes in waterfowl are impact, for example, with power lines, and shotgun wounds. Not infrequently birds are brought in with extensive skin wounds where the skin has peeled back revealing the underlying flesh; these injuries are most frequent on the breast and head. The breast wounds can usually be successfully sutured by a veterinary surgeon and mostly heal very well, but those on the scalp are rarely successfully treated as there is no underlying blood supply to assist healing and the skin tends to slough.

Fractures of legs and wings can be caused by either type of incident and vary greatly in location and severity. Treatment will depend on a number of factors, including the size of the bird and the accommodation available during convalescence. Quite frequently the only possible course of action is to amputate the leg or wing concerned, in which case it is probably out of the question to try and return the bird to the wild. However, most of these species do well in captivity and can be kept if a suitable home is available. However, it should be remembered that heavy birds like swans and geese cannot manage easily on one leg. Any amputation should be performed at, or above, the tarsal joint since dragging a stump about does seem more of a hindrance than the loss of the whole leg.

A bird suspected of having a fractured wing should be placed in a stockinette tube bandage of suitable size, wings folded over the back and holes cut for legs, until a veterinary surgeon has had an opportunity of examining it. Many wing fractures will heal quite well if the wing if kept close to the body in this way for 3–4 weeks but it is frequently difficult to obtain good alignment and the veterinary surgeon may prefer to repair the fracture by internal wiring or pinning. Even then, there is no guarantee the bird will fly again since often nerves and tendons have been damaged as well as the bone.

If the worse comes to the worst and a decision is made to amputate, the bird should be released into a large enclosed area as soon as possible. Such accommodation must include some cover in which the bird can hide if it so wishes; it will then adjust more quickly to a restricted life.

Skin wounds caused by gunshot can be treated as ordinary wounds (see Chapter 9). No attempt should be made to remove the pellets unless they are associated with infection or restricting movement; if left they will remain inert in the flesh and do no further harm.

Fishing hooks and lines often cause casualties among waterbirds. Usually it is a matter of unravelling the tangle but surgery may be necessary if the hook has entered the oesophagus or stomach. It must be remembered that hooks are best removed by pushing them on through and not by trying to pull them out.

THE CARE OF ABANDONED WATERFOWL CHICKS

All too often baby ducks and other species are picked up by well meaning people and brought in to be cared for when they have only temporarily been deserted by their mothers. Some species, like eiders and shelducks, are in fact deliberately abandoned by their parents quite soon after reaching the seashore; they form groups of 'crèches' with one or two 'aunties' vaguely in attendance. Unfortunately, very young ducklings have an innate tendency to follow moving objects and some get led well and truly astray.

Most ducklings can be reared under an infra-red lamp such as is used for chickens and will do well on chick-crumbs with the addition of as many worms and insects as possible. Their water dish should be partly filled with stones so that they cannot get themselves soaked and cold. Baby coots and moorhens are fed at first by the parents which bring waterweed and insects to the young in their bills. Herons, grebes and gulls are fed fish by their parents; small strips of herrings, eel, trout and minnows are usually successfully hand-fed to the young of these species. It must be remembered (see Chapter 13) that many other sorts of fish contain the enzyme thiaminase which destroys vitamin B1 so that either the fish mentioned above should be used or else vitamin supplements must be given. It is always easier to get very young birds to peck at red and green so any forceps or tongs used should be wrapped in red or green paper. Also, many will peck at anything moving, so small live earthworms or mealworms, grasshoppers or green caterpillars placed on the chick crumbs will usually encourage orphans to feed readily within a day or two.

Most of these species grow very rapidly and can do without a lamp after ten days; they are all very messy and require scrupulous cleanliness in their surroundings. A pen with a close mesh floor and some clean old towelling placed under the lamp helps to keep them in a satisfactory state. A supply of clean sand and small grit should not be forgotten either; as the babies grow, slightly coarser grit should be offered. Very young orphaned cygnets can be treated like ducklings except that they should be offered more waterweed and greenstuff.

Young ducks and many other birds that have been raised by man become very tame and may be very difficult to return to the wild; even then, they are easy prey for the casual shooter. It is really best to spend as little time as possible with youngsters of this sort and, once they are fairly well feathered, to release them on to a pond or stream where they will continue to be fed for a while longer but where they will have minimum contact with people. Precautions will still need to be taken against stoats, cats, foxes and other predators.

19 Captive breeding of birds of prey

L. H. Hurrell

Editors' note: The inclusion of a chapter on captive breeding in a book on wild bird casualties may come as a surprise to some readers. However, as has been mentioned throughout the text, not all disabled birds can be returned to the wild. Those that remain in captivity may prove of educational value but it is an added bonus if they can contribute to our understanding of avian biology. Attempting to breed casualty birds in captivity is one important way of making such contributions and is a field in which there is a dearth of scientific data. In this chapter the breeding of one group, the birds of prey, is considered. The author, who has been involved with raptor casualties for many years, has been extremely successful in his work on captive breeding. Other species are mentioned briefly elsewhere in the book and Brenda Marsault's article (see the 'Recommended Reading' section) gives an account of the successful breeding of guillemots after an oiling episode (see Plate 22).

Our wild raptor populations were threatened so seriously by the immensely destructive pressures of toxic agricultural chemicals in the mid-sixties that it was impossible then to predict whether the dramatic decline of these populations would be arrested in time. This was, without doubt, a desperate situation, but one small compensation on the positive side was that it did stimulate a great deal of important work on all aspects of raptor biology, including attempts to breed them in captivity. It was appreciated that captive breeding could be an important conservation tool, especially in the field of biological research. It could have a special significance where attempts were being made to restore a depleted wild bird population but clearly attention to the environment and to the causes of the decline would always need to be given priority.

Practically all the work in Great Britain in the field of captive breeding has, of necessity, been carried out using trained hawks and disabled wild casualties. It must be stressed that only wild casualties that cannot be released on account of permanent disability can legally be retained for captive breeding (see Chapter 2). Although it is possible to apply to the Department of the Environment for a licence to retain a bird that has fully recovered this is unlikely to be granted unless there are very special circumstances. Nevertheless, quite seriously disabled individuals may prove successful breeders provided they are capable of copulation and of carrying food up to the nest site.

Present indications are that in many species eyasses (young taken from the nest) are more likely to breed in artificial quarters than those that have lived for some time in the wild. However, young birds of prey that have been orphaned, have fallen from the nest or that have, through other adverse circumstances, been rescued during fledging must be released as soon as they are able to fend for themselves. It is therefore no easy matter to bring together a suitable pair that have some prospect of success, and it is most important to be aware that a great deal of thoughtful preparation must go into the provision of suitable quarters. On the whole, birds of prey do not thrive in wire-netting enclosures and such quarters often result in very serious injuries to plumage and soft parts. Although both hawks and falcons can be kept undamaged in barn or shed accommodation and some successful breeding has been achieved under such enclosed conditions, there may be problems over the provision of adequate light and ventilation. It may be necessary to augment the available light with electric light governed by a time-switch to coincide with the natural photoperiod. If windows are used to allow daylight to enter, they must on no account be covered with wire-netting but have smooth vertical rods 2–3cm apart (see Chapter 16). This will minimise damage to plumage and cere.

One of the most promising types of quarters is that which can be described as the 'skylight and seclusion enclosure'.[1, 2] In essence, the construction consists of opaque walls about 2.5m high on all four sides and the ceiling is formed by soft polythene or nylon netting (the heaviest gauge available and not larger than 4.5cm knot to knot). Quarters of this design expose the occupants to natural daylight, provide a healthy environment and conditions completely free from visual disturbance. To achieve total seclusion, attention must be paid to the design of the feeding hatch and of the water supply for the bath. It is a great advantage to incorporate a hide from which observations can be made through a two-way mirror. Up to the present time, six of the seven species of diurnal raptors that the author has paired in such quarters have laid eggs and five have reared youngsters. Since that notoriously sensitive and temperamental species the sparrowhawk is numbered amongst those which have reared youngsters successfully,

242

there is every likelihood that these conditions should prove generally suitable for breeding any of the diurnal raptors. Such enclosures are also proving eminently satisfactory for housing convalescent birds before a decision is made as to whether they are capable of returning to the wild.

The female diurnal raptor is larger than the male. In those species in which this sexual dimorphism is pronounced, it is desirable that the male shall not be more disabled than the female. There is an aggressive phase in the courtship of most raptors preceding mating when a female may prove lethal if she can too easily outfly the male. However, there is a great deal of variation in the character of birds of prey and some individuals are much less dominant than others. It may be possible for an amenable female to get along safely with a less able male if he is not particularly timid.

The author has had so many surprises when several injured sparrow-hawks have been together that he is hesitant about making unqualified generalisations. For instance, in the early part of 1974 his breeding pair of sparrowhawks lived amicably with two extra females which were awaiting conditions favourable for their release. One was an adult and the other an immature. The male was in no way threatened, though so heavily outnumbered, nor did he try to drive the extra females away. Instead he ignored the adult and courted the immature bird. However, as the old female came into breeding condition, she took great exception to the presence of one of the other females. During 1975, two different immatures were with the adult male and the old female was no longer present. This time the male clearly took to the female with serious flight impairment, but resented the presence of the other almost perfect bird. He chased her aggressively with increasing determination, and she gave the chitter of alarm and submission. It should be emphasised that if a male (which, in the sparrowhawk, is only half the weight of the female) is under pressure, such warning signs must be acted upon and the birds separated without delay, because a disaster can occur very swiftly. These incidents underline the need for caution and constant vigilance, especially during the weeks before the breeding season.

Then there is the need for a suitable food supply that must be of top quality for the adults and which needs to be backed up by a considerable reserve for the brood of nestlings. One soon learns how much food will satisfy the appetites of a pair without a surplus being left. For much of the year this can be supplied once a day. In frosty weather it is advisable to give unfrozen food twice a day, especially for the small species, and in really hot weather it is likewise sensible to offer morning and evening feeding. The most important points to bear in mind concerning the dietary requirements of a young brood are that they require only very small morsels during the first few days (usually given casting-free by the parents). The brood must certainly be provided with whole animal carcasses containing bone (whether laboratory mice, day-old chicks or road casualty birds) before the youngsters are one week old. The increasing demand for food reaches a level (in the case of the small hawks at about two weeks) when each individual's consumption of food is approximately double that needed by mature birds of the species. During the latter half of the fledging period, this consumption remains approximately constant and then steadily declines until the end of the period of feather growth. By that time, the food requirement is back to that of the adults of the species.

Release of young captive-bred hawks into the wild can be considered only with indigenous species and is itself a considerable undertaking. It should be attempted only in a habitat suitable for the particular species and the youngsters should be ringed by a person approved by the British Trust for Ornithology. Probably the best method of release is to establish the brood at hack and continue the supportive feeding until the youngsters succeed in capturing food for themselves and disperse.[3]

In order to hack off a brood they must be placed in an artificial stick nest or nestbox a few days before fledging. This method has been used for centuries by falconers but is not quite as easy to carry out successfully as these few brief sentences might suggest. One exceptionally long hack was with a kestrel. A brood of three raised in 1970[4] was hacked from a box on top of the breeding pen. One drowned in a water butt on the first day out. One went off as anticipated after the usual month or so at hack. The third one, called Van, continued to come in for regular feeds during the next seven and a half years and is still doing so at the time of writing. During recent years his visits have sometimes become infrequent, quite often after intervals of many weeks in summer and autumn. Apart from his continued willingness to return for occasional token feeds, he behaves and reacts to humans like a wild hawk.

Owls appear to breed more easily in captivity than diurnal birds of prey and several species have reared young successfully under a variety of conditions. Even so, the actual breeding chamber needs to be free from disturbance.

From the foregoing, it will be appreciated that many difficulties are likely to be encountered in attempts at captive breeding and that few people are likely to have suitable conditions. It is unlikely that bird hospitals will have the necessary spacious facilities and they would be especially vulnerable to the danger of cross infection. However, since they are likely to be the initial recipients of a considerable number of disabled raptors, it is important that they should be especially conscious of the breeding potential of such casualties, particularly of the rarer species, that do not recover sufficiently well for release. Bearing this in mind, it is a great advantage if they can keep in touch with people who are in a position to provide the most promising conditions. Indeed, such liaison is already established in some areas of the UK.

42 Female sparrowhawk with young

20 Cage and aviary design and construction

C. G. Jones

Man has kept birds in captivity for centuries; indeed, pigeons are believed to have been domesticated as long ago as 4500 BC by the civilisation of Arpachiya in modern Iraq. In one way or another captive birds have been intimately associated with man's culture for thousands of years.

The ways in which man has kept birds over the centuries have ranged from the enlightened to the barbaric. A careful scrutiny of these avicultural methods can give us tremendous insight into the requirements of captive birds. There are many excellent modern texts on this subject; however, these are mainly concerned with traditional cage and aviary birds. Few of these publications go into detail over the requirements of sick, injured or orphaned birds.

The housing requirements of birds vary greatly with regard to the species, age and the individual. A knowledge of the birds' natural history is very useful when one is trying to accommodate species which are infrequently kept in captivity.

To determine the needs of a captive bird the reader must attempt to identify the parameters that induce a feeling of well-being in the species or individual he is trying to care for. In perching birds the flight distance is less in a vertical plane than it is in a horizontal one. This can be exploited by placing cages high above the ground and by giving birds perches high in the corners of the aviaries. Many perching birds also respond to a gently swaying perch; hence the origin of the swing in a modern canary or budgerigar cage. All birds do better if allowed seclusion and low levels of light intensity during times of stress. Falconers have known and exploited this for centuries by the use of the hood, and oriental falconers by seeling, whereby the eyelids are closed with a fine silk thread. Other species of birds, such as grebes, and many species of waterfowl, feel safest and usually sleep in the middle of an expanse of water. Woodpeckers and treecreepers rest and sleep in a vertical position on the bark or hollow inside of a tree.

It is these differences in the behaviour and ecology of birds that have to be considered when birds are being kept in captivity for a long period of time.

It is unlikely that someone who has found a wild bird, whether it is sick, injured or orphaned, will be able to provide it immediately with correct accommodation. The requirements of a bird that has just come from the wild are also going to differ appreciably from a bird that has been in captivity for some time. The accommodation needed will reflect, in part, the mental and physical state of the bird. Most birds have a distrust of man and just being handled may have a psychologically traumatic effect upon them. The recently found wild bird will probably be shocked and stressed, a condition which can be exacerbated by examination, surgery or force-feeding.

The simplest, and in many ways the most effective, treatment and housing is to place the casualty in a cardboard box in which it can

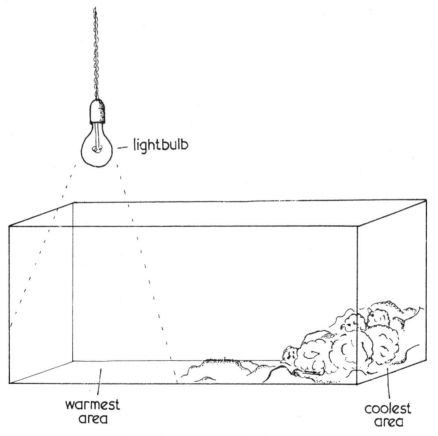

lightbulb

warmest
area

coolest
area

43 Accommodation for a nestling, showing temperature gradient

stand up and turn around if desired, but no more than this. Ventilation holes should be placed low down so that the patient cannot see through them; the bird should be kept warm, dark and quiet. Normally, even shy birds will feed soon after being found, provided the correct diet is supplied and enough light is entering the cardboard box for them to see the food.

Nestlings and birds that have suffered from exhaustion or haemorrhage may be hypothermic and need additional warmth; a temperature of 25–32°C will usually suffice. Warmth can be provided by a variety of means, and an aviculturist's hospital cage is the ideal; however, lacking this, an alternative approach is to hang an electric lightbulb over a long box, thereby setting up a temperature gradient along its length (see Fig 43). The bird will then move to the area of optimum warmth. A fuller discussion regarding nestlings can be found towards the end of the chapter.

After birds have recovered from the initial shock of captivity they may be placed in a cage or aviary to recuperate, until eventual release or rehabilitation. Birds that need to be kept relatively quiet as the result of fractures or other injuries should be placed in a box cage until they are fit enough to be housed in an aviary. Larger birds that are recuperating can be accommodated in a packing case. A door can be placed on the front, using vertical dowels or bamboo (about 5cm apart) mounted on to a wooden frame. The size of a recuperation cage is determined by the size of the bird but should be large enough for the bird to be able to stretch its wings comfortably without touching the sides and, if it is a perching bird, to be able to perch comfortably on a suitably positioned cross perch.

If the bird is highly strung and continually jumps at the front of the cage, the latter should be covered with a suitable piece of material that will allow light to enter the cage but will prevent the bird seeing out. A linen cloth serves the purpose admirably and it should be taut over the front of the cage. For larger birds, such as swans and herons, a shed, chicken house or stable may be used provided that it is dry, clean and draught-proof. Any additional heat can be provided by an infra-red lamp. Windows should be screened or barred with vertical dowels. The aim of any short-term accommodation is primarily to counter stress and to provide an environment conducive to the birds' recovery.

248

Cages

Robert Stroud, the famous 'Birdman of Alcatraz', wrote: 'I want to go on record against that very popular and very stupid abomination, the round canary cage . . . . Birds like corners for the same reasons you like them; they give a sense of protection.' It is indeed surprising that, even in today's animal-conscious society, the round all-wire, canary, budgerigar and parrot cages still persist. It is true that birds become accustomed to such cages and if they are correctly placed, in a corner or against a wall, up to 2m above the ground, they do suffice. The all-wire cage is a relic from the days when they were used to house finches. The old finch fancier understood how to use these cages to advantage. The cages were usually hung from a ceiling or placed high up on a wall, and if the occupant became in the least bit excited they were entirely or partly covered by a linen cloth. With highly excitable species, such as chaffinches, they used to employ another form of visual seclusion by blinding the bird in one eye.

The most suitable cage design is the box cage, so called because it is essentially a box with a wire front. The box cage has much to commend it. Birds feel secure in it and they can only be viewed from the front. All birds dislike being approached from either behind or above. When at rest birds usually face the direction which poses the greatest security threat, which in a box cage is the front; in a wire cage it could be all round and above as well!

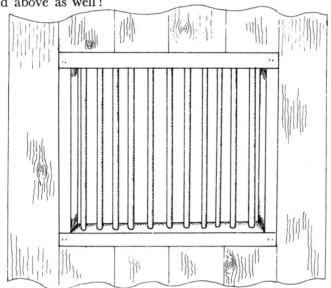

44 Window showing vertical bars which are circular in cross-section

The box cage can be easily constructed from any sound wooden box, and cage fronts can be procured from a good pet store in a number of different sizes with different bar spacings for different species. Failing this, a front can be made from wire netting. The cage should preferably have a removable tray so that it can be cleaned. The floor should be covered with a thick layer of newspaper to absorb droppings. It is advisable to place perches at either end of the cage, so that the bird is encouraged to take as much exercise as possible in flying or hopping back and forth. The perches should be far enough away from the walls so the bird can turn around without brushing its tail against the sides; they should also be of varying thicknesses, but not so thin that the toes meet when the bird perches.

A cage should be well positioned in a dry, light, draught-free place, and where the bird feels relaxed. The author used to keep an imprinted collared dove in a cage. The cage was well positioned but the dove continually fluttered at the bars trying to get out. There can be no sound more distressing to the ears of anyone who has the least sensitivity towards animals and in desperation the cage was placed so that it faced another direction – but to no avail. The bird's distressed attempts to escape only subsided when a nearby wireless was placed on the other side of the room. With the removal of the wireless the dove lapsed into its usual state of contentment. The wireless which had been playing close to the cage represented a threat to the dove.

Ideally cages should be used only for temporary accommodation. Some birds, such as many of the small insectivorous birds and other active or highly strung species, are not really suited to a cage life. However, some species positively thrive in a cage. Many finches, such as the goldfinch, greenfinch and siskin, will even breed in a cage although others, like the chaffinch, are only really suited to an aviary.

Hospital cages are a necessity for anyone who frequently looks after ailing birds and several excellent designs can be acquired from avicultural suppliers. An effective hospital cage can be constructed quite simply by placing an electric lightbulb or underfloor heating elements (like the ones often used by herpetologists) into a standard box cage. There should be only one perch which should be near to the floor. The most effective temperature is usually around 25–32°C but this should be adjusted to suit the needs of the bird. The hospital cage provides the optimum conditions for the recovery of an ailing bird, warmth and security. It should be kept as clean as possible and should periodically be washed out with hot soapy water or a suitable disinfectant, such as cetrimide.

Aviaries

By far the most effective and humane way of housing birds is in aviaries. Aviaries can range from the modest to the spectacular. Many Victorian and Edwardian aviaries were works of art, beautiful to the eye but totally impractical. Today, most birds in collections are housed in less spectacular but more practical aviaries, more thought being given to the birds' ecology and behaviour. Many modern zoological gardens have vast aviaries housing mixed collections of birds with each species exploiting differing niches within the captive environment. These aviaries have the advantage that a bird chooses the parts of the aviary that most suit it. It can behave in many respects like a wild bird, in avoiding stressful situations, by flying to the other end of the aviary or running under a bush. There are few people who could afford, let alone aspire to build, such a mini ecosystem.

More modest structures can be just as practical and efficient in meeting the requirements of many wild birds. Aviary design is dictated by the species of birds it is going to house. Many birds can be housed in aviaries that conform to a general plan, others cannot be kept successfully in captivity because their ecology and behaviour are not conducive to captivity. Species such as swifts, swallows, grebes, petrels and other birds with very exacting ecological requirements do not usually do well in captivity and should be retained only for short periods.

Many species that were once considered impossible to keep and breed in captivity now do so with some regularity (see Chapter 19) and, hopefully, the requirements of other exacting species will be met in the future.

Most aviaries are rectangular in design with a sheltered section and perches at either end to encourage the birds to fly the whole length of the interior. Many texts on the subject stress the need for length rather than height in aviary design. In small passerines that is indeed true and a 2m high aviary is usually adequate provided it offers shelter and seclusion to its inmates. For larger birds additional aviary height is often desirable. The bird flying vertically expends more energy than it would flying a similar distance horizontally, and where aviary space is lacking it is an efficient way to induce fitness. The height should not normally exceed the length of the aviary.

It is a regrettable fact that aviary size is often going to depend upon resources. In many instances aviaries can be constructed from already existing buildings. Most spare rooms and outhouses can be converted into suitable accommodation by arranging wire netting or closely placed vertical dowels over any window, by erecting perches at either end of the room, and by providing a suitably screened perch or area behind which a bird may hide. Indoor aviaries have the distinct advantage over outdoor ones in that they can be easily heated, and artificial light, or darkness, can be provided when necessary. All of these may be essential when one considers the care of a convalescing bird. On the other hand, for healthy birds, an outdoor aviary has many points in its favour as it provides a healthier atmosphere and has the added advantage that it can be planted with natural foliage.

Outdoor aviaries may be constructed from a variety of materials and are best placed on a well drained piece of ground. To economise on materials an aviary may be built against a wall or the side of an outhouse. The legal considerations when constructing an aviary are discussed in Chapter 2. It is often desirable to have at least the back of the aviary covered, for the same reason that box cages are preferred to wire ones. In some cases it is necessary for all the sides to be enclosed, with only the roof or part of the roof open to the elements, especially when highly strung birds are convalescing and need to be kept as quiet as possible. By keeping birds in total visual isolation from their keeper Dr L. H. Hurrell has consistently succeeded in breeding birds of prey in captivity (see Chapter 19). Seclusion of some form should be provided for all wild birds in captivity. Many aviaries have a dry, draught-proof shed attached to the aviary into which the bird can retreat when under stress or during inclement weather. For small passerines most aviculturists provide access to the shed via a hole about 30cm square. In the case of wild birds in the UK, as long as they can retreat from rain and draughts an open-fronted shed will suffice. For the larger hardier birds such a shelter is not really necessary so long as the aviary is in a sheltered position and has a covered section. Screening of some form or another should be present in every aviary and it is often advisable to cover certain of the aviary sides. Taut hessian stretched outside the aviary will serve the purpose admirably.

The highest perches in aviaries should be placed in corners because these are the perches that are most often used for roosting and it is advantageous if the roosting bird can, if necessary, hide behind a screen of some form. Most owls roost against a solid object, usually a tree trunk in the wild, but this could be the side of the aviary in captivity. Barn owls spend long periods in a nestbox and do not usually roost anywhere else. A nestbox should always be present into which they can retreat. A packing case with an entrance hole in the front serves the purpose. The retiring nature of the barn owl is probably the reason why it is so prolific in captivity; by spending most of its time in a nest-box it does not become stressed by people moving within its flight distance. A different approach is needed for ground birds and species that feed under cover; a board laid across the side of the aviary will allow plenty of room behind which the bird can retreat.

Several materials can be used as screens or aviary sides. Dr Hurrell has successfully used corrugated PVC sheets, although larch lap fencing or marine ply are almost as good. PVC sheets have the added advantage of allowing more light to enter the aviary, but they have the disadvantage of drawing the sun and as such should not be used for overhead cover. The author lost a clutch of fertile kestrel eggs because the nest box was placed beneath the covered PVC section of the aviary and the eggs became overheated.

By giving the bird an opportunity to hide, or conversely by screening the sides of the aviary, it is possible to approach within the flight distance of a bird without causing the bird any alarm. This can be done because birds do not have the ability to rationalise. As soon as something is no longer visible it no longer represents a threat or an attraction. A captive bird should not be sent into a state of panic at the approach of its keeper and must be able to move into a position of visual seclusion.

The aviary framework can be of any material provided it allows for the attachment of wire netting or solid sides. Sawn timber can be used, or even metal angle irons; spruce or larch poles are very useful and provide a sound structure. Wire netting can be very effectively used to cover most of the aviary and the mesh size is dependent upon the birds that are being kept and the pests or predators one wishes to exclude. 1cm mesh should be used for the smaller species of bird – or if one wishes to exclude sparrows – and this should be buried to a depth of 30cm to exclude rats. Mice will be most difficult to exclude and it may in some cases be necessary to have a strip of sheet metal 60cm high nailed to the uprights with the top turned over. For larger species weldmesh or chain-link fencing is excellent. Some species, especially the larger birds, may repeatedly fly into the wire and thus sustain feather, beak or foot damage. This can be rectified by placing vertical battens at least 5–6cm apart on the inside of the wire. This gives them a barrier through which they know they cannot fly. A similar procedure may be used for the roof.

The positioning of perches has already been briefly mentioned. The perches should be placed so that the bird is using the full height and length of the aviary by flying to them, and getting as much exercise as possible from the space available. Birds with wing injuries may be

253

unable to fly to the highest perches. To overcome this problem, perches should be placed to form a ladder arrangement, so that the bird can hop to the most desirable ones. They should be of varying thicknesses, well spaced and some should gently sway under the bird's weight. Rigid perches of the same thickness may give rise to foot problems (see Chapter 10). Larger aviaries should be planted with natural foliage; this provides natural shelter and perches, provides nesting sites and attracts insects which are a welcome supplement to the diet of many species.

Bathing is essential for maintaining the condition and insulatory properties of the bird's plumage. Baths, like feeding receptacles, should be placed away from the perches so they are not fouled by the droppings. Some birds will refuse to bathe unless the bath is sunk into the ground and the water increases in depth gradually. As a rough guide the bath should be no deeper than the bird's leg length. For larger species an upturned dustbin lid makes an ideal receptacle. Permanent baths may be dug into the aviary floor and lined with concrete. The water must always be clean and should be changed frequently; birds refuse to bathe in anything other than the cleanest water. There should be a perch or rock close to the bath, on which the bird can perch and dry itself after bathing. Many species of perching and gamebirds also dust-bath and this should be encouraged. In an outdoor, naturally planted aviary, most birds will make their own dust-baths on any exposed patch of soil, such dust-bathing being most prevalent during the summer.

With highly strung species it may be preferable not to enter the aviary unnecessarily, in which case feeding hatches should be fixed to the outside of the aviary. In extreme instances where it is undesirable for the birds even to see their keeper, feeding may be done through a letter-box type hatch or by pushing food down a length of drain pipe fixed to the outside of the aviary.

Aviary doors should, if possible, be double to avoid losses or, failing this, the door should be small and open inwards.

THE NESTLING

The nestling bird varies considerably from species to species. Most nestlings can be placed into two categories as was outlined in Chapter 5. The precocial nestling can run around soon after hatching and is quickly able to find its own food – an example is the chick of the domestic fowl. On the other hand, the altricial nestling is born blind, naked and helpless, and the young of passerine birds come into this group. In between there are the semi-altricial chicks which are the

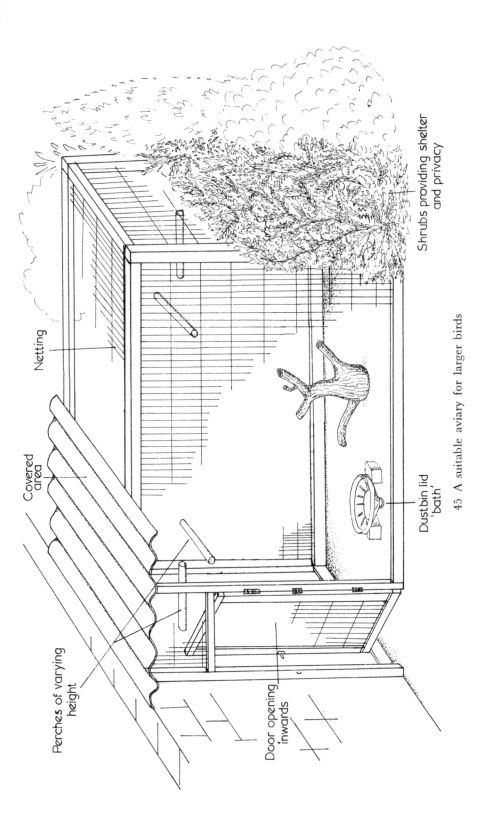

Netting

Covered area

Perches of varying height

Door opening inwards

Dustbin lid 'bath'

Shrubs providing shelter and privacy

45 A suitable aviary for larger birds

young of the birds of prey. Nearly all young birds are poikilothermic (unable to regulate their own temperature), and must therefore be given additional warmth, as described earlier under short-term accommodation. The amount of warmth needed will depend upon the age of the bird and the amount of precociality that the species shows. Precocial species soon move to the area of optimum warmth if placed in a temperature gradient, and the temperature requirements of precocial chicks are not as critical as those of altricial birds. It is best to place young altricial chicks at a temperature of 25–30°C and try to assess whether the temperature is too high or too low. If the temperature is too high the chick will be panting, with rapid throat palpitations, and the skin will appear flushed. If, on the other hand, the temperature is too low, the bird will be cold to the touch, lethargic and possibly shivering, although it should be noted that young altricial chicks can tolerate low temperature for an hour without marked effects.

The reactions of a nestling to its keeper will be dependent upon age. During a bird's development it passes through a critical period; before this stage the bird will be tame and trusting, while if obtained after this period the bird will be shy and defensive and in some cases difficulties will be encountered in getting it to feed. In kestrels this critical period is between ten and fourteen days. During this period the birds are thought to go through an imprinting process when they imprint upon their parents, siblings or, often, upon the person rearing them. Imprinting upon a keeper may be permanent if a young bird is reared in isolation and is not allowed access to its own species until maturity. An imprinted bird directs its reproductive behaviour towards its keeper and in many instances may be very aggressive towards humans. Imprints should not, in most circumstances, be released to the wild, although some species, such as the raven, eventually redirect their reproductive behaviour towards their own species. There is a school of thought that believes that imprinting to humans is reversed when birds are released to the wild, although this has yet to be conclusively proved.

A young bird is continually learning and it is now realised that many of the behaviour patterns that were once thought to be instinctive are learned. Some people have suggested that even the positioning of nest sites and the types of food birds eat are, in some cases, learned during their development. These points have to be carefully considered, especially if the birds are to be rehabilitated.

Nestlings should receive a great deal of stimulation during their development. The more stimulation young birds have, the more capable they are of adapting when they reach maturity. The author has

256

a buzzard that was bred in captivity; it was reared in an aviary from which it could not see out. The only movements it observed during its development were those of the parent birds. As a result the buzzard is extremely nervous and has a low tolerance level for movement. Similar observations have been noted by other aviculturists.

During a bird's development signs of neurosis may appear as the result of bad handling or management. The author has had several birds that, following forceful handling when young, developed an extraordinary fear of hands and yet remained extremely tame towards their keeper. In other cases, if the birds associate the approach of a human with an unpleasant stimulus, such as force-feeding or having to have an injury inspected, they may be sent into a panic at the sight of their keeper. Great care should always be taken in handling birds and they should not be chased around the aviary. Once the bird develops a fear it is very difficult to extinguish it.

REHABILITATION

The problem of re-introduction has been briefly mentioned throughout the text. The birds should only be released if 100 per cent fit and in perfect feather. Birds that have been in captivity a while and those that have been hand-reared should be hacked back to the wild gradually rather than just be taken to a suitable place and released. Perching species can be re-introduced by having part of the aviary front opened, so that the birds may fly back and forth at will. The author has used this method successfully with crows and raptors. Many people remove part of the roof, with similar success. Waterbirds can be released from an open-topped enclosure. Waterbirds soon become accustomed to a particular area and will be reluctant to leave it if it provides them with the security they require.

Birds that are being rehabilitated will gradually gain their independence over a period of weeks as their fitness and ability to find food improve. They will return at more protracted intervals until they finally become fully independent. Birds that are being released should always have food available and this can either be placed on the top of the aviary or inside their original enclosures. Some birds will become very shy on being given their freedom and may only feed some distance away from their original aviary. In these cases food can be placed on a shed roof or other vantage point. Before birds are released they should be ringed by someone with a BTO ringing licence. It is the duty of anyone involved in bird rehabilitation to ensure that the birds are marked in this way so that a body of information can be built up on this important and growing region of aviculture and ornithology.

The whole subject of rehabilitation warrants more research and it is probably true to say that it represents one of the biggest problems in wild bird care. There is a very clear legal obligation to release a wild bird when it is able to fend for itself but there are no guidelines as to how this is assessed. A wild bird may be 100 per cent fit in physical terms but its chances of survival in the wild may still be minimal on account of its tameness and affinity to man as a result of captivity. Conversely, a bird may have had a leg amputated – and thus not have 'recovered' from its disability – and yet be able to fend for itself very successfully. These two examples demonstrate that each case must be assessed separately and it is here that the combined knowledge and expertise of the wild bird hospital organiser, the veterinary surgeon and the field ornithologist might be best used to advantage.

The management of birds in captivity is dependent upon a large number of variables, some of which have been covered in this chapter; others can only be appreciated as a result of experience. The problem of accommodating and rehabilitating wild birds is a challenging one which should be tackled with commonsense and sensitivity regarding the bird's needs.

Appendices

1 *Ornithological, avicultural, veterinary and animal welfare organisations*
The Avicultural Society (Secretary), c/o Windsor Forest Stud, Mill Ride, Ascot, Berks
British Bird Fancy Council (Secretary), 35 Chatham Road, Kingston-upon-Thames, Surrey
British Ornithologists' Union (BOU), c/o Zoological Society of London, Regent's Park, London, NW1
British Trust for Ornithology (BTO), Beech Grove, Tring, Herts
British Veterinary Association, 7 Mansfield Street, London, W1
The Game Conservancy, Burgate Manor, Fordingbridge, Hants
The Hawk Trust, PO Box 1, Hungerford, Berks
International Society for the Protection of Animals (ISPA), 106 Jermyn Street, London, SW1
People's Dispensary for Sick Animals (PDSA), South Street, Dorking, Surrey
Royal Society for the Prevention of Cruelty to Animals (RSPCA), Causeway, Horsham, Sussex
Royal Society for the Protection of Birds (RSPB), The Lodge, Sandy, Beds
Universities' Federation for Animal Welfare (UFAW), 8 Hamilton Close, Potters Bar, Herts
The Wildfowl Trust, Slimbridge, Glos
World Wildlife Fund, 29 Greville Street, London, EC1

2 *Government departments (UK)*
British Museum (Natural History), Cromwell Road, London, SW7
Department of the Environment, 17–19 Rochester Row, London, SW1
Ministry of Agriculture, Fisheries and Food (Animal Health Division), Hook Rise South, Tolworth, Surrey
Nature Conservancy Council, 19–20 Belgrave Square, London, SW1

3 *Bird hospitals and similar organisations*
(Important note : inclusion of the names and addresses overleaf does not imply that the people involved are able to accept wild bird casualties. Nevertheless, practical advice may be available from them.)

Miss E. Anderson, 10 Barnstaple House, Devonshire Drive, Greenwich, London, SE10

Mr A. H. Bayes, 11 Winchester Avenue, Habberley, Kidderminster, Worcs

Mr J. H. Billingham, Lower Grove, Upton Snodsbury Road, Lower Peopleton, Pinvin, Nr Pershore, Worcs

Mr and Mrs C. Christie, 25 Main Road, Middleton Cheney, Banbury, Oxon

Mrs. M. Davidson, Trenoweth Mill, St Keverne, Nr Helston, Cornwall

Mrs E. Engholm, Lame Ducks, Catsfield, Nr Battle, East Sussex

Mr and Mrs J. R. Lewington, 17 Weald View Road, Tonbridge, Kent

Mrs. B. Marsault, 1 Redgate, Salterton Road, Exmouth, Devon

Mousehole Wild Bird Hospital and Sanctuary, Raginnis Hall, Mousehole, Penzance, Cornwall.

Mrs P. Talbot, Idyates Farm, Shatterford, Bewdley, Worcs

Three Owls Bird Sanctuary, Wolstenholme Fold, Norden, Rochdale, Lancs

Mr K. Williams, Penrhos Nature Reserve, Holyhead, Wales

4   *Veterinary advice*
Veterinary advice should always be sought from a local veterinary surgeon. Even if he or she does not have experience of wild birds such a contact will enable medicines and basic advice to be obtained. In addition a local veterinary surgeon should be able to suggest a laboratory to which wild birds may be sent for post-mortem examination and can refer health problems to a veterinary college or a colleague with specialised knowledge of birds.

RECOMMENDED EQUIPMENT AND MEDICINES FOR BIRD HOSPITALS

Gentian violet
Antibiotic or sulphonamide powder*
Insecticidal preparation (see Chapter 11)
Kaolin suspension
Liquid paraffin (or cod-liver oil)
Sterile saline
Distilled water
Empty gelatin capsules
Calcium injection*

Multivitamin injection*
Atropine injection*
Glucose saline solution (small bottles)
Glucose powder
Vitamin/mineral supplements
Sterilised bonemeal
Oil or moisturising cream for feet
Vacuum flasks and ice for samples
Bottles for samples
Swabs and transport medium
Formalin (or formol-saline) solution 10 per cent
Quaternary ammonium or ampholytic disinfectant, for example cetrimide
Alcohol 70 per cent (or methylated spirit)
Scalpel blades

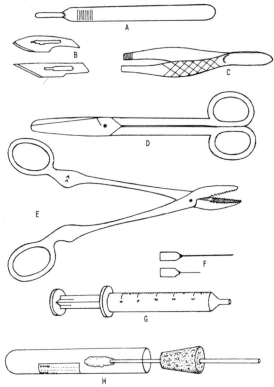

46 Some useful equipment: A Scalpel handle, B Scalpel blades, C Forceps, D Scissors, E Artery forceps, F Hypodermic needles, G Syringe, H Bacteriological swab.

Pair of artery forceps
Emergency suture set*
Needles and syringes
Scissors
Forceps
Stomach tube (rubber or plastic)
Wooden ice lolly sticks
Material for splints
Plaster of Paris
Towels, stockings
Tubular gauze
Cotton wool
Surgical gauze
Adhesive plaster
Sticky tape
Bandages
Hotwater bottles
Lightbulbs
Hospital cages
Baskets, cardboard boxes and other containers
Nets
Falconers' hoods or small cloth bags
Leather gloves for handling birds
Rubber gloves
Small torch
Food and water containers
Supplies of newspaper

All medicines should be stored in a refrigerator or cool place and this must not be accessible to children or unauthorised persons. Those products marked with an asterisk must be obtained from a veterinary surgeon and, in general, should only be used under his direction.

Certain of the items listed below may be kept at a bird hospital in order to be available for an emergency but *should not be used by an unqualified person.*

Veterinary attention
In addition to the items listed above, the following are likely to prove useful in the treatment of bird casualties and should be stocked by veterinary surgeons involved in such work.

Ketamine hydrochloride (10mg/ml and 50mg/ml)
CT 1341 (Saffan) anaesthetic

Pentobarbitone sodium
Methoxyflurane anaesthetic
Water for injection
Spiramycin injection
Tylosin injection
Ampicillin capsules (50mg and 250mg)
Cloxacillin/ampicillin injection
Lincomycin injection
Ophthalmic ointment
Levamisole or tetramisole
Piperazine tablets
Thiabendazole tablets or suspension
Bunamidine hydrochloride tablets
Sulphaquinoxaline or sulphadimidine solution
Dimetridazole or metronidazole tablets
Adrenaline solution
Corticosteroid injection and tablets
Phenobarbitone tablets
Avian tuberculin
Newcastle disease inactivated vaccine
Pigeon-pox vaccine
Surgical appliances
Anaesthesia/euthanasia chamber

DRUGS AND DOSAGES

NB : not all drugs mentioned in the text are included in this Appendix.
The list is intended to be a guide to those agents commonly used in the
treatment of wild birds. The doses of therapeutic substances intended for
specialised treatment are either given in the text or included in the
reference section, p264–266.

The following drugs should *not* be used in the treatment of wild
birds :
    streptomycin by injection
    neomycin by injection
    procaine penicillin
    local analgesics (but see Chapter 15)

Many chemicals may also prove hazardous to birds and should be
avoided. Examples include the chlorinated hydrocarbon insecticides,
(for example, DDT and BHC) and creosote. Further information on
toxic agents is available in Chapter 12.

All therapeutic agents must be used cautiously and, where appropriate, in accordance with the manufacturer's instructions. Neither the number of doses to be given nor their frequency is listed below; veterinary advice must be sought on these and other queries.

Type of compound	Drug	Route	Dose
Antibacterial	Tetracyclines	oral	250mg/kg
		injection	15mg/kg
	Tylosin	oral	250mg/kg
		injection	15mg/kg
	Spiramycin	oral	250mg/kg
		injection	20mg/kg
	Lincomycin	oral	50mg/kg
		injection	15mg/kg
	Ampicillin	oral	250mg/kg
		injection	100mg/kg
	Cloxacillin	oral	250mg/kg
		injection	100mg/kg
	Streptomycin	oral	15mg/kg
	Neomycin	oral	15mg/kg
	Sulphonamides	oral	500mg/kg
	Furazolidone	oral	50mg/kg
Antifungal	Amphotericin B	intra-tracheal	1mg/kg
Antiparasitic	Piperazine	oral	100mg/kg
(endoparasites)	Thiabendazole	oral	500mg/kg
	Bunamidine hydrochloride	oral	25mg/kg
	Niclosamide	oral	150mg/kg
	Levamisole	oral or subcutaneous injection	15mg/kg
	Tetramisole	oral	100mg/kg
Antiparasitic (ectoparasites)	Pyrethrum (or pyrethrins) Piperonyl butoxide Derris powder Flowers of sulphur	external application	as required (with caution)
	Benzyl benzoate (10 per cent)	topical	as required (with caution)
	Trichlorphon (0.15 per cent)	external application	as required (with caution)

264

Type of compound	Drug	Route	Dose
Antiprotozoal	Sulphadimidine	oral	500mg/kg
	Dimetridazole ⎫ Metronidazole ⎭	oral	100mg/kg
Nutritional or metabolic supplements	Glucose saline	oral or injection	4 per cent of body weight
	Complan	oral	up to 10ml/kg
	Glucose solution (10 per cent)	oral or subcutaneous injection	up to 5ml/kg
	Vitamin preparations (for example, Abidec, SA37 and Vionate)	oral	small quantities on food
	Vitamin preparations	injection	as recommended by manufacturers (usually the same as for cats and small dogs)
	Sterilised bonemeal	oral	small quantities on food
	Calcium boragluconate (10 per cent)	injection	up to 5ml/kg
Anaesthetic and sedative	CT 1341 (Saffan)	intravenous injection	10mg/kg
	"	intramuscular injection	36mg/kg
	Metomidate	intramuscular injection	10mg/kg
	Ketamine	intramuscular injection	50mg/kg
	Diazepam	intramuscular injection	10mg/kg
	"	intravenous injection	up to 2mg/kg
	Phenobarbitone	oral	up to 20mg/kg
Hormonal or similar	Betamethasone	oral or intramuscular injection	up to 0.05mg/kg
	Thyroxine	oral	up to 1mg/kg
	Atropine	intramuscular injection	0.05mg/kg

Type of compound	Drug	Route	Dose
Purgative	Liquid paraffin (or cod-liver oil)	oral	up to 5ml/kg
	Magnesium sulphate (5 per cent)	oral	in drinking water
Antidiarrhoeal	Kaolin suspension	oral	up to 15ml/kg
Disinfectant	Washing soda (2–5 per cent)	for disinfection of inanimate objects only	as required
	Formalin (1–2 per cent)	as above	as required
	Phenol compounds (1–5 per cent)	as above	as required
	Methyl or ethyl alcohol (70 per cent)	for disinfection of instruments or skin surface	as required
	Cetrimide (1 per cent)	for disinfection of inanimate objects, instruments or skin wounds	as required

LIST OF PRODUCTS MENTIONED BY TRADENAME IN TEXT (MANUFACTURERS OR SUPPLIERS)

Seeds and birdfood (mentioned in Chapter 8) can be obtained from: John E. Haith, Park Street, Cleethorpes, Lincolnshire. Other items may be obtained from: Lowe's Animal Products, F. C. Lowe and Son, Sittingbourne, Kent.

Other compounds (listed alphabetically) are:
Abidec: Parke-Davis and Company, Usk Road, Pontypool, Gwent
Alevaire: Winthrop Laboratories, Surbiton-upon-Thames, Surrey
Complan: Glaxo-Farley Foods, Glaxo Laboratories Limited, Torr Lane, Plymouth, Devon
Equithesin: Jansen-Salsbery Laboratories, Kansas City, Missouri, USA

Farex: Glaxo-Farley Foods, Glaxo Laboratories Limited, Torr Lane, Plymouth, Devon

Forgastrin: Willington Medicals Limited, Lancaster Road, Shrewsbury, Shropshire

Fungizone: E. R. Squibb and Sons, Regal House, Twickenham, Middx

Mysteclin F: E. R. Squibb and Sons, Regal House, Twickenham, Middx

Nutri-cal paste: Evsco Pharmaceutical Corporation, Long Island, New York, USA

SA 37: Intervet Laboratories Limited, Viking House, Viking Way, Bar Hill, Cambridge

Saffan: Glaxo Laboratories Limited, Greenford, Middlesex

Saval: Spillers Foods Limited, Old Change House, Cannon Street, London, EC4

Sluis: Produced by Royal Sluis, NV—Etten-Leur (Holland) and distributed in the UK by E. W. Coombs Limited, Frindsbury Road, Strood, Kent

Terramycin: Pfizer Limited, Sandwich, Kent

Velcro Ltd, Biddulph, Stoke-on-Trent, Staffs

Vionate: E. R. Squibb and Sons Limited, Animal Health Division, Regal House, Twickenham, Middx

Weetabix: Weetabix Limited, Burton Latimer, Kettering, Northants

Zimmer splint: Zimmer Orthopaedics, Bridgend, Glam

SCIENTIFIC NAMES OF IMPORTANT ANIMALS
AND PLANTS REFERRED TO IN TEXT

1 *Birds*

Budgerigar	*Melopsittacus undulatus*
Canary	*Serinus canarius*
Cockatiel	*Nymphicus hollandicus*
Domestic duck	*Anas platyrhynchos*
Domestic fowl	*Gallus domesticus*
Domestic pigeon	*Columba livia*
Japanese quail	*Coturnix coturnix*
Turkey vulture	*Cathartes aura*

2 *Mammals*
   Domestic cat   *Felis catus*
   Domestic dog   *Canis familiaris*
   Fox   *Vulpes vulpes*
   Lion   *Panthera leo*
   Stoat   *Mustela erminea*

3 *Lower vertebrates*
   Brown trout   *Salmo trutta*
   Carp   *Cyprinus carpio*
   Chub   *Leuciscus cephalus*
   Cod   *Gadus morhua*
   Herring   *Clupea harengus*
   Plaice   *Pleuronectes platessa*
   Sardine   *Sardina pilchardus*
   Smelt   *Atherina presbyter*
   Sole   *Solea solea*
   Sprat   *Sprattus sprattus*
   Turbot   *Scophthalmus maximus*
   White bass   *Dicentrarchus labrax*
   Whiting   *Trisopterus luscus*

4 *Invertebrates*
   African migratory locust   *Locusta migratoria*
   Flour moth   *Ephistia cautella*
   Fruit fly   *Drosophila melanogaster*
   Earthworm   *Lumbricus* sp
   Greater wax moth   *Galeria mellonella*
   Honey bee   *Apis mellifera*
   House cricket   *Acheta domestica*
   House fly   *Musca domestica*
   Lesser wax moth   *Achroia grisella*
   Mealworm   *Tenebrio molitor*
   Mediterranean flour moth   *Anagasta kuhnella*
   Rust red flour beetle   *Tribiolum casteneum*
   Whiteworms   *Euchytraeus albiclus*

5 *Plants*
   Blackberry   *Rubus fructicosus*
   Chickweed   *Stellaria media*
   Dandelion   *Taraxacum officinale*

Dock	*Rumex* sp
Elderberry	*Sambucus nigra*
Groundsel	*Senecio vulgaris*
Millet	*Panicum miliaceum*
Niger	*Guizotia abyssinica*
Shepherd's purse	*Capsella bursa-pastoris*
Sow thistle	*Sonchus oleraceus*
Sunflower	*Helianthus* sp
Teasel	*Dipsacus fullonum*
Wheat	*Triticum* sp

HEALTH HAZARDS IN VOLUNTEER BIRD HOSPITALS

J. E. Cooper

There is considerable public interest in the welfare of wild birds in countries on both sides of the Atlantic, particularly for those individuals that are found sick, injured, oiled or orphaned. In the UK such sentiments are very strong and as a result a number of wild bird hospitals have been started to house and treat wild birds. Such hospitals pose certain management problems, especially when they are staffed by laymen who have limited experience of veterinary medicine. Well-meaning people such as these are often very sincere; however, a few tend to be over sentimental. This, coupled with their limited operating funds, can prove to be a headache for any veterinary surgeon attempting to assist their work.

In the UK the legal position of such hospitals is not entirely clear. Under the Protection of Birds Act 1954, and subsequent legislation, a protected wild bird may be retained in captivity 'for the purpose of tending it and releasing it when no longer disabled', but the Veterinary Surgeons' Act 1966 may cast some doubt on the legality of laymen accepting wild birds from the public and then 'treating' them on their premises.

The subject of treatment of wild birds is a controversial one and many people feel that all injured or sick wild birds should be destroyed. The author does not subscribe to this view. A variety of diseases can be successfully treated and the wild patients released; other birds, although unfit for release, can be retained in captivity for educational or scientific

269

purposes. A number of species may even be propagated in captivity using casualty birds as a breeding nucleus.

In addition, the attempted treatment of wild birds can prove a direct benefit by advancing clinical and pathological knowledge of avian diseases. An example is oiled seabirds where attempted rehabilitation has taught us a great deal about the pathological effects of oiling. However, this is not to suggest that hopeless cases should not be destroyed on humane grounds.

Some of the veterinary aspects involved in the treatment of wild birds were described in an earlier publication.[1] In that paper brief mention was made of the danger of zoonoses from captive wild birds. This is a subject that has not, in the author's opinion, received sufficient attention though Keymer[2] discussed the dangers of maintaining exotic mammals and birds in captivity and Irvin and colleagues[3] drew attention to the hazards of handling dead avian material. It is also worth noting that Macdonald and Brown[4] recorded four human cases of salmonellosis in which the phage types of *S typhimurium* responsible were those commonly found in house sparrows and greenfinches. A number of US and UK authors refer to the dangers of such zoonoses as salmonellosis associated with the feeding of wild birds in the garden or backyard. However, apart from these papers, the emphasis has tended to be on the danger of zoonoses from mammals and domestic birds with little or no reference to captive wild birds.

In order to reduce the risks of zoonoses the author has produced the following guide for those working in wild bird hospitals. It should be stressed that it is designed for the layman, not the veterinarian. The guide is reproduced in the Journal of Zoo Animal Medicine in order to bring it to the attention of US colleagues and, where possible, to stimulate their comments and criticisms.

Introduction
Several diseases of wild birds are a potential hazard to human health. Under normal circumstances the danger of transmission is slight but in the intensive atmosphere of a bird hospital an accident can more easily occur. The aim of this guide is not to alarm, but to remind all persons associated with wild birds of the possible hazards. Good hygiene practices will reduce considerably the risk to hospital personnel. The writer feels strongly that all bird hospitals should be aware of such hazards both for their own safety and for that of visitors.

Potential dangers associated with wild birds may be classified as follows:

270

1 Mechanical injury from beaks and claws. Infection may result if wounds are not cleaned and dressed.

2 Infectious disease. Some diseases are common to both man and birds and transmission from one to the other may occur. In other cases a bird may act as a mechanical carrier or exhibit 'silent' infection showing no signs of illness itself but being able to infect a human being. These latter cases pose particular problems. (Infectious disease will be discussed in more detail later).

3 Hypersensitivity or 'allergy' to bird feathers or excreta. Such a syndrome is well recognised and is often termed 'bird fancier's lung'. The symptoms vary but may resemble asthma or hay fever; they are usually exacerbated in the presence of birds. Adequate ventilation of bird rooms may help reduce its incidence.

4 Parasites. Very few internal parasites, such as worms or flukes, can establish themselves in humans and the risks are negligible. External parasites, for example fleas, may temporarily transfer themselves to humans but are not considered a disease risk. Mites and ticks from birds may bite humans and there is some slight danger of disease from them.

5 Chemical poisons in or on the bird may cause toxicity to people handling them. Examples are mercury, arsenic and chlorinated hydrocarbons. Some internal chemical poisons are irritants and will cause enteritis in addition to nervous signs. Handling of a bird with clinical signs of diarrhoea or fits should, therefore, always be followed by washing of the hands.

Infectious diseases

Psittacosis/Ornithosis Both diseases are caused by the same organism. The term psittacosis is applied to the syndrome when it appears in psittacine birds (such as parrot, budgerigar and cockatiel) and was responsible for legislation controlling the importation of such birds into Great Britain. Ornithosis refers to the disease from other types of birds (including domestic poultry and pigeons) and usually takes a milder form in man. Classical psittacosis in man produces a pneumonic disease but may resemble influenza. Cases can readily be treated if diagnosed early.

In birds, clinical signs may be variable; advanced cases show diarrhoea, emaciation, and nasal discharge. Apparently clinically healthy carriers exist. These present a potential danger to humans.

Fortunately the psittacosis agent is killed by most common disinfectants and the risks may, therefore, be reduced if hygienic measures are taken. Psittacine birds should not be kept near the birdroom and, if sick, should be treated with caution.

Avian tuberculosis This disease appears to be on the increase in wild birds in Britain. It is now realised that it can occasionally infect man.

Carrier birds are rare. A bird infected with tuberculosis shows loss of weight and other signs, such as paralysis and enteritis, related to the location of tubercular lesions in the body. Infected wood pigeons may show a darker plumage than usual.[5] Diagnosis of avian tuberculosis in live birds may be assisted by:

1 A tuberculin test – a simple skin test like the Mantoux test in humans. This is far from reliable but can be tried when dealing with suspected cases.
2 A sample of faeces can be examined in a laboratory and in some cases the tuberculosis bacilli can be seen. These tests must be carried out by a suitably experienced person.

Tuberculous birds can excrete organisms in their faeces and thus may infect other birds or man. The organisms are extremely resistant and therefore one infected bird can be responsible for contamination of a bird hospital for a long time. For this reason any suspect case should be isolated, examined by a veterinary surgeon and, if necessary, humanely destroyed. Thorough disinfection is then essential, using such agents as formalin or lysol.

Pseudotuberculosis This disease has some similarities to avian tuberculosis. It can also infect man but, fortunately, the causal bacteria are far more susceptible to disinfectants. Enteritis is not often a clinical sign but the bird shows general malaise and lethargy, and in acute cases sudden death may be the first indication of its presence.

Enteric infection Most of the bacteria causing avian enteric disease are specific to birds but some of them, for example certain *Salmonella* spp can infect man. Enteritis is often seen in affected birds though carriers may also exist. Hygiene is again important in control, including disinfection and washing of hands.

Less common diseases which may affect humans include listeriosis, aspergillosis and Newcastle disease (fowl pest). Aspergillosis is a fungal disease which usually affects the respiratory tract, and may be a hazard to human health. In the live bird few spores are exhaled and there is relatively little danger but there is a greater risk when a case is examined post mortem since the operator can be exposed to a heavy challenge.

This is a common fungus and spores are present in small numbers in most normal air samples but their numbers may build up if ventilation in the birdroom is poor.

Newcastle disease is a notifiable disease of poultry. It can also affect game and other birds. Disease in man is rare. Affected humans often show only a conjunctivitis but occasionally a more general syndrome (including headache and swollen lymph nodes) may result. A possible precaution is to avoid keeping poultry near the birdroom.

Suggested hospital measures to reduce health hazards

1 Always wash the hands after handling birds and be sure that equipment, such as food dishes, is kept clean.
2 Ensure birdrooms are well ventilated and disinfected (or fumigated) at regular intervals. Discuss suitable disinfectants with a veterinary surgeon; the quaternary ammonium group is particularly recommended.
3 Avoid smoking in the birdroom; keep all human food carefully covered and free from exposure.
4 Destroy bedding and disinfect cages regularly; protect the floor with polythene sheeting or paper.
5 Treat all sick birds with caution, especially if they show diarrhoea or if there is reason to suspect that their condition is infectious. Isolate such cases and, if available, wear washable or disposable gloves when handling these birds. *Seek professional advice.*
6 Burn or bury all birds which die or, preferably, have a post-mortem examination carried out by a veterinary surgeon. Never open the carcass of a dead bird in the birdroom and avoid feeding them to birds of prey.
7 Report to your doctor immediately if you are unwell, especially if suffering from a fever, a cough, watering eyes or a skin rash; or if an apparently mild condition (for example, influenza) fails to improve. Always mention to your doctor that you are in close contact with birds.

(Reproduced, with permission, from the Annual Proceedings of the American Association of Zoo Veterinarians 1972, Houston, Texas and 1973, Columbus, Ohio)

PATHOLOGICAL SPECIMENS

Articles sent for Medical Examination or Analysis

Deleterious liquids or substances, though otherwise prohibited from transmission by post, may be sent for medical examination or analysis to a recognised medical laboratory or institute, or to a qualified medical practitioner or a registered dental practitioner or veterinary surgeon by first-class letter post, but on no account by parcel post, under the following conditions :

1   Any such liquid or substance must be enclosed in a receptacle, hermetically sealed or otherwise securely closed, and this receptacle must itself be placed in a strong wooden or metal case (or other case which has been approved by the Post Office) in such a way that it cannot shift about, and with a sufficient quantity of some absorbent material (such as sawdust or cotton-wool) so packed about the receptacle as absolutely to prevent any possible leakage from the package in the event of damage to the receptacle. The packet so made up must be conspicuously marked FRAGILE WITH CARE and bear the words PATHOLOGICAL SPECI-MEN.

2   Any packet of this kind found in the parcel post, or found in the letter post not packed and marked as directed, will be at once stopped and destroyed with all its wrappings and enclosures. Further, any person who sends by post a deleterious liquid or substance for medical examination or analysis otherwise than as provided by these regulations is liable to prosecution.

3   Receptacles supplied by a laboratory or institute must be submitted to Postal Headquarters (PMk 1), St. Martin's-le-Grand, London, EC1 1HQ in order to ascertain whether they are regarded as complying with the regulations.

(Extracted, with permission, from UK Post Office Regulations)

References and Recommended Reading

CHAPTER 1

References
1 Kirk, R. W. (Editor), *Current Veterinary Therapy V. Small Animal Practice*, W. B. Saunders Company, Philadelphia, London and Toronto (1974)
2 Petrak, M. L. (Editor), *Diseases of Cage and Aviary Birds*, Lea and Febiger, Philadelphia (1969)
3 Arnall, L. and Keymer, I. F. (Editors), *Bird Diseases*, Baillière Tindall (1975).
4 Davis, J. W., Anderson, R. C., Karstad, L. and Trainer, D. O. (Editors), *Infectious and Parastic Diseases of Wild Birds*, The Iowa State University Press, Iowa (1971)
5 Greenwood, A. 'The role of disease in the ecology of British raptors', *Bird Study*, 24 (1977), 259–65

Recommended Reading
Ash, J. S., 'Post-mortem examinations of birds found dead during the cold spells of 1954 and 1956', *Bird Study*, 4 (1957), 159–66.
Baker, J. R. 'The results of post-mortem examination of 132 wild birds', *British Veterinary Journal*, 133 (1977), 327–33.
Cooper, J. E. 'First aid and veterinary treatment of wild birds', *Journal of Small Animal Practice*, 16 (1975), 579–91.
Engholm, E. *Company of Birds*, Neville Spearman (1970)
Hurrell, H. G. *Wildlife: Tame but Free*, David and Charles, Newton Abbot (1968)
Jennings, A. R. 'An analysis of 1,000 deaths in wild birds', *Bird Study*, 8 (1961), 25–31
Knight, M. *A Cuckoo in the House*, Methuen and Co Ltd (1955)
Knight, M. *Taming and Handling Animals*, G. Bell and Sons Ltd (1959)
Macdonald, J. W. 'Mortality in wild birds', *Bird Study*, 10 (1963), 91–108
Royal Society for the Protection of Birds, *Treatment of Sick and Injured Birds*, RSPB, Sandy, Beds (1976)

CHAPTER 2

Recommended Reading
Anon. *Wild Birds and the Law*, The Royal Society for the Protection of Birds, Sandy, Beds (1971)
Anon. *Legislation affecting the Veterinary Profession in Great Britain*, The Royal College of Veterinary Surgeons (1975)
Anon. *Cruelty to Animals and the Law*, The Royal Society for the Prevention of Cruelty to Animals, Horsham, Sussex (nd)
Boyd, H. 'Legal requirements', *Laboratory Animal Handbook*, 5 (1972), 91–100
Field-Fisher, T. G. *Animals and the Law*, Universities Federation for Animal Welfare (1964)
Halsbury, Lord (Editor) *Laws of England*, Vol 2, 4th ed, Butterworths (1973)
The Law Society's Gazette 'Charity and Appeals Supplement', The Law Society (nd)
North, P. M. *The Modern Law of Animals*, Butterworths (1972)
Porter, A. R. W. 'Pet animals and the law', in Anderson, R. S. (Editor), *Pet Animals and Society*, Ballière Tindall (1975)
Thomas, J. L. *Diseases of Animals Law*, Police Review Publishing Co Ltd (1975)

Note: Acts of Parliament and statutory instruments may be obtained from Her Majesty's Stationery Office, London or branches elsewhere.

CHAPTER 3

Recommended Reading
Arnall, L., and Keymer, I. F. *Bird Diseases*, Baillière Tindall (1975)
Dorst, J. (Editor) *The Life of Birds*, 2 vols, Weidenfeld and Nicholson (1971)
Evans, H. E. 'Anatomy of the budgerigar' in Petrak, M. L. (Editor), *Diseases of Cage
    and Aviary Birds*, Lea and Febiger, Philadelphia (1969)
Farner, D. S., and King, J. R. (Editors) *Avian Biology*, in several volumes, Academic
    Press (1970 and continuing)
Matthews, L. H., and Knight, M. *The Senses of Animals*, Museum Press Ltd (1963)
Thomson, A. L. (Editor) *A New Dictionary of Birds*, Thomas Nelson, London and
    Edinburgh (1964)
Welty, J. C. *The Life of Birds*, W. B. Saunders (1962)

CHAPTER 4

Reference
1 Stoll, N. R. (Editor) *International Code of Zoological Nomenclature*, International
    Trust for Zoological Nomenclature, London (1964)

Recommended Reading
Hafez, E. S. E. (Editor) *The Behaviour of Domestic Animals*, Baillière Tindall (1975)
Thomson, A. L. (Editor) *A New Dictionary of Birds*, Thomas Nelson, London and
    Edinburgh (1964)

CHAPTER 5

References
1 Cooper, J. E. 'First-aid for birds', *Pedigree Digest*, 4, (1977–8), 12–13
2 Yglesias, D. *The Cry of a Bird*, William Kimber (1962)

Recommended Reading
Arnall, L. and Keymer, I. F. *Bird Diseases*, Baillière Tindall (1975)
Anderson, E. 'Orphaned sparrows', *Cage and Aviary Birds*, 6 July (1978)
Batten, L. A. 'The seasonal distribution of recoveries and çauses of blackbird
    mortality', *Bird Study*, 23 (1978), 23–32
Carins, M. 'Sick and injured birds', *The Australian Bird Bander*, 9 (1971), 60–1
Dolphin, R. E. and Olsen, D. E. 'The feeding and care of orphan birds', *Veterinary
    Medicine/Small Animal Clinician*, 72 (1977), 1868–9
Petrak, M. L. (Editor) *Diseases of Cage and Aviary Birds*, Lea and Febiger, Phila-
    delphia (1969)
Royal Society for the Protection of Birds, *Treatment of Sick and Injured Birds*,
    RSPB, Sandy, Beds (1976)
Tottenham, K. *Bird Doctor*, T. Nelson, Edinburgh (1969)

CHAPTER 6

References
1 Cooper, J. E. and Kreel, L. 'Radiological examination of birds', *Journal of Small
    Animal Practice*, 17 (1976), 799–808
2 Cooper, J. E. 'Haematological investigations in East African birds of prey',
    Journal of Wildlife Diseases, 11 (1975), 389–94
3 Leonard, J. L. 'Clinical laboratory examinations', in Petrak, M. L. (Editor),
    Diseases of Cage and Aviary Birds, Lea and Febiger, Philadelphia (1969)
4 Guy, C. 'Exmouth bird hospital', *Devon Birds*, 25 (1972), 2–6

Recommended Reading
Arnall, L. and Keymer, I. F. *Bird Diseases*, Baillière Tindall (1975)
Cooper, J. E. 'First aid and veterinary treatment of wild birds', *Journal of Small
    Animal Practice*, 16 (1975), 579–91
Petrak, M. L. (Editor) *Diseases of Cage and Aviary Birds*, Lea and Febiger,
    Philadelphia (1969)

REFERENCES AND RECOMMENDED READING

CHAPTER 7

References
1 Engholm, E. *Company of Birds*, Neville Spearman (1970)
2 Cooper, J. E. 'The role of vaccination in the maintenance of captive birds of prey', *Raptor Research*, 9 (1975), 21–6
3 Chu, H. P., Trow, E. W., Greenwood, A. G., Jennings, A. R. and Keymer, I. F. 'Isolation of Newcastle disease virus from birds of prey', *Avian Pathology*, 5 (1976), 227–33

Recommended Reading
Stone, R. M. 'Clinical examination and methods of treatment', in Petrak, M. L. (Editor), *Diseases of Cage and Aviary Birds*, Lea and Febiger, Philadelphia (1969)

CHAPTER 8

References
1 Low, R. *Beginner's Guide to Birdkeeping*, Pelham Books Ltd (1974)
2 Morse, R. *Wild Plants and Seeds for Birds*, Cage and Aviary Birds (1926 and later editions)
3 Meaden, F. 'Meating off', *ASPEBA Occasional Publications*, 2 (1968), 9–11
4 Hanley, H. 'Observations on breeding the nightingale', *Proceedings of the Zoological Society of London* (1951), 196–7 (reprinted in *ASPEBA Occasional Publications*, 5 p6, (1971))
5 Smith, G. R., Hime, J. M., Keymer, I. F., Graham, J. M., Olney, P. J. S. and Brambell, M. R. 'Botulism in captive birds fed commercially bred maggots', *Veterinary Record*, 97 (1975), 204–5
6 Hunter-Jones, P. *Rearing and Breeding Locusts in the Laboratory*, Anti-Locust Research Centre (now Centre for Overseas Pest Research), London (1966)
7 Anon. 'Culturing insects for bird food', *ASPEBA Occasional Publications*, 1 (nd), 5–10
8 Anon. 'Culturing house flies', *ASPEBA Occasional Publications*, 2 (1968), 11–12
9 McCluskey, R. 'Breeding grey wagtails using fish as food', *Avicultural Magazine*, 78 (1972), 20–2
10 Hitchin, H. E. and Harrison, C. J. O. 'Improving maggots for bird food', *ASPEBA Occasional Publications*, 1 (1967), 10–11
11 Ivor, H. R. *I Live With Birds*, The Ryerson Press, Toronto, and Souvenir Press, London (1968)
12 Lanyon, W. E. and Lanyon, V. H. 'A technique for rearing passerine birds from the egg', *Living Bird*, 8 (1969), 81–93

Recommended Reading
Cage and Aviary Birds published weekly by IPC Specialist and Professional Ltd, London
Graham, J. M. '*Clostridium botulinum* type C and its toxin in fly larvae', *Veterinary Record*, 102 (1978), 242–3
Martin, R. D., Rivers, J. P. W. and Cowgill, U. M. 'Culturing mealworms as food for animals in captivity', *International Zoo Yearbook*, 16 (1976), 63–70
Muller, K. A. 'Maintaining insectivorous birds in captivity', *International Zoo Yearbook*, 16 (1976), 32–8
Royal Society for the Protection of Birds *Treatment of Sick and Injured Birds*, RSPB, Sandy, Beds (1976)

CHAPTER 9

References
1 Wallach, J. D. and Flieg, G. M. 'Frostbite and its sequelae in captive exotic birds', *Journal of the American Veterinary Medical Association*, 155 (1969), 1035–38
2 Altman, I. E. 'Disorders of the skeletal system', in Petrak, M. L. (Editor), *Diseases of Cage and Aviary Birds*, Lea and Febiger, Philadelphia (1969)

Recommended Reading
Arnall, L. and Keymer, I. F. *Bird Diseases*, Baillière Tindall (1975)

CHAPTER 10

References
1 McDiarmid, A. 'Tuberculosis in wild birds', *Proceedings of the Royal Society of Medicine*, 57 (1964), 480-1
2 Macdonald, J. W. and Cornelius, L. W. 'Salmonellosis in wild birds', *British Birds*, 62 (1969), 28-30
3 Cooper, J. E. and Needham, J. R. 'An investigation into the prevalence of *S.aureus* on avian feet', *Veterinary Record*, 98 (1976), 172-4
4 Halliwell, W. H. 'Bumblefoot infections in birds of prey', *Journal of Zoo Animal Medicine*, 6 (1975), 8-10
5 Bird, D. M. and Lague, P. C. 'Treatment of bumblefoot by radiotherapy', *Hawk Chalk*, 15 (1976), 57-60
6 American Association of Avian Pathologists *Isolation and Identification of Avian Pathogens*, Texas A & M University (1975)

Recommended Reading
Burtscher, H. and Sibalin, M. 'Herpesvirus strigis: host spectrum and distribution in infected owls' *Journal of Wildlife Diseases*, 11 (1975), 164-9
Cooper, J. E. *Veterinary Aspects of Captive Birds of Prey*, The Hawk Trust, Hungerford, Berks (1972) (2nd, revised, edition, The Standfast Press, Glos (1978))
Davis, J. W., Anderson, R. C., Karstad, L. and Trainer, D. O. (Editors) *Infectious and Parasitic Diseases of Wild Birds*, Iowa State University Press (1971)
Graham, D. L., Maré, C. J., Ward, F. P. and Peckham, M. C. 'Inclusion body disease (herpesvirus infection) of falcons (IBDF)', *Journal of Wildlife Diseases*, 11 (1975), 83-91
Hall, R. F., Waldhalm, D. G., Meinershagen, W. A. and DuBose, D. A. 'Isolation of *Salmonella* spp. from dead gulls (*Larus californicus* and *Larus delawarensis*) from an Idaho irrigation reservoir', *Avian Diseases*, 21 (1977), 452-4
Hofstad, M. S., Calnek, B. W., Helmboldt, C. F., Reid, W. M. and Yoder, H. W. (Editors) *Diseases of Poultry*, 6th ed, Iowa State University Press (1972)
Jensen, W. I. and Cotter, S. E. 'An outbreak of erysipelas in eared grebes *Podiceps nigricollis*', *Journal of Wildlife Diseases*, 12 (1976), 583-6
Karstad, L. Diseases diagnosed in free-living wild birds', *Ontario Bird Banding*, 6 (1970), 6-17
Keymer, I. F. 'Ornithosis in free-living and captive birds', *Proceedings of the Royal Society of Medicine*, 67 (1974), 733-5
Zinkl, J. G., Dey, N., Hyland, J. M., Hurt, J. J. and Heddleston, K. L. 'An epornitic of avian cholera in waterfowl and common crows in Phelps Country, Nebraska, in the Spring, 1975', *Journal of Wildlife Diseases*, 13 (1977), 194-8

CHAPTER 11

References
1 Rothschild, M. and Clay, T. *Fleas, Flukes and Cuckoos*, Collins (1952)
2 Arnall, L. and Keymer, I. F. *Bird Diseases*, Baillière Tindall (1975)
3 Keymer, I. F. 'Parasitic diseases', in Petrak, M. L. (Editor), *Diseases of Cage and Aviary Birds*, Lea and Febiger, Philadelphia (1969)
4 Macdonald, J. W. and Gush, G. H. 'Knemidokoptic mange in chaffinches', *British Birds*, 68 (1975), 103-7
5 Cooper, J. E. 'Trichlorphon as a safe insecticide for use on birds of prey', *Veterinary Record*, 94 (1974), 455
6 Zumpt, F. *Myiasis in Man and Animals in the Old World*, Butterworths (1965)
7 Woodard, J. C., Forrester, D. J., White, F. H., Gaskin, J. M. and Thompson, N. P. 'An epizootic among knots (*Calidris canutus*) in Florida I, Disease syndrome, histology and transmission studies, *Veterinary Pathology*, 14 (1977), 338-50

278

8 Simpson, C. F., Woodard, J. C. and Forrester, D. J. 'An epizootic among knots (*Calidris canutus*) in Florida II. Ultra structure of the causative agent, a *Besnoitia*-like organism', *Veterinary Pathology*, 14 (1977), 351–60

Recommended Reading
Ash, J. S. 'Post-mortem examinations of birds found dead during the cold spells of 1954 and 1956', *Bird Study*, 4, (1957) 159–166
Messent, P. R. 'Birds', in Cowie, A. F. (Editor) *A Manual of the Care and Treatment of Children's and Exotic Pets*, British Small Animal Veterinary Association (1976)
Soulsby, E. J. L. *Helminths, Arthropods and Protozoa of Domesticated Animals*, Baillière, Tindall and Cassell (1968)

CHAPTER 12

References
1 Kalmbach, E. R. and Gunderson, M. F. 'Western Duck Sickness a form of Botulism', *US Dept of Agriculture Technical Bulletin* (1934)
2 Fish, N. A., Mitchell, W. R. and Barnum, D. A. 'A report of a natural outbreak of botulism in pheasants', *Canadian Veterinary Journal*, 8 (1967), 10–16
3 Blandford, T. B., Roberts, T. A. and Ashton, W. L. G. 'Losses from botulism in mallard duck and other waterfowl', *Veterinary Record*, 85 (1969), 541–2
4 Keymer, I. F., Smith, G. R., Roberts, T. A., Heaney, S. I. and Hibberd, D. J. 'Botulism as a factor in waterfowl mortality at St James's Park, London', *Veterinary Record*, 90 (1972), 111–4
5 Kalmbach, E. R. 'American vultures and the toxin of *Clostridium botulinum*', *Journal of the American Veterinary Medical Association*, 94 (1939), 187–91
6 Gorham, P. R. 'Toxic algae', in Jackson ,D. F. (Editor), *Algae and Man*, Plenum Press, New York (1964)
7 Hartung, R. 'Effects of toxic substances', in Davis, J. W., Anderson, R. C., Karstad, L. and Trainer, D. O. (Editors), *Infectious and Parasitic Diseases of Wild Birds*, Iowa State University Press (1971)
8 Hammer, U. T. 'Toxic blue-green algae in Saskatchewan', *Canadian Veterinary Journal*, 9 (1968), 221–9
9 Deem, A. W. and Thorp, F. 'Toxic algae in Colorado', *Journal of the American Veterinary Medical Association*, 95 (1939), 542–4
10 Schantz, E. J. 'Paralytic shellfish poisoning and saxitoxin', in Simpson, L. L. (Editor), *Neuropoisons: their Pathophysiological Actions* Vol 1, Plenum Press, New York (1971)
11 McKernan, D. L. and Scheffer, V. B. 'Unusual numbers of dead birds on the Washington coast', *Condor*, 44 (1942), 264–6
12 Coulson, J. C., Potts, G. R., Deans, I. R. and Fraser, S. M. 'Exceptional mortality of shags and other seabirds caused by paralytic shellfish poisoning', *British Birds*, 61 (1968), 381–404
13 Forsyth, A. A. 'British Poisonous Plants', *MAFF Bulletin*, 161, HMSO (1954)
14 North, P. M. *Poisonous Plants and Fungi*, Blandford Press (1967)
15 Nestler, R. B. and Bailey, W. W. 'The toxicity of *Crotalaria spectabilis* seeds for quail', *Journal of Wildlife Management*, 5 (1941), 309–13
16 MacGregor, W. G. 'Cyanide poisoning of song-birds by almonds', *Condor*, 57 (1955), 370
17 Clarke, E. G. and Clarke, M. L. *Veterinary Toxicology*, 3rd ed, Baillière Tindall and Cassell (1967)
18 Department of the Environment 'Lead in the Environment and its Significance To Man', *Pollution Paper*, 2, HMSO (1974)
19 Bazell, R. 'Lead poisoning: zoo animals may be first victims', *Science*, 173 (1971), 130–1
20 Olney, P. J. S. 'Lead poisoning in waterfowl', *Bulletin of the British Ornithological Club*, 80 (1960), 35–40 and 53–9
21 Bellrose, F. C. 'Lead poisoning as a mortality factor in wildfowl populations', *Illinois Natural History Survey Bulletin*, 27 (1959), 235–88
22 Del Bono, G. and Bruce, G. 'Lead poisoning in domestic and wild ducks', *Avian Pathology*, 2 (1973), 195–209

23 Beer, J. V. and Ogilvie, M. A. 'Mortality', in Scott, P. and the Wildfowl Trust (Editors), *The Swans*, Michael Joseph (1972)

24 Irby, H. D., Locke, L. N. and Bagley, G. E. 'Relative toxicity of lead and selected substitute shot types to game farm mallards', *Journal of Wildlife Management*, 31 (1967), 252–7

25 Irwin, J. C. and Karstad, L. H. 'Toxicity for ducks of disintegrated lead shot in a simulated marsh environment', *Journal of Wildlife Diseases*, 8 (1972), 149–54

26 Mackle, W. 'Lead absorption from bullets lodged in the tissues', *Journal of the American Medical Association*, 115 (1940), 1536

27 Bagley, G. E. and Locke, L. N. 'The occurrence of lead in the tissues of wild birds', *Bulletin of Environmental Contamination and Toxicology*, 2 (1967), 297–305

28 Bates, F. Y., Barnes, D. M. and Higbee, J. M. 'Lead toxicosis in mallard ducks', *Bulletin of Wildlife Disease Association*, 4 (1968), 116–25

29 Trainer, D. O. and Hunt, R. A. 'Lead poisoning of whistling swans in Wisconsin', *Avian Diseases*, 9 (1965), 252–63

30 Barclay-Smith, P. 'Oil pollution – an historical survey', Journal of Devon Trust for Nature Conservation Supplement, *Conservation and the Torrey Canyon* (1967), 3–7

31 Cramp, S. 'The threats to seabirds', in the Seabird Group (Editors), *The Seabirds of Britain and Ireland*, Collins (1974)

32 Mayer-Gross, H. 'The Torrey Canyon disaster', *British Trust for Ornithology News*, 23 (1967), 2–4

33 Clark, R. B. and Kennedy, J. R. 'Rehabilitation of oiled seabirds', *Report to Advisory Committee on Oil Pollution of the Sea*, University of Newcastle-upon-Tyne (1968)

34 O'Connor, R. J. 'The Torrey Canyon. A census of breeding auks in Cornwall, June 1967', *Seabird Bulletin*, 4 (1967), 38–45

35 Nero, R. W. 'Detergents – deadly hazard to water birds', *Audubon Magazine*, 66 (1964), 26–7

36 Risebrough, R. W., Rieche, R., Herman, S. G., Peakall, D. B. and Kirven, M. N. 'Polychlorinated biphenyls in the global ecosystem', *Nature*, 220 (1968), 1098–102

37 Bogan, J. A. and Bourne, W. R. P. 'Organochlorine levels in Atlantic seabirds', *Nature*, 240 (1972), 358

38 Prestt, I., Jefferies, D. J. and Moore, N. W. 'PCBs in wild birds in Britain and their avian toxicity', *Environmental Pollution*, 1 (1970), 3–26

39 Harvey, G. R., Steinhower, W. G. and Miklas, H. P. 'Decline of PCB concentration in North Atlantic surface water', *Nature*, 252 (1974), 387–8

40 Mellanby, K. *Pesticides and Pollution*, Collins (1967)

41 Cramp, S. 'The effect of pesticides on British wildlife', *British Veterinary Journal*, 129 (1973), 315–23

42 Moore, N. W. (Editor) 'Pesticides in the environment and their effect on wildlife', *Journal of Applied Ecology*, 3 (Supplement) (1966)

43 Scott, W. N. 'Pesticides and animal poisoning', *Veterinary Record*, 76 (1964), 964–73

44 Cramp, S. and Conder, P. J. *The Deaths of Birds and Mammals connected with Chemicals in the First Half of 1960*, Report No 1 of the BTO/RSPB Committee on Toxic Chemicals (1961)

45 Jefferies, D. J. and Prestt, I. 'Post-mortems of peregrines and lanners with particular reference to organochlorine residues', *British Birds*, 59 (1966), 49–64

46 Lockie, L. D. and Ratcliffe, D. A. 'Insecticides and Scottish golden eagles', *British Birds*, 57 (1964), 89–102

47 Hickey, J. J. (Editor) *Peregrine Falcon Populations – Their Biology and Decline*, University of Wisconsin Press (1969)

48 Ratcliffe, D. A. 'Decrease in eggshell weight in certain birds of prey', *Nature*, 215 (1967), 208–10

49 Borg, K., Wanntrop, H., Erne, K. and Hanko, E. 'Alkyl mercury poisoning in terrestrial Swedish wildlife', *Viltrevy*, 6 (1969), 301–79

50 Bailey, S., Bunyon, R. J., Hamilton, G. A., Jennings, D. M. and Stanley, P. I. 'Accidental poisoning of wild geese in Perthshire, Nov. 1971', *Wildfowl*, 23 (1972), 88–91

51 Macmillan, A. T. 'Whooper deaths', *Scottish Birds*, 5 (1968), 111–2

52 Schafer, E. W. 'The acute oral toxicity of 369 pesticidal pharmaceutical and other

280

chemicals to wild birds', *Toxicology and Applied Pharmacology*, 21 (1972), 315–30
53 St. Omer, V. V. 'Chronic and acute toxicity of the chlorinated hydrocarbon insecticides in mammals and birds', *Canadian Veterinary Journal*, 11 (1970), 215–26
54 Tucker, R. K. and Haegele, M. A. 'Comparative acute oral toxicity of pesticides to six species of birds', *Toxicology and Applied Pharmacology*, 20 (1971), 57–65
55 James, O. D. 'Metaldehyde poisoning of ducks', *Veterinary Record*, 67 (1955), 248
56 Coburn, D. R., Dewitt, J. B., Derby, J. V. and Ediger, E. 'Phosphorus poisoning in waterfowl', *Journal of the American Pharmaceutical Association*, 39 (1950), 151–8
57 Murton, R. K., Isaacson, A. J. and Westwood, N. J. 'The use of baits treated with a-chloralose to catch wood pigeons', *Annals of Applied Biology*, 52 (1963), 271–93
58 Thearle, R. J. P. 'Urban bird problems', in Murton, R. K. and Wright, E. N. (Editors), *The Problems of Birds as Pests*, Institute of Biology Symposium 17, Academic Press (1965)
59 Lees, P. 'Pharmacology and toxicology of a-choralose – a review', *Veterinary Record*, 91 (1973), 330–3
60 Knapp, M. and Russell, H. A. 'Detection of a poisoning of buzzards', *Deutsche Tierärztliche Wochenschrift*, 80 (1973), 573–5
61 Trainer, D. O. and Karstad, L. 'Salt poisoning in Wisconsin wildlife', *Journal of the American Veterinary Medical Association*, 136 (1960), 14–17
62 Field, H. I. and Rees-Evans, E. T. 'Acute salt poisoning in poultry', *Veterinary Record*, 58 (1946), 253–4
63 Anon. 'Polymer fume fever syndrome', *State Veterinary Journal*, 29 (1974), 206

Recommended Reading
Blandford, T. B., Seamon, P. J., Hughes, R., Pattison, M. and Wilderspin, M. P. 'A case of polytetrafluoroethylene poisoning in cockatiels accompanied by polymer fume fever in the owner', *Veterinary Record*, 96 (1975), 175–6
Cutler, J. R., Muttrie, M. P., Papworth, D. S. and Taylor, J. K. 'The use of pesticides by local authorities in Great Britain', *Royal Society of Health Journal*, 1 (1976), 45–9
Higuchi, K. *PCB Poisoning and Pollution*, Academic Press, New York (1976)
Hunt, A. E. 'Lead poisoning in swans', *British Trust for Ornithology News*, 90 (1977), 1–2
Institute of Terrestrial Ecology Annual Report 1976, HMSO (1977)
Peakall, D. B. 'The peregrine falcon (*Falco peregrinus*) and pesticides', *Canadian Field-Naturalist*, 90 (1976), 301–7
Peckham, M. C. 'Poisons and toxins', in Hofstad, M. S., Calnek, B. W., Helmboldt, C. F., Reid, W. M. and Yoder, H. W. (Editors), *Diseases of Poultry*, 6th ed, Iowa State University Press (1972)
Shlosberg, A. 'Treatment of monocrotophos-poisoned birds of prey with pralidoxime iodide', *Journal of the American Veterinary Medical Association*, 169 (1976), 989–90

CHAPTER 13

References
1 Clark, R. B. and Kennedy, R. J. *Rehabilitation of Oiled Seabirds*, Department of Zoology, University of Newcastle-upon-Tyne (1968)
2 Joensen, A. H. 'Danish seabird disasters in 1972', *Marine Pollution Bulletin*, 4 (1973), 117–8
3 Bibby, C. J. and Bourne, W. R. B. 'More problems for threatened seabirds', *Birds*, 3 (1971), 307–9
4 Bibby, C. J. and Bourne, W. R. B. 'Trouble on oiled waters', *Birds*, 4 (1972), 160–2
5 Bibby, C. J. and Bourne, W. R. B. 'Pollution still kills', *Birds*, 5 (1974), 30–1
6 Hunt, G. S. *Waterfowl Losses on the Lower Detroit River due to Oil Pollution*,

Publication No 7, Great Lakes Reservation Division, Institute of Science and Technology, University of Michigan (1961)

7 Hartung, R. and Hunt, G. S. 'Toxicity of some oils to waterfowl', *Journal of Wildlife Management*, 30 (1966), 565–9

8 Snyder, S. B., Fox, J. G. and Soave, O. A. *Mortalities in Waterfowl following Bunker C. Fuel Exposure*, Standard Medical Center, Stanford, California (1973)

9 Clark, R. B. and Kennedy, R. J. *How Oiled Seabirds are Cleaned*, Department of Zoology, University of Newcastle-upon-Tyne (1971)

10 Beer, J. V. 'Post-mortem findings on oiled auks dying during attempted rehabilitation' in Carthy, J. D. and Arthur, D. R. (Editors), 'The Biological Effects of Oil Pollution on Littoral Communities', *Field Studies Supplement*, 2 (1968), 123–9

11 Bibby, C. J. 'The attempted rehabilitation of oiled seabirds', *Wildfowl*, 19 (1968), 120–4

12 Clark, R. B. and Croxall, J. P. 'Rescue operations for oiled seabirds', *Marine Pollution Bulletin*, 3 (1972), 123–7

13 Research Unit on the Rehabilitation of Oiled Seabirds Third Annual Report, 1972, Department of Zoology, University of Newcastle-upon-Tyne (1973)

14 Research Unit on the Rehabilitation of Oiled Seabirds Fourth Annual Report, 1973, Department of Zoology, University of Newcastle-upon-Tyne (1974)

15 Naviaux, J. L. *Aftercare of Oil-covered Birds*, National Wildlife Health Foundation, California (1972)

16 Kennedy, R. J. 'Directional water-shedding properties of feathers', *Nature*, 227 (1970), 736–7

17 Rijke, A. M. 'Wettability and phylogenetic development of feather structure in waterbirds', *Journal of Experimental Biology*, 52 (1970), 469–79

18 Clark, R. B. and Gregory, K. G. 'Feather-wetting in cleaned birds', *Marine Pollution Bulletin*, 2 (1971), 78–9

19 Croxall, J. P. 'Cleaning oiled seabirds', *Petroleum Review*, 26 (1972), 362–5

20 Research Unit on the Rehabilitation of Oiled Seabirds Second Annual Report, 1971, Department of Zoology, University of Newcastle-upon-Tyne (1972)

21 Naviaux, J. L. and Pittman, A. 'Cleaning of oil covered birds', *Biological Conservation*, 5 (1974), 292–3

22 Research Unit on the Rehabilitation of Oiled Seabirds, *Recommended Treatment of Oiled Seabirds*, Department of Zoology, University of Newcastle-upon-Tyne (1972)

23 Jarvis, C. (Editor) 'A Symposium on the Subject of Penguins in Captivity', *International Zoo Yearbook*, 7 (1967), 1–44

24 Stanton, P. B. *Operation Rescue: Cleaning and Care of Oiled Waterfowl*, American Petroleum Institute, Washington DC (1972)

Recommended Reading

Anon. 'Oil – a question of faster actions', *Birds*, 6 (1977), 14–15

Anon. 'Dispatch from one oil front', *Birds*, 7 (1978), 9

Anon. 'Conference. The changing seabird populations of the North Atlantic. Aberdeen University: 26–28 March 1977', *Ibis*, 120 (1978), 102–36

International Bird Rescue Research Center, *Saving Oiled Seabirds*, American Petroleum Institute, Washington (1978)

Marsault, B. 'To kill or not to kill', in Gooders, J. (Editor), *The Third Bird-Watchers' Book*, David and Charles, Newton Abbot (1976)

Tottenham, K. 'Oil pollution', in Petrak, M. L. (Editor), *Diseases of Cage and Aviary Birds*, Lea and Febiger, Philadelphia (1969) .

CHAPTER 14

References

1 Voitkevich, A. A. *The Feathers and Plumage of Birds*, Sidgwick and Jackson (1969)

2 Woodford, M. H. *A Manual of Falconry*, A. & C. Black (1960)

3 Wallach, J. D. 'Nutritional diseases of exotic animals', *Journal of the American Veterinary Medical Association*, 157 (1970), 583–99

4 Tollefson, C. I. 'Nutrition', in Petrak, M. L. (Editor), *Diseases of Cage and Aviary Birds*, Lea and Febiger, Philadelphia (1969)
5 Cooper, J. E. 'Osteodystrophy in birds of prey', *Veterinary Record*, 97 (1975), 307
6 Wallach, J. D. and Flieg, G. M. 'Cramps and fits in carnivorous birds, *International Zoo Yearbook*, 10 (1970), 3–4
7 Blackmore, D. K. 'Diseases of the endocrine system', in Petrak, M. L. (Editor), *Diseases of Cage and Aviary Birds*, Lea and Febiger, Philadelphia (1969)
8 Hasholt, J. 'Gout', in Petrak, M. L. (Editor), *Diseases of Cage and Aviary Birds*, Lea and Febiger, Philadelphia (1969)
9 Von Faber, H. 'Stress and general adaptation syndrome in poultry', *World's Poultry Science Journal*, 20 (1964), 175–82
10 Murton, R. K., Isaacson, A. J. and Westwood, N. J. 'The significance of gregarious feeding behaviour and adrenal stress in a population of woodpigeons Columba palumbus', *Journal of Zoology, London* 165, (1971), 53–84
11 Jennings, A. R. 'Tumours of free-living wild mammals and birds in Great Britain', *Symposia of The Zoological Society of London*, 24 (1968), 273–87
12 Petrak, M. L. and Gilmore, C. E. 'Neoplasms', in Petrak, M. L. (Editor), *Diseases of Cage and Aviary Birds*, Lea and Febiger, Philadelphia (1969)
13 Macdonald, J. W. 'Chaffinches with papillomas', *British Birds*, 58 (1965), 346–7
14 Lina, P. H. C. 'Viral particles in chaffinch papilloma cells', *Ardea*, 59 (1971), 47–9

Recommended Reading
Blackmore, D. K. and Keymer, I. F. 'Cutaneous diseases of wild birds in Britain', *British Birds*, 62 (1969), 316–31
Bourne, W. R. P., Bogan, J. A., Bullock, D., Diamond, A. W. and Feare, C. W. 'Abnormal terns, sick sea and shore birds, organochlorines and arboviruses in the Indian Ocean', *Marine Pollution Bulletin*, 8 (1977), 154–8
Cooper, J. E. *Veterinary Aspects of Captive Birds of Prey*, The Hawk Trust, Hungerford, Berks (1972) (2nd, revised, edition, The Standfast Press, Glos (1978))
Gochfeld, M. 'Prevalence of subcutaneous emphysema in young terns, skimmers and gulls', *Journal of Wildlife Diseases*, 10 (1974), 115–20
Macdonald, J. W. 'Cutaneous salmonellosis in a house sparrow', *Bird Study*, 25 (1978), 59
Messent, P. R. 'Birds', in Cowie, A. F. (Editor), *A Manual of the Care and Treatment of Children's and Exotic Pets*, British Small Animal Veterinary Association (1976)
Minsky, L. 'Obesity, abdominal rupture, senility and shock', in Petrak, M. L. (Editor), *Diseases of Cage and Aviary Birds*, Lea and Febiger, Philadelphia (1969)

CHAPTER 15

References
1 Arnall, L. 'Aspects of anaesthesia in cage birds', in Graham-Jones, O. (Editor), *Small Animal Anaesthesia*, Pergamon Press, Oxford (1964)
2 Stunkard, J. A. and Miller, J. C. 'An outline guide to general anesthesia in exotic species', *Veterinary Medicine/Small Animal Clinician*, 69 (1974), 1181–6
3 Whittow, G. C. and Ossorio, N. 'A new technic for anesthetizing birds', *Laboratory Animal Care*, 20 (1970), 651–6
4 Andrews, C. J. H. 'Pentobarbitone as an anesthetic agent in the Adelie Penguin (Pygoscelis adeliae)', *Journal of Small Animal Practice*, 16 (1975), 515–22
5 Delius, J. D. 'Pentobarbital anaesthesia in the herring and lesser blackbacked gull', *Journal of Small Animal Practice*, 7 (1966), 605–9
6 Sanford, J. 'Avian anesthesia', in Soma, I. R. (Editor), *Veterinary Anesthesia*, Williams and Wilkins Company, Baltimore (1971)
7 Kittle, E. L. 'Ketamine HC1 as an anesthetic for birds', *Modern Veterinary Practice*, 52 (1971), 40–1
8 Redig, P. T. and Duke, G. E. 'Intravenously administered ketamine HC1 and diazepam for anesthesia of raptors', *Journal of the American Veterinary Medical Association*, 169 (1976), 886–8
9 Cooper, J. E. 'Use of the hypnotic agent methoxymol in birds of prey', *Veterinary Record*, 87 (1970), 751–2

10 Cooper, J. E. and Frank, L. 'Use of the steroid anaesthetic CT 1341 in birds', *Veterinary Record*, 92 (1973), 474–9
11 Anon. *Humane Killing of Animals*, Universities Federation for Animal Welfare, Potter's Bar, Herts (1978)

Recommended Reading
Camburn, M. A. and Stead, A. C. 'Anaesthesia in wild and aviary birds', *Journal of Small Animal Practice*, 19 (1978), 395–400
Cooper, J. E. 'First aid and veterinary treatment of wild birds', *Journal of Small Animal Practice*, 16 (1976), 579–91
Gandal, C. P. 'Avian anesthesia', *Federation Proceedings*, 28 (1969), 1533–4
Graham-Jones, O. 'Restraint and anaesthesia of small cage birds', *Journal of Small Animal Practice*, 6 (1965), 31–9
Holt, P. E. 'The use of a steroid anaesthetic in a long-eared owl (Asio otus)', *Veterinary Record*, 101 (1977), 118

CHAPTER 16

References
1 Williams, M. H. 'Some notes and comments on birds that have been treated by the Hawk Trust', *Annual Report of the Hawk Trust*, 2 (1971), 17–20
2 Wheeldon, E. B., Bogan, J. A. and Taylor, D. J. 'Dieldrin poisoning in a captive bird of prey', *Veterinary Record*, 97 (1975), 412
3 Cooper, J. E. 'Osteodystrophy in birds of prey', *Veterinary Record*, 97 (1975), 307
4 Mendelssohn, H. and Paz, U. 'Mass mortality of birds of prey caused by azodrin, an organophosphorus insecticide', *Biological Conservation*, 11 (1977), 163–70
5 Anon. 'RSPB anti-poisoning campaign', *British Trust for Ornithology News*, 91 (1978), 7

Recommended Reading
Clarke, A. 'Contamination of peregrine falcons (*Falco peregrinus*) with fulmar stomach oil', *Journal of Zoology, London*, 181 (1977), 11–20
Cooper, J. E. *Veterinary Aspects of Captive Birds of Prey*, The Hawk Trust, Hungerford, Berks (1972) (2nd, revised, edition, The Standfast Press, Glos (1978))
Cooper, J. E. and Kenward, R. E. (Editors) *Papers on the Veterinary Medicine and Domestic Breeding of Diurnal Birds of Prey*, British Falconers' Club (1977)
Greenwood, A. (Editor) *Veterinary Medicine of Birds of Prey*, Proceedings of the 1973 British Falconers' Club Conference (1973)
Greenwood, A. 'The role of disease in the ecology of British raptors', *Bird Study*, 24 (1977), 259–65
Hamerstrom, F. *An Eagle to the Sky*, Iowa State University Press (1970)
Jones, D. M. 'The occurrence of dieldrin in sawdust used as a bedding material', *Laboratory Animals*, 11 (1977), 137
Keymer, I. F. 'Diseases of birds of prey', *Veterinary Record*, 90 (1972), 579–94
Ratcliffe, E. J. 'Injured and orphaned birds of prey reared and returned to the wild', *Annual Report of the Hawk Trust*, 5 (1974), 17–32
Williams, M. H. 'The red kite – six weeks in its company', *Annual Report of the Hawk Trust*, 3 (1972), 18–20
Wingfield, W. E. and DeYoung, D. W. 'Anesthetic and surgical management of eagles with orthopedic difficulties', *Veterinary Medicine Small Animal Clinician*, 67 (1972), 991–3

CHAPTER 17

Recommended Reading
Goodwin, D. *Crows of the World*, British Museum (Natural History) (1976)
Richards, P. R. 'Breeding the rook in captivity', *Avicultural Magazine*, 79 (1973), 19–23
Richards, P. R. 'The nesting and hand rearing of the red billed occipital blue pie', *Avicultural Magazine*, 82 (1976), 2–4

CHAPTER 18

References
1 Evans, M. and Kear, J. 'A jacket for holding large birds for banding', *Journal of Wildlife Management*, 36 (1972), 1265–7

2 Kear, J. and Duplaix-Hall, N. (Editors) *Flamingos*, T. and A. D. Poyser, Berk-hamsted (1975)
3 Clegg, F. G. and Hunt, A. E. 'Salmonella infection in mute swans (*Cygnus olor*)', *Veterinary Record*, 97 (1975), 373

Recommended Reading
Bicknell, E. J., Greichus, A., Greichus, Y. A., Bury, R. J. and Knudtson, W. U. 'Diagnosis and treatment of aspergillosis in captive cormorants', *Sabouraudia*, 9 (1971), 119–22
Humphreys, P. N. 'Problems of keeping ornamental waterfowl', *Journal of Small Animal Practice*, 17 (1976), 607–16
Duplaix-Hall, N. (Editor) 'Waterfowl in captivity' *International Zoo Yearbook*, 13 (1973), 1–100
Scott, P. *A Coloured Key to the Wildfowl of the World*, The Wildfowl Trust, Slim-bridge, Glos (1957)

CHAPTER 19

References
1 Hurrell, L. H. 'The kestrel (*Falco tinnunculus*) breeds in captivity', *The Falconer* 5, (1969) 168–72, (reprinted in the *Journal of the Devon Trust for Nature Conservation*, 2 (September 1970)
2 Hurrell, L. H. 'On breeding the sparrow-hawk in captivity', in Mavrogordato, J. G,. *A Hawk for the Bush*, revised edition, Neville Spearman (1973)
3 Mavrogordato, J. G. *A Falcon in the Field*, Knightly Vernon Ltd (1966)
4 Hurrell, L. H. 'The kestrel (*Falco tinnunculus*) breeds in captivity Part II', *The Falconer*, 5 (1970), 228–30

Recommended Reading
Marsault, B. M. 'Auks breeding in captivity', *Bird Study*, 22 (1975), 44–5
Rutgers, A. and Norris, K. A. *Encyclopaedia of Aviculture*, 3 vols, Blandford Press, Poole, Dorset (1970 and continuing)

CHAPTER 20

Recommended Reading
Fuller, M. R., Redig, P. T. and Duke, G. E. 'Raptor rehabilitation and conservation in Minnesota', *Raptor Research*, 8 (1974), 11–19
Hediger, H. *Wild Animals in Captivity*, Butterworths Scientific Publications, London (1950)
Lewis, W. *Breeding British Seedeaters and their Hybrids for Exhibition*, Walter Lewis, Milnsbridge, Bicton, Shrewsbury, Shropshire (1977)
Lorenz, K. *King Solomon's Ring*, Methuen and Co Ltd (1953)
Rogers, C. H. *Encyclopaedia of Cage and Aviary Birds*, Pelham Books Limited (1975)
Royal Society for the Protection of Birds *Treatment of Sick and Injured Birds*, RSPB, Sandy, Beds (1976)
Rutgers, A. and Norris, K. A. *Encyclopaedia of Aviculture*, 3 vols, Blandford Press, Poole, Dorset (1970 and continuing)
Snyder, H. A. and Snyder, N. F. R. 'Increased mortality of Cooper's hawks accustomed to man', *Condor*, 76 (1974), 215–6

APPENDIX

References
1 Cooper, J. E. and Rubenis, J. 'Veterinary care for sick and wounded wild birds', *Veterinary Practice*, 2 (1970), 10–13
2 Keymer, I. F. 'The unsuitability of non-domesticated animals as pets', *Veterinary Record*, 91 (1972), 373–81
3 Irvin, A. D., Cooper, J. E. and Hedges, S. R. 'Possible health hazards associated with the collection and handling of post-mortem zoological material', *Mammal Review*, 2 (1973), 43–54
4 Macdonald, J. W. and Brown, D. D. 'Salmonella infection in wild birds in Britain', *Veterinary Record*, 94 (1974), 321–2
5 McDiarmid, A. 'The occurrence of tuberculosis in the wild wood-pigeon', *Journal of Comparative Pathology*, 58 (1948), 128–33

Index

This index does not include the names of authors of references or species of birds, unless particularly relevant to the text.
Page numbers in **bold** type denote Plates; page numbers in *italics* denote Figures.